Southern
New England

Anna Mundow
Photography by James Marshall

COMPASS AMERICAN GUIDES
An Imprint of Fodor's Travel Publications, Inc.

Southern New England
First Edition

ISBN : 0-679-00184-0

Editors: Kit Duane, Lesley Bonnet, Michael Oliver
Managing Editor: Kit Duane
Food & Lodging Editor: Julia Dillon

Creative Director: Christopher Burt
Designers: Christopher Burt, Julia Dillon
Map Design: Mark Stroud, Moon Cartography
Cover Design: Siobhan O'Hare

Compass American Guides, Inc., 5332 College Ave., Suite 201, Oakland, CA 94618, USA
10 9 8 7 6 5 4 3 2 1
Production House: Twin Age Ltd., Hong Kong; Manufactured in China

All photographs are by James Marshall unless otherwise credited below.
American Antiquarian Society, Worcester, Mass. p. 24; **Arcadia Publishing Comp.**, courtesy of **Joseph Garland** p. 117, courtesy of **Joe Fuoco** p. 296; **Bowdoin College Museum of Art**, Brunswick, Maine p. 105; **Columbus Museum of Art, Ohio** gift of Ferdinand Howland p. 264; **Devin-Adair Publishers, Old Greenwich, Conn.**, from The Captain's Daughters of Martha's Vineyard p. 148; **Carol Glover** pp. 297, 319; **Robert Holmes** pp. 224, 229, 233, 248, 260, 270; **Isabel Stewart Gardner Museum** pp. 70, 71; **Markham Johnson** pp. 149, 150; **Library of Congress** pp. 20, 43, 108, 302; **Marblehead Historical Society** p.90; **Massachusetts Historical Society** pp. 27, 29, 31; © **Metropolitan Museum of Art, NY**, Arthur Hoppock Hearn Fund, 1950 p.40; Gift of Mrs. Russell Sage, 1908 p. 190; **Museum of Fine Arts, Boston** M. and M. Karolik Collection p.69; bequest of Martha C. Karolik for the M. and M. Karolik Collection of American Paintings, 1815-1865 p. 97; gift of Mr. and Mrs. Daniel S. Wendel, Thomkins Collection, and Seth K. Sweetser Fund by exchange p. 100; **The Museum of Modern Art, NYC**, Mrs. Simon Guggenheim Fund p. 137; **New Bedford Whaling Museum, Mass.** p. 125; **New Britain Museum of American Art**, John Butler Talcott Fund p. 273; **The Norman Rockwell Museum at Stockbridge**, © 1999 **The Norman Rockwell Family Trust** pp. 182-183; **Peabody Essex Museum, Salem, Mass.** p. 83; **Pilgrim Hall Museum, Plymouth, Mass.**, p. 115; **Rhode Island School of Design Art Museum** gift of Mr. Robert Winthrop p. 19; Museum Works of Art Fund p. 283; **Shelburne Museum, Shelburne, Vermont** p. 84; **Timken Museum of Art, San Diego**, The Putnam Foundation p. 159; **Underwood Photo Archives**, San Francisco pp. 42, 118, 239, 285; **Wadsworth Atheneum, Hartford** the Ella Gallup Sumner and Mary Catlin Sumner Fund p.91; purchased from the artist before 1850 p. 208; **Whitney Museum of American Art**, Josephine N. Hopper Bequest p. 96; **Yale University Art Gallery**, Mabel Brady Garvan Collection p. 199.

The publisher would also like to thank **Ellen Klages** for proofreading, **Julie Searle** for indexing, **James A. Smith** and **Ruth Owen Jones** for professional reading, **Judy Anderson** of the Marblehead Historical Society for her valuable assistance, and John Groton of Stonington, Conn., for his local insights.

For my parents

AUTHOR'S ACKNOWLEDGMENTS

I am grateful to Kit Duane at Compass American Guides for her patience, precision, and sense of humor; to photographer Jim Marshall for being an inspired and inspiring co-conspirator; to Jim Aaron, Daniel Aaron, Katherine A. Powers, and Julie Graham for advice and assistance; to Annabel Davis-Goff for encouragement; to Trisha Howells for technical and moral support.

Thanks to the staff of the following libraries and research institutions: **Jones Library**, Amherst; **University of Massachusetts Library**, Amherst; **Forbes Library**, Northampton; **Redwood Library**, Newport; **Connecticut Historical Society**, Hartford; **Rhode Island Historical Society**, Newport; **Providence Athenaeum**, Providence; **Wadsworth Athenaeum**, Hartford; **Nantucket Athenaeum**, Nantucket; **Society for the Preservation of New England Antiquities**, Boston; **Mystic Seaport**, Connecticut.

Thanks also to Nina Stack at Block Island Tourism; Evan Smith at Newport County Convention & Visitors Bureau; Michelle Hatem Meehan, North of Boston Convention & Visitor Bureau.

CONTENTS

Maps

Literary Extracts and Essays

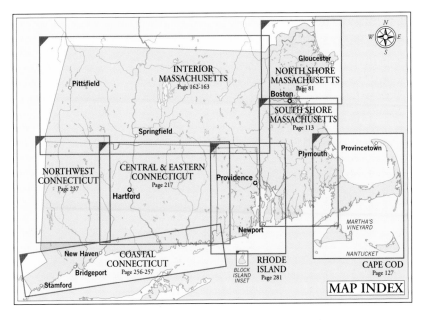

INTERIOR MASSACHUSETTS
Page 162-163

Pittsfield

Springfield

NORTH SHORE MASSACHUSETTS
Page 81

Gloucester

Boston

SOUTH SHORE MASSACHUSETTS
Page 113

Plymouth

Provincetown

NORTHWEST CONNECTICUT
Page 237

CENTRAL & EASTERN CONNECTICUT
Page 217

Hartford

Providence

Newport

MARTHA'S VINEYARD

NANTUCKET

New Haven

COASTAL CONNECTICUT
Page 256-257

Bridgeport

Stamford

BLOCK ISLAND INSET

RHODE ISLAND
Page 281

CAPE COD
Page 127

MAP INDEX

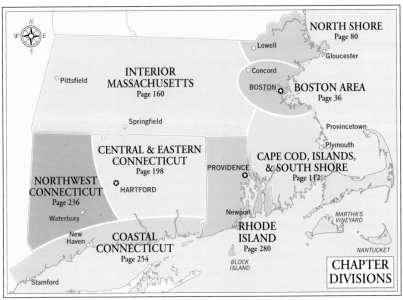

NORTH SHORE
Page 80

Lowell

Gloucester

INTERIOR MASSACHUSETTS
Page 160

Pittsfield

Concord

BOSTON

BOSTON AREA
Page 36

Springfield

Provincetown

Plymouth

CENTRAL & EASTERN CONNECTICUT
Page 198

CAPE COD, ISLANDS, & SOUTH SHORE
Page 112

PROVIDENCE

NORTHWEST CONNECTICUT
Page 236

HARTFORD

Waterbury

Newport

MARTHA'S VINEYARD

New Haven

COASTAL CONNECTICUT
Page 254

RHODE ISLAND
Page 280

BLOCK ISLAND

NANTUCKET

Stamford

CHAPTER DIVISIONS

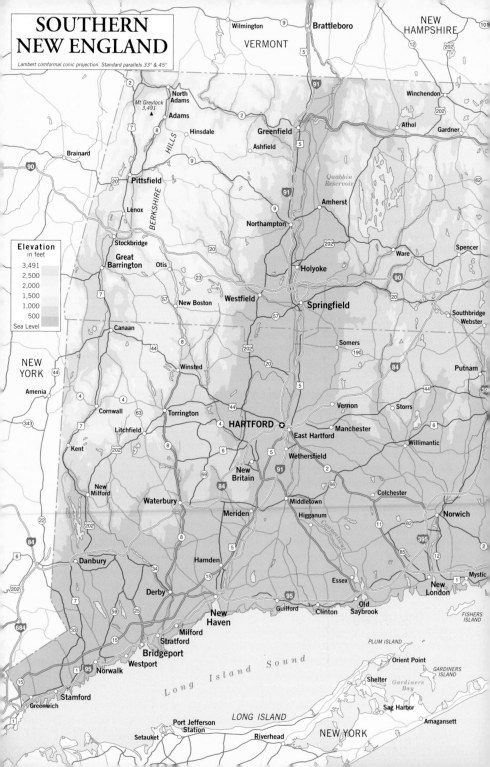

SOUTHERN NEW ENGLAND

Lambert comformal conic projection. Standard parallels 33° & 45°

Elevation
in feet

3,491
2,500
2,000
1,500
1,000
500
Sea Level

NEW HAMPSHIRE

VERMONT

Wilmington · 9 · Brattleboro

NEW YORK

101

North Adams
Mt Greylock 3,491 ▲
Adams
Hinsdale

12

202

Winchendon

Athol · Gardner

2

Greenfield
Ashfield

Spencer

Quabbin Reservoir

91

Amherst

Ware

Northampton

202

Holyoke

90

Southbridge
Webster

Pittsfield

Lenox

BERKSHIRE HILLS

Stockbridge

Great Barrington · Otis

20

23

New Boston

57

Westfield

Springfield

57

Somers

190

NEW YORK

Amenia

44

Canaan

8

202

Winsted

20

202

84

Putnam

44

Cornwall

63

Torrington

44

Vernon

Storrs

6

Litchfield

Kent

7

202

8

4

HARTFORD ✦

East Hartford

Manchester

Willimantic

New Milford

69

New Britain

Wethersfield

2

66

Colchester

Norwich

Waterbury

84

Middletown

Higganum

11

82

395

Meriden

Danbury

34

Derby

15

Hamden

5

Guilford

85

12

6

684

33

New Haven

95

Clinton

Old Saybrook

Essex

1

New London

Mystic

2

Milford
Stratford

Bridgeport

Westport

Norwalk

95

1

15

Stamford

Greenwich

1

Long Island Sound

Orient Point

Shelter

FISHERS ISLAND

PLUM ISLAND

GARDINERS ISLAND

Gardiners Bay

Sag Harbor

Amagansett

LONG ISLAND

Port Jefferson Station

Setauket

Riverhead

NEW YORK

Milford · 13
Nashua · 13 · Hudson
Haverhill · Newburyport
Lawrence · 1
Lowell · 93
Fitchburg · 495 · 95 · Reading · Essex · Rockport · CAPE ANN
Leominster · 2 · 114 · Gloucester · 128
Maynard · Concord · Salem · MARBLEHEAD NECK
90 · 110 · Marlborough · Cambridge · Lynn · DEER ISLAND
Worcester · 290 · 20 · ☆ BOSTON · POINT ALLERTON
Natick · 115 · Quincy · Boston Bay
Milford · 109 · 93 · 3A · Scituate
Franklin · 24 · 3
16 · Easton · Brockton · 18 · 106
Woonsocket · 146 · 95 · 495 · 44
scoag · 44 · 1 · Plymouth · GURNET POINT · Plymouth Bay · Provincetown · RACE POINT · CAPE COD
PROVIDENCE · ☆ · 44 · 44 · 3 · Cape Cod Bay · Eastham
6 · Fall River · 105 · 140 · 3A · Sandwich · Yarmouth · 6
195 · 28 · Hyannis · 28 · Chatham
New Bedford · 24 · MONOMOY ISLAND
95 · Wickford · 138 · Falmouth · Woods Hole · Nantucket Sound
Wakefield · Newport · ELIZABETH ISLANDS · Vineyard Haven · Oak Bluffs · GREAT POINT
esterly · POINT JUDITH · Rhode Island Sound · CUTTYHUNK I · Edgartown · Nantucket
GAY HEAD · MARTHA'S VINEYARD · Muskeget Channel · NANTUCKET ISLAND
NO MANS LAND

Massachusetts Bay · Buzzards Bay · Vineyard Sound

Block Island Sound · Block Island · BLOCK ISLAND · AUK POINT

SOUTHERN NEW ENGLAND

VERMONT · NEW HAMPSHIRE · Portland · MAINE
Albany · Concord
NEW YORK · MASSACHUSETTS · Boston
Hartford · Providence
CONNECTICUT · RHODE ISLAND
Newark · NEW JERSEY · NEW YORK
Philadelphia

0 · 10 · 20 Miles
0 · 10 · 20 · 30 Kilometers

N · W · E · S

CLIMATE CHART	TEMPERATURES				RECORDS		PRECIPITATION				ANNUAL	
Weather Station	Jan	Apr	Jul	Oct	High	Low	Jan	Apr	Jul	Oct	Rain	Snow
Boston	36/23	56/41	81/65	63/48	104°	-18°	4.0"	3.7"	2.7"	3.4"	44"	40"
Provincetown	38/25	52/37	78/62	61/46	104°	-6°	3.9"	3.5"	2.7"	3.4"	40"	39"
Nantucket	38/25	51/38	75/61	61/48	100°	-6°	4.3"	4.0"	2.7"	3.1"	44"	32"
Stockbridge	32/13	56/33	79/56	61/37	97°	-29°	3.8"	3.8"	4.5"	2.9"	43"	67"
Hartford	33/16	59/37	84/61	62/36	102°	-26°	3.4"	3.9"	3.2"	3.6"	44"	46"
New Haven	37/22	56/38	81/63	64/44	101°	-15°	4.0"	3.9"	3.4"	3.5"	46"	37"
Norfolk	30/13	53/37	78/57	58/38	101°	-37°	4.3"	4.5"	4.2"	4.1"	54"	101"
Providence	36/21	57/38	81/63	64/43	104°	-17°	3.9"	4.2"	3.2"	3.6"	45"	39"
Block Island	37/25	52/39	76/64	61/48	95°	-10°	4.0"	4.2"	3.1"	3.3"	42"	21"

INTRODUCTION

A FRIEND OF MINE, A JAZZ MUSICIAN living in Western Massachusetts, recently returned from an engagement at three in the morning. Two hours later he was woken by his ringing telephone. It was the neighboring farmer calling for a chat. "Do you have any idea what time it is?" the musician snarled. "Sure," the 80 year-old Yankee replied. "Time to get up." New England had just disciplined another newcomer.

Over the centuries this small place has grown not only layers of history but barnacles of character. It knows what it is and—just as importantly—what it is not. It is not, for instance, California. New Englanders may tell you to have a nice day, but they would prefer you to have a productive one. Preferably with a little adversity thrown in to stiffen your spine. When the temperature drops to 20 below and New Englanders say, "Bit nippy," they are celebrating not complaining.

Like some of the region's other emblems—the white spire on the Common, the red barn in the snow, Boston's rigidity, Connecticut's ingenuity—the obstinate New England character is now only part of the story in a place deluged by mass culture. But living here is, for the most part, still a serious business. Winter sees to that, tipping the equation of work + adversity = virtue clearly in weather's favor.

Winter is not, however, the real test of Yankee application. Autumn is—September and October days so perfect that they immobilize the busiest worker, vaporizing his intentions and condemning him to stare helplessly at the golden world around him.

Visitors may, of course, stare in any season. And this book encourages the practice, whether you are contemplating a Federal mansion or an island sunset. It largely avoids the shopping malls, suburbs, and major highways of Massachusetts, Connecticut, and Rhode Island—wastelands indistinguishable from thousands of others across the country—instead choosing byways where surprises lurk and people still know what time it is. So don't be alarmed if you find yourself in a dreamy hilltop graveyard picnicking among the winged skull headstones. And when a local farmer drives by, try not to look as if you're enjoying yourself too much.

O V E R V I E W

SOUTHERN NEW ENGLAND
Massachusetts, Connecticut, and
Rhode Island together form one of the
nation's richest regions, historically and
culturally. They also offer a wide variety
of landscapes and coastal settings, street
life and wildlife. Drive for just a couple
of hours and you can trade cultural
urban pleasures for a wilderness inhabited by black bear or for a rugged Atlantic seashore.

OVERVIEW

1 BOSTON AREA

Site of pivotal events in America's history, Boston's historic neighborhoods
are vibrantly intact, retaining their distinctive immigrant stamp just as the
Isabella Stewart Gardner Museum still
projects its founder's vision. The towns
of Lexington and Concord preserve
Revolutionary War sites alongside literary shrines like Walden Pond.

2 NORTH SHORE

The coast north of Boston, encompassing rocky Cape Ann, packs a
wealth of natural beauty and good
food into its small area. Salem preserves its witch trial history in several
sites and its seafaring glory on beautiful Chestnut Street and in the Peabody
Essex Museum. An afternoon's drive
takes you through fishing towns, ele-
gant Ipswich, and treasure-filled Marblehead, leaving time for a walk on the beach.

3 SOUTH SHORE, CAPE COD, ISLANDS

Plimoth Plantation, south of Boston, is living history at its most intelligent and engrossing, while Cape Cod is a popular holiday destination with 50 spectacular miles of protected national seashore. Here you may watch birds or whales and enjoy solitary beach walks, ethereal Wellfleet ponds, or the exotic pleasures of Provincetown. The lovely islands of Martha's Vineyard and Nantucket have a lively tourist trade, an exceptionally rich seafaring history, and a sizeable amount of open land.

4 INTERIOR MASSACHUSETTS

With its forested wilderness, historic villages, gentle hills, and empty backroads, the Massachusetts interior is one of the region's best-kept secrets. Drive west beyond the Boston suburbs, and you reach the Connecticut River Valley and the Berkshire Hills, where you may explore historic Deerfield and Old Sturbridge Village, hike the slopes of Mount Greylock, or discover museums offering a variety of art from Renaissance masters to Norman Rockwell.

5 & 6 INTERIOR CONNECTICUT

With the commercial city of Hartford at its core, central Connecticut has some of the state's loveliest historic towns—Wethersfield being the most notable—as well as exceptional art museums. Noticeably rural by contrast, the northeast corner encloses the undulating Woodstock Valley, a quiet retreat ideal for hiking, biking,

and picnicking. To the west, the Litchfield Hills are not only beautiful but sophisticated, offering pretty hill towns and picturesque river valleys; exquisite flower farms and nature preserves; plus summer arts festivals and general stores that sell gourmet foods.

7 CONNECTICUT COAST

Stretching along Long Island Sound from the Rhode Island border to the New York suburbs, the Connecticut coast provides a variety of urban, seafaring, and even semi-rural pleasures. Contrasts are remarkable. A short drive takes you from a charming fishing village like Stonington to the neo-Tudor cocoon of Yale University; or from the salty past at Mystic Seaport, the nation's most remarkable maritime museum, to the bucolic landscape around picture-perfect Old Lyme. There are numerous beaches of both the family-filled and the bird-filled kind.

8 RHODE ISLAND

A small jewel tucked away in New England's southeastern pocket, Rhode Island encircles bewitching Narragansett Bay and draws you to the ocean whatever your route. But there is more to the tiny state than pristine beaches, dreamy marshland, and outstanding seafood. In Newport, history comes alive in Gilded Age mansions and is palpable on the town's busy wharves and elegant streets. The Tiverton–Little Compton peninsula is a quiet green delight, while Providence is a charmingly eccentric city with sublime historic neighborhoods and a distinct Italian accent. Then there is the gem within the jewel: glorious Block Island.

LANDSCAPE & HISTORY

SOUTHERN NEW ENGLAND IS BOTH THE THRESHOLD and the edge of the North American continent. Approach the region from the east and you arrive on the nation's doorstep, from the west and you soon run out of land. Either way, you will notice the sudden change in scale. After the broad sweep of the Atlantic or the numbing expanse of the heartland, this compact corner of the Northeast seems improbably small, too modest a patch to contain a major slice of the nation's history and culture.

■ RIVER VALLEYS AND PLEATED COASTLINES

Massachusetts, Connecticut, and Rhode Island combined are less than half the size of neighboring New York State. What these three states lack in spaciousness, however, they make up for in complexity. The pleated coastline of Narragansett Bay in Rhode Island or Buzzard's Bay in Massachusetts doubles back on itself every few miles, like the creation of a demented fretworker, intent on fitting in just one more cove, one more inlet, before the tide turns. The course of the Connecticut River is straightforward by comparison, but its valleys and tributaries perform their own impressive contortions. Folding in on each other, they swallow time and schedules, conspiring to lose you in their undulating switchbacks.

With its often jagged seashore and its dreamy interior, this is a subversive place that slows you down and undermines first impressions. From the summit of Mount Wachusett in central Massachusetts, for example, you see mature forest in every direction, but you are looking at land that was open pasture just a hundred years ago. Today, much of the landscape is dominated by trees that gradually reclaimed the fields abandoned by disillusioned farmers. In a region known for its human achievement and endurance, even the vegetation is a study in persistence.

The setting for so much of the nation's historical drama was itself shaped by ancient cataclysm and upheaval. Eight million years ago, molten rock expelled from the Earth's core formed the Appalachian Mountain Range, which extends from northern Maine south to Georgia. Cycles of erosion and accretion followed, the most significant occurring in the twilight of the last ice age, some 11,000 years ago, when the glacier covering New England retreated, strewing boulders, gouging ponds, and shaping the land we see today.

(opposite) "Something there is that does not love a wall," wrote Robert Frost, but stone walls served not only as boundaries but as a convenient place to pile the rocks that filled New England's fields.

The region's most distinctive landmarks are consequently some of the continent's most ancient formations. The 65-mile-long Cape Cod peninsula, for example, is the glacier's handiwork, as are the islands of Martha's Vineyard and Nantucket. Bunker Hill is a glacial drumlin and Thoreau's Walden Pond a glacial pothole. The ice sheet even favored tiny Rhode Island with altitude in the form of demure but charming Badger Mountain, which kept its head 700 feet above sea level when the glacial meltdown raised the surrounding ocean. There are more dramatic peaks to the north—Mount Washington in New Hampshire, for instance—but they are young upstarts compared to their venerable southern cousins.

The most insulated visitor, cocooned in an automobile, cannot help noticing that Southern New England is chiefly a place of water and rock. Whatever your route, you will find yourself tracing the arc of the ocean, the meanderings of a river or stream in a region that has over 2,000 miles of coastline and is bisected by the major waterways of the Connecticut, the Merrimack, and the Housatonic Rivers. Even solid Boston is an amphibian city that started life as a humble peninsula and grew by accumulating marshy landfill that still feels soggy underfoot.

Rock is the other key player here. At its most benevolent it forms two groups of rolling hills: the Berkshire Hills in Massachusetts and the Litchfield Hills in Connecticut, both rising close to the eastern border with New York State. These are tasteful rather than grandiose protuberances, substantial enough to give the region beauty and backbone, but gradual enough to inspire affection rather than awe.

Sailors and farmers alike, however, will vouch for the malevolence of New England rock. At its most treacherous, it spikes the coastline and surrounding ocean and has been lethal to shipping, particularly in the 19th-century maritime heyday. Inland, rock presents a different challenge. Each spring, in all but the most fertile river valleys, groundfrost propels a fresh crop of stones and mini-boulders to the surface—a reminder that ice can still rearrange things.

This small, defiant place is an oddity on the continent. Here the American dictum that bigger is better never took hold. Instead a more subtle theory is demonstrated: that landscape shapes the people who shape history.

■ FIRST PEOPLE

A crude version of Southern New England's history rests on what might be called the motion-sensor theory. The first Pilgrim sets foot on Plymouth Rock in 1620, trips the motion sensor, and a dormant landscape is suddenly flooded with light and humming with activity. The soundtrack is activated and—surprise—it's in English! Historical fact is not that tidy, however.

The first people to discover New England came not by sea but overland, descendants of nomadic hunters who had crossed from Asia to Alaska in a series of migrations beginning thousands of years ago. These groups merged, evolved, multiplied, and broke apart into subgroups, eventually making their way from the Pacific to the Atlantic seaboard. Archaeological evidence has concluded that the early tribal groups which established themselves in New England were composed of nomadic hunters and fishermen who used very basic stone implements, but had not yet developed pottery or more refined tools such as axes.

By the end of the 15th century, perhaps as many as 100,000 Native Americans had established settlements east of the Hudson River, where they introduced pottery making and agriculture. Charting the New England coast in 1615, Capt. John Smith reported "large fields of corn and great troops of well-

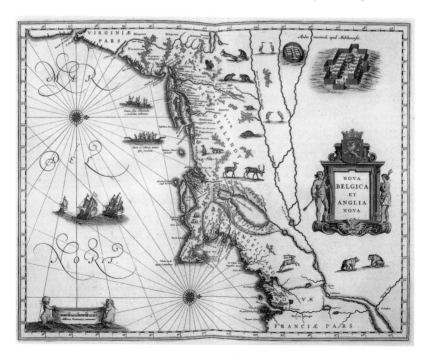

This 1635 Dutch map is drawn from an unusual perspective: with west at the top of the map, and north to the right.

proportioned people." Encounters between Europeans and Native Americans had increased throughout the previous century. In 1578, for example, roughly 400 vessels from France, Portugal, England, and Spain were busy fishing and whaling off New England, and most traded with the natives.

At their peak, tribes belonging to the Algonquian language group covered an area ranging from the Florida coast to the Canadian Maritimes and west to the Mississippi. New England, in its early colonial period, was inhabited by 10 Algonquian tribes, and today's place names commemorate some of them—the Massachusetts, Narragansetts, Penobscots, and Pocumtucs, for example. Others like the Mohicans, Abenakis, Pequots and Nipmucks were immortalized by James Fenimore Cooper, the 19th-century novelist who founded what Mark Twain derisively termed "the broken twig school of realism."

◆ WAMPANOAG LAND

The Pilgrims who came ashore on Cape Cod in 1620, stepping onto Wampanoag land, had little reason to anticipate serious opposition. In his 1616 "Description of New England"—surely the region's first tourist brochure—Capt. John Smith had downplayed native hostility to English encroachment, preferring to dwell on New England's bountiful seas and invigorating climate.

As it turned out, the Pilgrims were met by a severely weakened people. The plague of 1616 and 1617 had reduced the native population to such an extent that by 1631, the dominant Massachusett tribe would number only about 500. Even at their healthiest, the New England tribes had never centralized their power as the Iroquois did in New York. Recurring intertribal warfare consequently made a unified defense against the settlers unlikely. A small band of Wampanoags did fire arrows at Myles Standish and his exploring party while the Mayflower rode at anchor off Provincetown. They were doubtless recalling the English slave traders who, just six years earlier, had kidnapped their kin, selling them in Spain. That brief resistance is commemorated today by a modest plaque on the dunes outside Eastham.

Weakness alone cannot explain the Native American response to the early settlers, however. Goodwill and trust—however misplaced—also played a part.

A portrait of Ninigret, chief of Rhode Island's Niantic Indians, relatives of the Narragansett tribe. He was made chief of the Narragansetts by the English for aiding them in 1675 during King Philip's War. Ninigret refused to become a Christian, instead telling the missionaries to "go and make the English good first." (Museum of Art, Rhode Island School of Design)

◆ SAMOSET AND SQUANTO

On a March day in 1621, a lone Native American appeared on Leyden Street, Plymouth, greeting the alarmed citizens with the words "Welcome, Englishmen." Thanks to Samoset, that respected Massachusett, and to Squanto, a Pawtuxet, a 50-year peace treaty was drawn up the following month between the settlers and Massasoit, chief of the Wampanoags. Squanto, who had been taken to England by George Weymouth in 1605, had returned to New England in 1615 and six years later offered himself as an interpreter and guide to the Pilgrims. Showing them where to plant, hunt, and fish, equipping them for life in the wilderness, Squanto became a shining example of the "Good Indian" who even converted to Christianity on his deathbed.

◆ NARRAGANSETTS AND PEQUOTS

Not all Native Americans were cooperative. The Narragansetts of interior Massachusetts and the formidable Pequots in eastern Connecticut remained hostile, launching sporadic raids on frontier settlements. The English response was predictable. In 1636, the citizens of Boston, Hartford, Wethersfield, and Windsor, aided by the Mohicans, mounted an attack on the Pequots and largely exterminated them. Survivors were sold to the Bermudans who complained that as slaves the Pequots were "sullen and treacherous." They subsequently became known as fearless sailors and whalers.

The brutal Pequot War and the relentless expansion of settlements across New England ended the honeymoon between the English and Native Americans. Even some colonists were enraged by European imperialism. "Why lay such stress upon your patent from King James?" Rhode Island founder Roger Williams demanded in a letter to Governor Bradford. "James has no more right to give away or sell Massasoit's lands and cut and carve his country than Massasoit has to sell King James' kingdom or to send Indians to colonize Warwickshire."

◆ KING PHILIP'S WAR

While Williams protested, Metacom (or King Philip), the Wampanoag leader, prepared for war. As he saw it, only a simultaneous attack by all tribes of the North Atlantic seaboard would end the encroachment that threatened to eradicate the native population. To that end, Philip built tribal alliances and planned a concerted offensive. War was precipitated in June 1675, however, when Sassamon,

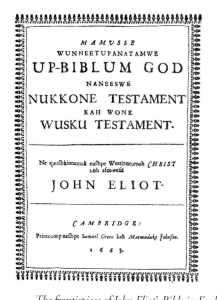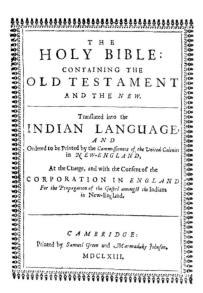

The frontispiece of John Eliot's Bible in English and that of his Algonquian translation.

who had leaked Philip's plans to the Governor at Plymouth, was killed and six Wampanoags were convicted of the murder and executed. Philip attacked Swansea, Massachusetts, and appeared unstoppable until he traveled to enlist the Narragansetts' support. In a swamp outside present-day Kingston, Rhode Island, he and the entire Narragansett nation were encircled and defeated.

Before the outbreak of King Philip's War, the native people of Southern New England has been largely, if superficially, Christianized. John Eliot, the Algonquian-speaking "Apostle to the Indians," established centers of Christian education in which tribal leaders held town offices. The first of these "praying towns" was founded at Natick, Massachusetts, in 1651 and Eliot later promoted higher education for his converts. Harvard's first brick building was constructed for Native American students, and Caleb Cheeshahteamuck graduated from that university in 1665. But Eliot's brand of Christian idealism was another casualty of King Philip's War. Six years after that conflict, just four out of 30 praying towns survived.

Today, approximately 12,000 Native Americans remain in New England. The Wampanoags inhabit ancestral land at Gay Head on Martha's Vineyard, and in Mashpee, Massachusetts. The Connecticut tribes use their special status to override state anti-gambling laws and operate the nation's largest casino.

■ COMMONWEALTH OF THE ELECT: 1614–1690

Throughout most of the 17th century, England was more interested in bypassing than settling the American continent. Visions of the fabled Northwest Passage to the golden East drew English explorers who doubtless regarded the rocky coast of Southern New England as a poor consolation prize.

◆ CAPTAIN JOHN SMITH

Giovanni Caboto (known as John Cabot) did think New England worth claiming in 1497 for his patron, King Henry VII of England, and Bartholomew Gosnold, commanding the *Concord,* explored the coast from Maine to Rhode Island in 1602. But Capt. John Smith, exploring the area in 1614, was the first to call it New England and to advertise its charms.

A shameless self-promoter, Smith is best known from the Pocahontas episode, which he surely embellished. His equally colorful "Description of New England" was not an immediately successful sales pitch, however. Most English adventurers preferred the well-established Virginia colony, which promised instant tobacco fortunes. "I am not so simple to think," Smith wrote in his description, "that ever any other motive than wealth, will ever erect there a Commonweale; or draw companie from their ease and humours at home, to stay in New England."

There he was mistaken. The settlement of New England was, above all, a religious act, begun when the *Mayflower* set sail from Plymouth, England, in August 1620 and consolidated with the formation of the Massachusetts Bay Colony nine years later and the subsequent settlement of Connecticut and Rhode Island. The *Mayflower's* 102 passengers were not fortune hunters but religious separatists who came ashore at Provincetown, Cape Cod, on a bleak November day in 1620 with a mission. Having rejected "decadent" English Protestantism, they would establish a settlement based on God's ordinance as revealed in the Bible. We identify them as Puritans, a term they would have regarded as an insult.

◆ PILGRIM FOUNDERS

The Pilgrim Founders, as they became known, expected hardship and were not disappointed. Even after the move from Provincetown to the more sheltered Plymouth, half of the group died during that first bitter winter, most from scurvy and exposure. The "Plimoth Plantation" survived, however, with the help of the Native

Americans and under the leadership of William Bradford, who would govern the colony until his death in 1657. A three-day feast in the autumn of 1621 celebrated the first corn crop and gave the nation what is still, appropriately, its least commercial holiday: Thanksgiving.

◆ JOHN WINTHROP

Plymouth was both a toehold and an example. By 1629, English settlers of all religious persuasions (or none) had established fishing and trading stations along much of the coast. That same year the Massachusetts Bay Colony, a solidly Puritan enterprise, was formed as a joint-stock corporation, with its office in London, its colonial base at Salem, and 41-year-old John Winthrop at its head.

Winthrop's account of the *Arabella's* 1630 voyage to New England reveals, among other things, the Puritan cure for seasickness. A rope was slung from the steerage to the mainmast and those who "lay groaning in their cabins" were required to "sway it up and down till they were warm, and by this means they soon grew well and merry." Human frailty—like nature itself—was to be conquered, not indulged. That principle was both enshrined and enforced in early New England.

The wilderness had already seduced some colonists, however—most notably Thomas Morton, who erected a maypole at hedonistic Merrymount near Quincy, Massachusetts, in 1627. What followed, according to Governor Bradford, was "drinking and dancing aboute it many days togeather, inviting the Indean women for their consorts, dancing and frisking togither…and worse practises." Morton was shipped back to England in 1628, when even non-Puritan settlers became alarmed by his casual trade in firearms with the Native Americans. After Merrymount, bountiful seas and native temptations continued to derail many Christian zealots. In 1641, John White even complained that New Englanders were becoming "exceedingly rude, more likely to turne heathen than to turne others to the Christian faith."

◆ LEARNING AND PIETY

Occasional backsliding could not undermine a vigilant society that believed, above all, in its own perfectibility. By 1630, Boston had become the vigorous center of the Massachusetts Bay Colony. As 17th-century historian Thomas Fuller wrote of the Puritan enterprise, "Knowledge caused piety, and piety bred industry." Citizens had to be able to read the Bible in order to follow God's law, and in 1649

The first governor of the Massachusetts Bay Colony, John Winthrop.
(American Antiquarian Society, Worcester, Mass.)

Massachusetts required every town of 50 householders to maintain a grammar school. The idea of vanquishing Satan with education produced the country's first college—Harvard University, founded in 1636—and one of the most literate populations in history. Toward the end of the 17th century, the literacy rate in New England is estimated to have been between 89 and 95 percent for men and around 62 percent for women.

Not all publications were religious. Mary Rowlandson's account of her captivity among the Indians appeared in 1682, histories of the settlement began to appear as early as 1622, and Anne Bradstreet's remarkable poems—many prefiguring the work of Emily Dickinson—were first published in 1650.

The belief that literacy was not only everyone's duty but everyone's right certainly prepared the ground for the seeds of democracy. Germination would, however, be slow. Winthrop and his associates replaced English feudalism not with democracy but with theocracy. The secret ballot was permitted in 1635, but in the early years only church members or "visible saints" were eligible to elect the governor, deputy governor, and assistants who ran the colony. The practice was hardly egalitarian. It did, however, make social status irrelevant. While a rich man rejected by a congregation could not vote, the most indigent church member could elect his rulers. The following year a row over taxation ushered in representative government in Massachusetts Bay when freemen demanded representation in the legislating body of the Great and General Court.

COMMON COASTERS, UNPROFITABLE FOWLERS, AND TOBACCO TAKERS

*I*t is ordered by this Court and the Authorite therof, that no person, housholder or other, shall spend his time idlely or unproffitably under pain of such punishment as the Court of Assistants or County Court shall think meet to inflict. And for this end it is ordered that the Constable of everie place shall use speciall care and diligence to take knowledge of offenders in this kinde, especially of common coasters, unprofitable fowlers, and tobacco takers.

—*Laws and Libertyes,* taken from *Builders of the Bay Colony,* 1648

◆ DISSENTERS

Fiscal dissent was one thing; theological dissent, however, was another. Depending on their brazenness, those who expressed "new and dangerous opinions" in the colony were banished, beaten, or hanged. As the Puritans saw it, the execution of Quaker Mary Dyer was as necessary as the "divine slaughter" of whole tribes in the Pequot War of 1636 and King Philip's War of 1675-1676. Both were, after all, impediments to God's work.

Transplanted dissenters quickly marked out their own territory. "Forced worship stinks in God's nostrils," Roger Williams declared before fleeing Salem in 1635 to establish a remarkably tolerant settlement at Providence, Rhode Island. "Purchased with love" from the natives, the new colony insisted on the separation of church and state. Thomas Hooker and his congregation left Cambridge in 1636 to establish a more open community at Hartford, Connecticut. Two years later, heretical Anne Hutchinson, who, according to one follower "Preaches better Gospell than any of your black-coates that have been at the Ninneversity," established her community at Portsmouth, Rhode Island. William Coddington, another religious exile, in 1639 settled in Newport, a town that soon became a haven for Quakers and Jews. Connecticut and Rhode Island received royal charters permitting the colonists to administer their political and financial affairs in 1662 and 1663 respectively.

◆ SALEM'S PARANOIA

The 17th century drew to a close in a spasm of paranoia in Massachusetts at tiny Salem village, and it is not entirely fanciful to interpret its Witch Trials in 1690 as the hysterical reaction of religious zealots besieged by uncontrollable change.

Whatever the interpretation, it is unfortunate that Salem Village gave the world its crude image of the Puritan: a humorless, guilt-racked man with a tall hat and tortured conscience. Often ignored is the independence of spirit, commitment to self-rule, and plainness of expression that contributed so much to American political and cultural life.

Boston cleric Cotton Mather, author of The Wonders of the Invisible World *(right), initially supported but later helped to end the witchcraft hysteria of 1692. (Massachusetts Historical Society)*

The Wonders of the Invisible World.

OBSERVATIONS

As well *Historical* as *Theological*, upon the NATURE, the NUMBER, and the OPERATIONS of the

DEVILS.

Accompany'd with,

I. Some Accounts of the Grievous Molestations, by DÆMONS and WITCHCRAFTS, which have lately annoy'd the Countrey; and the Trials of some eminent *Malefactors* Executed upon occasion thereof: with several Remarkable *Curiosities* therein occurring.

II. Some Counsils, Directing a due Improvement of the terrible things, lately done, by the Unusual & Amazing Range of EVIL SPIRITS, in Our Neighbourhood: & the methods to prevent the *Wrongs* which those *Evil Angels* may intend against all sorts of people among us; especially in Accusations of the Innocent.

III. Some Conjectures upon the great EVENTS, likely to befall, the WORLD in General, and NEW-ENGLAND in Particular; as also upon the Advances of the TIME, when we shall see BETTER DAYES.

IV A short Narrative of a late Outrage committed by a knot of WITCHES in *Swedeland*, very much Resembling, and so far Explaining, *That* under which our parts of *America* have laboured!

V. THE DEVIL DISCOVERED: In a Brief Discourse upon those TEMPTATIONS, which are the more Ordinary *Devices* of the Wicked One.

By **Cotton Mather.**

Boston Printed by *Benj. Harris* for *Sam. Phillips.* 1693.

■ REVOLUTION AND THE
REPUBLIC OF REASON: 1701–1789

"A Bostonian would seek his fortune in the bottom of hell," Felix de Beaujoir declared in 1712 as New England's wealth and commercial appetite grew and economics replaced theology as the region's motivating force.

Boston's population reached 12,000 by the mid-18th century, and a new merchant class established itself, chiefly on the booming West Indies trade. With fair winds and the right connections, a merchant's fortune could be made on one voyage. In the "Triangle Trade" for example, New England products—chief among them rum—were exchanged for slaves on Africa's west coast. Those slaves were then sold or traded in the West Indies for molasses and sugar, vital for rum distillation. Maritime supplies and fish were also sold to West Indian slave plantations. The Rhode Island ports of Bristol and Newport reaped huge profits from the Caribbean slave-trade. Even minor towns like Salem, Marblehead, and Essex grew rich on shipbuilding and mackerel and cod fishing, while later in the 19th century whaling outposts like New Bedford, New London, Provincetown, and the islands of Nantucket and Martha's Vineyard profited from the demand for lighting and lubricating oils.

◆ INTELLECTUAL GROWTH AND PERSONAL CONFIDENCE

Southern New England was also growing intellectually. Harvard University expanded. Yale University was established at New Haven, Connecticut, in 1701 and Brown University at Providence, Rhode Island, in 1764, both as religious institutions. A highly literate populace soon demanded a selection of newspapers and periodicals, the first of which was *The Boston News Letter*, published in 1704. Gradually a vibrant, homegrown culture replaced the transplanted English variety.

The combination of deeply rooted defiance and newfound confidence was incendiary. "I am as good flesh and blood as you…you may goe out of the way," a carter replied when Governor Dudley ordered the man and his load of wood out of the road one December day in 1705. The individual was jailed for a year, but his kind would have the last word in the ensuing conflict between a willful populace and an exploitative monarchy.

A view of Harvard Yard in 1726. (Massachusetts Historical Society)

◆ REVOLUTIONARY WAR

Direct taxes levied between 1764 and 1772—the Sugar Act, Currency Act, and Stamp Act among them—sparked widespread boycotts and mob violence. In 1770, British soldiers opened fire after being attacked by a crowd in Boston, killing five protesters in what became known as the Boston Massacre. Three years later, agitators boarded the East India Company's vessels in Boston Harbor and dumped their tea cargo overboard to protest the Tea Act of 1773. The British responded in 1774 with a series of punitive measures known as The Intolerable Acts, which struck at the heart of Massachusetts self-government and prompted the colonists to consider united resistance in the First Continental Congress.

Events soon overtook policy, however. By the time the Second Continental Congress assembled in 1775, the Massachusetts "Minutemen" had faced the British at Lexington and Concord, the first fatalities had occurred on both sides, and 16,000 New England colonists held the British forces under siege in Boston. New England's drama intensified demands for independence throughout the American colonies. Radical members of the Second Continental Congress in Philadelphia, prevailing over strong conservative opposition, moved to transform the colonial force into a Continental Army with Gen. George Washington in command, to introduce a separate currency, to form foreign alliances, and to issue a "Declaration of Causes for Taking up Arms."

On May 4, 1776, the Rhode Island colony and Providence Plantation renounced allegiance to King George III, provoking the British to occupy the region. Compromise was unthinkable, and the Declaration of Independence, formulated by Thomas Jefferson, was adopted on July 4, 1776.

Washington's victory in Boston (the British withdrew on March 17, 1776) was a decisive event, and key Boston figures such as Samuel Adams, John Hancock, and John Adams became leaders in the Revolutionary cause. Having ignited the conflict, however, New England subsequently played a backstage role, harassing British shipping and supplying the Continental Army with men, ships, and munitions.

(above) British troops open fire on a civilian mob in Paul Revere's classic illustration of the Boston Massacre. (Massachusetts Historical Society)

(opposite) Colonists dressed as Indians throw English tea overboard in the Boston Tea Party.

■ REPUBLIC OF INDUSTRY AND VIRTUE

Southern New England's fortunes had always been shaped by the ocean. In the 19th century, however, the region's newest form of wealth would be generated by the rivers. When Samuel Slater built the first water-powered cotton mill, beside the Blackstone River in Pawtucket, Rhode Island, in 1793, American textile manufacturing was transformed. A home craft industry became one of mass production, and Southern New England's industrial revolution had begun. In 1805, the mill town of Slatersville was founded, and soon river banks across the three states were dotted with communities built around the factory rather than the meeting house. Even after the 1803 introduction of the high-pressure steam engine, 90 percent of New England manufacturing remained water powered.

Ralph Waldo Emerson, Henry David Thoreau, Thomas Fuller, and their colleagues

The Ayer Mill in Lawrence was one of the largest textile mills in New England. Today, it boasts the second largest clockface in the world, after Big Ben.

Private signals of the sea merchants of Boston, circa 1840. Some of the merchants identified are still in business today. (Private collection.)

were among the sharpest critics of the industrial age that now defined New England. "This invasion of Nature by Trade with its Money, its Credit, its Steam, its Railroad, threatens to upset the balance of man," Emerson wrote in 1836 when the Transcendental Club first assembled in his Concord, Massachusetts house. Inspired by Goethe, Wordsworth, and other Romantic poets, the transcendentalists regarded nature as the savior of man's spiritual vision. That belief did not require complete withdrawal from society, however. Emerson, for example, hosted large luncheon and dinner parties in his comfortable Concord house while sharpening his indictments of the material world.

◆ THOREAU'S WALDEN POND

Thoreau, on the other hand, built a cabin on Emerson's wood lot at nearby Walden Pond in 1845, planted a two-and-a-half-acre garden, perplexed his hardworking neighbors, and defied the tax collectors. "I did not wish to live what was not life, living is so dear," he wrote in *Walden, or Life in the Woods* (1854). Though an extreme practitioner of the transcendentalist creed, Thoreau was neither as reclusive nor as politically disengaged as is often imagined. He did dismiss the Lowell economic miracle, saying: "I cannot believe that our factory system is the best mode by which men may get clothing." But his opposition to the 1850 Fugitive Slave Law, which required Americans to return escaped slaves as chattel, was more provocative. "I would remind my countrymen that they are to be men first, and Americans only at a late and convenient hour," he wrote. "This law rises not to the level of the head or the reason, its natural habitat is in the dirt."

◆ CONFIDENT, PRACTICAL IDEALISTS

The society from which Thoreau seceded was buoyantly confident, secure in its position as the nation's cultural capital, and immune to the idealist's subversive judgments. To the rest of the world, after all, New England in the mid-19th century represented not just industrial and commercial ingenuity but literary and intellectual vitality. Herman Melville, Henry Wadsworth Longfellow, James Russell Lowell, William Dean Howells, Louisa May Alcott, Harriet Beecher Stowe, Richard Henry Dana, and Francis Parkman were just some of the writers associated with Boston. In the fine arts, James Abbott McNeill Whistler of Lowell and Bostonian Winslow Homer drew international acclaim while John Singer Sargent's portraits immortalized Boston's upper class. Mark Twain, living in Hartford, Connecticut, became a literary celebrity and Emily Dickinson, writing poetry in

Amherst, Massachusetts, remained an unknown genius.

Like transcendentalism, labor unrest barely ruffled the new commercial aristocracy. Agitation for a 10-hour factory day, spearheaded chiefly by the Lowell women workers, did prompt the first government investigation of labor conditions in the United States, begun in Massachusetts in 1845. The findings, however, were splendidly abstract. "The remedy," the committee finally concluded, "is not with us. We look for it in the progressive improvement in art and science, in a higher appreciation of man's destiny, in a less love for money." Practical reform would be postponed until the end of the century.

New England, the birthplace of abolitionism, was also the first region to answer President Lincoln's call to arms in 1861, after Southern states began to secede from the Union and form the Confederate States of America, a new nation pledged to defend the institution of slavery. Within four days of the President's call on April 15, Massachusetts sent 1,500 men to Fort Monroe, and on the 86th anniversary of the battles of Lexington and Concord, the first Massachusetts blood was shed in the Civil War. Fueled by industrialism as well as idealism—it was the first war in history to draw on the inventiveness of an industrial society—the conflict propelled New England into the modern age.

■ MOVING INTO MODERN TIMES

After the Civil War, New England society was transformed by rapid industrialization. Fishing was still a viable occupation in Southern New England, but whale oil was no longer needed and New Bedford launched its last whaler in 1869.

Profits from large-scale manufacturing created an affluent middle-class for whom Emerson's vision was as irrelevant as John Winthrop's theology of self-denial and rigid authority. The new age needed engineers, and technical institutions such as the notable Massachusetts Institute of Technology and Worcester Polytechnic Institute were founded to produce them.

New England's industry declined at the turn of the 19th century when steam power and lower wages made the South a more profitable manufacturing base, and despite the manufacturing booms of the two world wars, the region never regained its primacy as an industrial center. In the 1980s, however, computer research, development, and manufacturing, along with the biotechnology and defense industries, revitalized Massachusetts and Connecticut in particular. Southern New England's colleges and coastline, along with a tradition of adaptability, continue to be the area's most profitable assets.

B O S T O N   A R E A

■ HIGHLIGHTS

■ TRAVEL BASICS

Boston's winding streets and historic neighborhoods are compact and easily explored on foot. Some of America's most revered historic sights and finest museums are here, while adjacent Cambridge contains famous Harvard University and the Massachusetts Institute of Technology. Water is omnipresent, the Atlantic Ocean lapping the waterfront and the Charles River brimming with sailboats and skiffs. Nearby Lexington and Concord witnessed the legendary first shot of the Revolutionary War and Paul Revere's ride. America's literary history is preserved in sites associated with Ralph Waldo Emerson, Henry David Thoreau, and Louisa May Alcott.

Getting Around: Driving through Boston is challenging and rush hour an endurance test. Travel the city by subway, catching the occasional taxi, and visit outlying towns by car or commuter rail in off-peak hours.

Climate: Summer temperatures range from the comfortable 70s to the muggy 90s. Bostonians prefer seersucker slacks and skirts to shorts, but visitors are excused. Carry a sweater for chilly air conditioning. Spring and autumn are unpredictable but glorious, while winter temperatures typically hover around freezing with an Atlantic bite. Ice makes quaint pavements treacherous, dictating sensible (not sleek) footwear.

Food & Lodging: Restaurants are excellent, from those run by top-name chefs to tiny ethnic enclaves; lodging is mostly hotels, with a few B&Bs or inns. Massachusetts listings begin on page 328; towns are listed in alphabetical order. Listings map page 327; listings chart 375.

■ BOSTON OVERVIEW

In 1699 Edward Ward issued Boston's first tourist advisory:

> The Inhabitants seem very Religious….But tho' they wear in their Faces the Innocence of Doves, you will find them in their Dealings as Subtle as Serpents. Interest is their Faith, money their God, and Large Possessions the only Heaven they covet."

Boston has never been what it seems to be. And that is part of its charm. On paper, the city comes across as a worthy rather than an entirely pleasurable destination. There's all that history and all that good taste to be absorbed. At first glance it may appear statically quaint, like a theme park designed by Ralph Lauren.

But the most fleeting tour destroys both impressions. Just when you conclude that the pale, thin man sitting opposite you on the T—the one in the bow tie who got on at Harvard Square—is a direct *Mayflower* descendant, he greets a friend in Russian. The *Mayflower* descendant is the one with the pin through her nose. Walk through the North End to visit Paul Revere's house, and you will hear more Italian than English spoken. An Irish woman will serve your cannoli in the Sicilian bakery, and that's Cantonese they're speaking outside the Old State House. Boston is all it purports to be: historic, academic, literary, politically liberal, self-consciously stodgy. But it would still give Edward Ward reason to complain. This intimate, surprising city never lost the art of wrong-footing its visitors.

■ BOSTON HISTORY

In *The Flowering of New England,* critic Van Wyck Brooks noted that there were books in Boston when wolves still howled in the hills, thanks to William Blaxton, who first settled the Shawmut peninsula in 1624, bringing with him a library of some 200 volumes. He was joined in 1630 by John Winthrop's colonists, who had quit marshy Charlestown and named their new hillside Trimountaine (the origin of Tremont Street), then later Boston after a Lincolnshire town. It was an unimposing site: 783 acres of glacial bumps connected to the mainland by a narrow causeway, with good fishing and unpredictable weather. Even today—after centuries of leveling, land reclamation, and expansion—the city covers just 46 square miles.

Boston's early survival and later prosperity depended on the sea, a fact that is recognized in the representation of the "Sacred Cod" that still hangs in the State

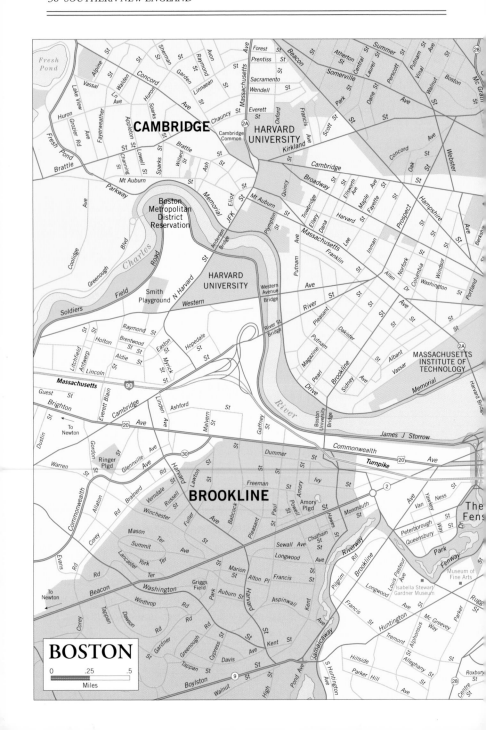

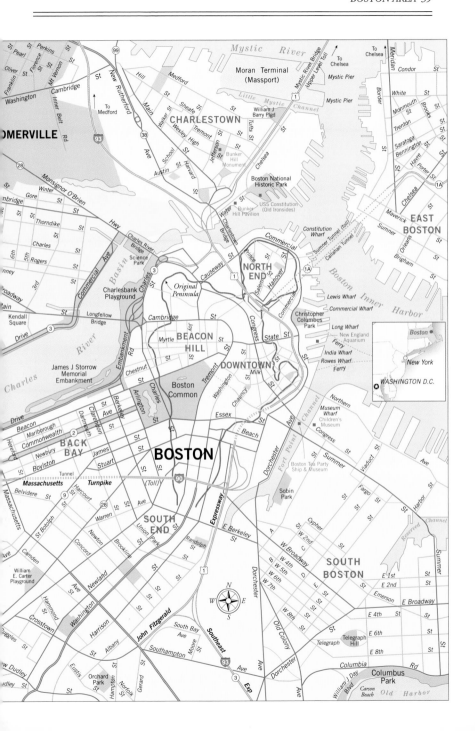

House. The settlement's destiny, in the view of Winthrop and those who governed after him, hinged on its ability to rule itself. When England twice attempted to revoke the colony's charter in the 17th century, Bostonians armed themselves to defend it. A royal governor was appointed in 1691, but Boston merchants enjoyed virtual free trade until 1764 when punitive tariffs were enforced and at first covertly, then violently, opposed.

◆ REVOLUTION IN THE AIR

In 1768, rioting forced the British to dispatch troops to patrol the city's crooked streets, and in 1770 a brawl that became known as the Boston Massacre resulted in the deaths of five colonists on King Street, now State Street. Three years later, tax protesters dumped three shiploads of tea into the harbor, and the British, by turning Boston into a military stronghold, ensured that the city would also become the epicenter of the American Revolution.

In April 1775, news of the British advance on Lexington and Concord was semaphored to Paul Revere by lamplight from the Old North Church, and

Grant Wood's painting Midnight Ride of Paul Revere, *1931. (Metropolitan Museum of Art, Arthur Hoppock Hearn Fund, 1950; 50.117. Photo © 1988, Metropolitan Museum of Art.)*

Civil War woodcarver John Haley Bellamy cut the most famous warship figureheads of his day.

Bunker Hill in nearby Charlestown became one of the war's early battle sites. When George Washington seized Dorchester Heights overnight, the British were faced with defeat and evacuated Boston on March 17, 1776.

Following a brief postwar depression, Boston's prosperity was reactivated by the China trade in silks, spices, and porcelain. The clipper ship dominated the trade route in the 1850s, but the development of steam-powered, iron ships ended its reign. Boston shipyards refused to build the new models, and the harbor went into decline as capital was shifted from trade to manufacturing.

◆ "THINKING CENTER OF THE CONTINENT"

Boston officially became a city in 1822, and between 1824 and 1858 the peninsula was enlarged by leveling the hills and filling in Back Bay and the coves. The causeway, or Neck, was also raised and widened. From 1830 onward, the railroads hastened urban development, and as Boston's industrial empire expanded so did its attitudes. Beacon Hill, home to the magnates of the Industrial Revolution, also became the headquarters of free-thinking and social reform.

"All I claim for Boston," physician and writer Oliver Wendell Holmes declared, "is that it is the thinking center of the continent, and therefore of the planet." The city and immediate areas certainly housed the country's leading 19th-century intellectuals, among them abolitionist William Lloyd Garrison (1805–1879), psychologist William James (1842–1910), and philosopher George Santayana (1863–1952). Edgar Allan Poe was born here in 1809, and Ralph Waldo Emerson gave Walt Whitman literary advice on Boston Common while William Dean Howells, editor of the *Atlantic Monthly*, experimented with literary realism.

◆ IDEALISTS AND IMMIGRANTS

The Boston Draft Riots of 1863 expressed one attitude toward the Civil War, but aristocrat Robert Gould Shaw embraced another. A Beacon Hill abolitionist, Shaw commanded the Union Army's famous Massachusetts 54th black regiment, half of whom fell, along with Shaw, outside Charleston, South Carolina in 1863. Shaw's sister later wrote of her 26-year-old brother's departure: "His face was as the face of an angel, and I felt perfectly sure he would never come back."

The post-Civil War era was one of tremendous industrial and commercial growth. In 1898, the first subway in America opened at Tremont Street and in 1901, ships leaving Boston Harbor carried goods valued at $143 million while imports amounted to just $80 million. Meanwhile, Irish immigrants who first

Mayor James Michael Curley (second from left), ascends the steps of the State House. The quintessential Irish politician, he was first elected in 1914, and he dominated city politics for the next 30 years. (Underwood Photo Archives, San Francisco)

A bird's-eye view of Boston, circa 1877. (Library of Congress)

flooded the city in 1846, the year of Ireland's potato blight, had increased their numbers and their power sufficiently to dominate Boston's politics. Yankee political ascendancy ended in 1914 with the election of mayor James Michael Curley, and the consolidation of Boston Irish power would culminate in the 1960 presidential victory of John Fitzgerald Kennedy.

◆ "PROGRESS" AND URBAN "RENEWAL"

The 2.5-mile Freedom Trail *(see pages 60-61)*, linking 16 historic sites, first appeared in 1958. But "progress" also made its mark. Urban renewal—a policy or an abomination, depending on your preservationist views—began in the 1960s with accelerated construction of highways, brutalist government buildings and parking garages and the Prudential Center. The financial district was further expanded in the 1970s and 1980s, and waterfront buildings were converted to house the Children's Museum, among other institutions. Despite the upheavals, Boston remains a walkable city with a relatively low skyline where a one-mile stroll in any direction takes you through 300 years of architecture.

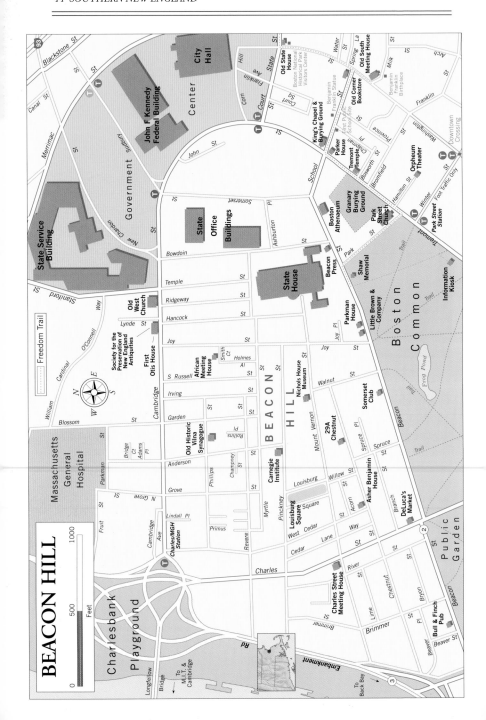

BEACON HILL

Feet
0   500   1000

The city's ongoing—and most lavish—street theater is the Big Dig, or Central Artery Project, which became the costliest highway project in history when estimates passed $10.4 billion in 1996. Viewing hours: anytime, especially when you're stuck in traffic. Admission: free or $10.4 billion-plus, depending on residency.

■ BOSTON COMMON

Boston Common is the city's birthplace, the country's oldest public park and most charming crossroads. William Blaxton built a cabin here in 1624, then sold the 48 acres to John Winthrop's Puritans, who set the land aside as cattle pasture and militia drill field in 1634. Criminals, Quakers, adulterers, and witches were pilloried and hanged here throughout the 17th century. In the 18th century, Back Bay's waves still broke on the Common, and boats that were launched from the banks carried British soldiers to march on Lexington and Concord and to attack Bunker Hill. The park is a natural rallying point. Here patriot Samuel Adams railed against British interference, Martin Luther King Jr. drew vast crowds, and Pope John Paul II celebrated Mass. And the fervent still preach at Brimstone Corner on everything from alien abductions to Tibetan liberation.

Getting there: The green pentangle is bounded today by Tremont, Boylston, Charles, Beacon, and Park Streets and abuts the 24-acre Public Garden. The city's Visitor Information Booth is on the Common at Tremont Street, near Park Street subway station (a national historic landmark). From here you can walk uphill to the wealth of Beacon Hill or downhill to the crooked streets where that wealth was created.

■ BEACON HILL

Beacon Hill has been Boston's most prestigious address for two centuries. This preserved 19th-century district is bounded by Boston Common, Charles Street, and Cambridge Street and is one of America's finest architectural treasures. The Hill's gradient and architectural detail defy you to cram its brick-paved, gaslit streets into an efficient hour.

There are numerous starting points for a leisurely exploration. The following ramble begins at Park Street Station, but you should consult the walking tour map (opposite) to chart your own course.

◆ NEAR THE COMMON

State House

The golden-domed, Bulfinch-designed State House presides over the Common, its cornerstone laid in 1795 by Revolutionaries Samuel Adams and Paul Revere. Wings added in 1917 lessen but cannot destroy Bulfinch's design, and the interior is as majestic as Revolutionaries could stand to make it. A double staircase from the magnificent Doric Hall leads to the chamber of the House of Representatives, with its 1784 Sacred Cod. The basement museum contains the state's royal charter and the Mayflower Compact, among other items. *617-727-3676. Weekday tours.*

Boston Athenaeum

Visitors are admitted to the first two floors of the Athenaeum (just to the east of the State House, at 10$^{1}/_{2}$ Beacon Street), which was established in 1807 as "a retreat for those who enjoy the humanity of books" and which is still splendidly hushed; *617-227-0270.*

Shaw Memorial

Across from the State House is the Shaw Memorial, an arresting bas relief by Augustus Saint-Gaudens, commemorating Col. Robert Gould Shaw and the all-black 54th Massachusetts Regiment.

◆ SOUTH SLOPE

Mount Vernon, Chestnut, and Beacon Streets, along with Louisburg Square and Acorn Street, are the Hill's jewels.

Parkman House

No. 33 Beacon Street is open to the public, and here you may hear the 1849 Parkman-Webster murder story that shook upper-class Boston and sent a Harvard professor to the gallows.

Somerset Club

The private Somerset Club, once described as "that reservoir of Boston blue blood," is at 42 Beacon.

Spruce Street links Chestnut to Beacon Street, which overlooks the Common and once housed the merchant and industrial

elite. Frederic Tudor, the "Ice King" who made his fortune shipping New England ice to the Far East, gave his name to the apartment building at 34$^{1}/_{2}$ Spruce, at the intersection with Beacon.

39 Spruce Street

Built in 1819, this was the home of Nathan Appleton, one of the Lowell mill developers, whose daughter, Fanny, married the poet Henry Wadsworth Longfellow here in 1843.

Chestnut Street

In a neighborhood that legally enforces good taste, Chestnut Street exudes it. **No. 29A** is the area's oldest house, as its rippled 1820 window glass attests. Richard Henry Dana lived at No. 43 before choosing the sea over Harvard and describing his experiences in *Two Years Before the Mast*. Historian Francis Parkman lived at 50 Chestnut from 1863 to 1895, during which time he completed *The Discovery of the Great West* and other histories.

Follow Chestnut to West Cedar Street.

Asher Benjamin House

West Cedar Street cuts across Beacon Hill from Chestnut Street to Cambridge Avenue. Asher Benjamin, the architect whose vision, along with that of Bulfinch, marks this area, lived at 9 West Cedar.

Acorn Street, West Cedar's offshoot, supplies undiluted Beacon Hill charm, with original cobblestones and a slight overabundance of window boxes.

Return to West Cedar and proceed north to Mount Vernon Street.

Mount Vernon Street

Charles Bulfinch, who was funded by Harrison Otis and Otis's colleague Jonathan Mason, was the chief architect of this harmonious street.

Henry James finished the novel *Daisy Miller* in number 131 Mount Vernon Street, where he lived for a brief time. Daniel Webster lived at number 57 from 1817 to 1819, and Rose Standish Nichols at number 55, which became the **Nichols House Museum** in accordance with her

Green grass grows from between cobblestones in early summer on Acorn Street.

1960 will. A bizarre collection of Nichols's possessions includes a chair once owned by John Winthrop. *55 Mount Vernon Street; 617-227-6993.*

Louisburg Square

Louisburg Square runs between Mount Vernon and Pinckney Streets. The Greek Revival block, built between 1834 and 1847, faces onto a handkerchief of greenery that hardly deserves the term "park" but is private—and therefore coveted real estate. Louisa May Alcott lived at No. 10 from 1885 to 1887, suffering from the poisonous effects of mercury ingested while nursing in the Civil War. Jenny Lind, the "Swedish Nightingale," was married in No. 20, and more recent residents include Senators Edward Kennedy and John Kerry.

Charles Street

Charles Street is downhill but hardly downmarket. Originally the neighborhood's shoreline, the pretty thoroughfare is lined with restaurants and antique shops. A couple of grocery stores and a hardware store keep terminal cuteness at bay.

Charles Street Meeting House, erected in 1807, was a center of abolitionism. Across the walkway from Charles Street, through the Red Line station, is **Massachusetts General Hospital.** Its 1817 Bulfinch Pavilion was the architect's last Boston job. The hospital's Ether Dome commemorates the first use of ether as an anaesthetic, which took place here in 1846.

Across Embankment Road is the Charles River Esplanade and the Hatch Memorial Shell, home of the Boston Pops Orchestra, July 4th fireworks, and other extravaganzas.

◆ NORTH SLOPE

Joy Street preserves the humble face of Beacon Hill in its 19th-century tenements. African-Americans moved here first, and Smith Court, off Joy, is the site of the **African Meeting House.** Built in 1806, this was an important stop on the "Underground Railroad" for fugitive slaves. Boston's first black school was started in the basement, where the New England Anti-Slavery Society was founded in 1832. Narrow thoroughfares like **Holmes Alley** are typical of the North Slope's 17th- and 18th-century streets, while nearby **Rollins Place** presents a 19th-century architectural

tease: a false portico concealing a 20-foot fall to Phillips Street. Pinckney Street once divided white from black, rich from poor. The 1791 house at Pinckney and Joy Streets is one of the Hill's oldest.

If you follow Joy to Cambridge Street you'll reach the first Otis House.

First Harrison Gray Otis House

Designed by Charles Bulfinch in 1796, this is the birthplace of Beacon Hill high society and is the prototype for the Federal-style residences that characterize the area.

(previous pages) A view of Beacon Hill as seen from the Charles River. The gold dome of the State House rises in the background.

Rescued by the Society for the Preservation of New England Antiquities in 1916, this is the only Otis-Bulfinch house open to the public, and one of its many surprises is the exuberance of the colonial and early Federal decoration. *141 Cambridge Street; 617-227-3956.*

Old West Church
Also on Cambridge, practically next door to the Otis House, the 1806 Old West Church that replaced a 1737 wood-frame structure stages recitals on its Fisk tracker-action pipe organ.

■ DOWNTOWN BOSTON

Boston's downtown streets date from the late 17th century and still define the city's scale. The towering slabs of the financial and government districts may cast a shadow over the old labyrinth, but in most places, pedestrians and motorists alike must submit to the city's original curves. **The Freedom Trail** winds through this area. *(See pages 60–61.)*

Park Street runs along the north side of the Common. The main landmark here is the 1809 **Park Street Church**, which replaced a huge granary that was used as a sail loft for the USS *Constitution*. Next door is the **Granary Burying Ground**, established in 1660 and named for that earlier building. Its 1,600 or so graves include those of Paul Revere, Samuel Adams, John Hancock, and victims of the Boston Massacre.

Cherry blossoms obscure the Granary Burying Ground and the spire of the Park Street Church.

Tremont Temple and Parker House

At 88 Tremont Street is Tremont Temple, America's first racially integrated church, and at 60 School Street (at the intersection with Tremont) is the Parker House, the oldest continually operating hotel in the country. The Saturday Club of 19th-century intellectuals met here with visitors like Charles Dickens, and mementos are exhibited in the foyer; *617-227-8600.*

King's Chapel and Burying Ground

The King's Chapel and Burying Ground occupy the corner opposite the Parker House. Originally Anglican, then Unitarian after the Revolution, the church was founded in 1686, although the present structure was built between 1749 and 1754. The altar table was presented by William and Mary in 1696 and the bell cast by Paul Revere in 1816. The 1631 Burying Ground is the city's oldest and contains the graves of the first colonists as well as that of Elizabeth Pain, buried in 1704, who was branded with the letter "A" for adultery and may have been the model for Hester Prynne in Hawthorne's *The Scarlet Letter.* The exquisitely strange headstones are the closest thing we have to snapshots of the Puritan soul.

Old Corner Bookstore

Past the 1635 site of the nation's first public school—Boston Latin—and the 1865 Old City Hall is the Old Corner Bookstore (renamed the Globe Corner Bookstore), opening onto School and Washington Streets. This may be the oldest brick structure in the city, built for the apothecary Thomas Crease on the site of the heretic Anne Hutchinson's house after the 1711 fire. From 1845 to 1865, it was the office of Ticknor and Fields, publisher of Hawthorne, Emerson, Thoreau, Longfellow, and Stowe, as well as of *The Atlantic Monthly* magazine. *3 School Street; 617-523-6658.*

Old South Meeting House

Old South Meeting House, the shrine of American independence, stands at the corner of Washington and Milk Streets. The original 1670 wooden building was replaced in 1729 by Joshua Blanchard's redbrick church. "Who knows how tea will mingle with salt water?" Samuel Adams shouted to the 5,000 tea-tax protesters who assembled there on December 16, 1773, launching the Boston Tea Party. The British subsequently used the church as an indoor riding arena and officers' bar. Plans to demolish Old South in 1876 were blocked by Emerson and others. *310 Washington Street; 617-482-6439.*

Old State House

The Old State House looks fragile beside its modern, multistory neighbors. Built in 1713 to replace a townhouse that burned in 1711, Boston's oldest public building was the epicenter of rebel activity. A cobblestone circle outside marks the **site of the Boston Massacre**, and on July 18, 1776, the Declaration of Independence was read from the balcony. The Old State House was first restored in 1881, having been a firehouse and newspaper office. It now shares its territory with the Downtown Visitors Center of the Boston National Historic Park. *206 Washington Street; 617-720-3290.*

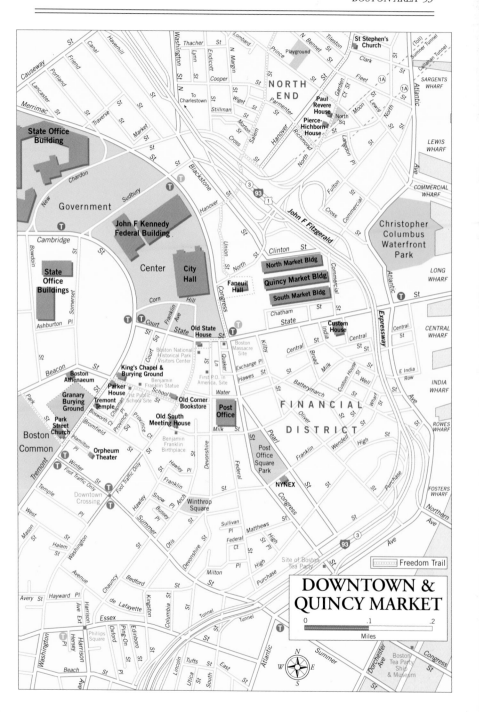

DOWNTOWN & QUINCY MARKET

0   .1   .2

Miles

⬡⬡⬡⬡ Freedom Trail

■ FINANCIAL DISTRICT AND MARKETS

Close to State Street is Boston's financial district, where the generally dull architecture is redeemed by the inspiring art deco post office, the murals and exhibits in the New England Telephone Building, and the N. C. Wyeth paintings in the Congress Street bank building. Government Center, an 11-acre concrete wind tunnel between Cambridge and Congress Streets, has no such redeeming features.

Faneuil Hall Marketplace

The adjacent market district is all about food on one end, where produce markets operate under the expressway, and tourism on the other end at Faneuil Hall Marketplace. "Real" Bostonians are contemptuous of the Faneuil Hall/Quincy Market 1970s makeover, and "about as Boston as Faneuil Hall" is a common insult. Nevertheless, the 19th-century market and warehouse building are impressive and inside they are not entirely given over to souvenir shops. The top floor of Faneuil Hall houses the Ancient and Honorable Artillery Company of Massachusetts, America's oldest military group, founded in 1638. Rebuilt in 1805 on the site of the original 1742 market, Faneuil Hall was the site of Revolutionary

Quincy Market building (left) stands opposite the North Market building (right); Faneuil Hall can be seen in the background.

Chinatown street scene.

and later abolitionist meetings. Quincy Market was opened in 1827; the adjacent Blackstone Building is Boston's oldest commercial block, built before 1714. *For tours call 617-242-5689.*

Boston Stone

The Boston Stone—a granite lump embedded in the wall of 9 Marshall Street, off Union Street—was transported from England in the late 17th century. Used as a paint grinder by Thomas Child in his shop here, the stone was set in the present building in 1737 and used as a starting point to measure distances from Boston.

Filene's Basement

A short distance from Faneuil Hall, at the junction of Summer, Winter, and Washington Streets, grittier commerce is carried on in Filene's Basement, the birthplace (in 1908) of the "automatic markdown." *426 Washington Street; 617-357-2400.*

Combat Zone and Chinatown

Grittier still is the Combat Zone on Washington Street, Boston's shrunken "adult entertainment zone," today a shadow of its former sleaze. The adjoining Chinatown is small—comprising Beach, Oxford, Tyler, and Hudson Streets—but lively. Originally called South Cove, the area was a 19th-century Chinese neighborhood, the residents having been shipped in to break a strike at a Lawrence shoe factory in the 1870s. Garment-making developed, and by 1931, Chinatown had a population of 1,200. Today much of that population is Southeast Asian.

Leather District and Bay Village

The nearby Leather District and Bay Village were manufacturing centers through the 1940s but were later truncated by the Expressway. In 1809, Edgar Allan Poe was born in Bay Village at 62 Carver Street, now demolished. Only the Haynes Flute and Piccolo Company at 12 Piedmont Street hints at past productivity.

■ THEATER DISTRICT

Boston's Theater District centers on Tremont and Boylston Streets. Theater did not exist in the city until 1792, thanks to the legacy of the Puritan ban, but stage entertainment flourished in the 19th century. Censorship unwittingly aided this expansion, as "Banned in Boston" became a guarantee of box-office success. At its healthiest, the theater district boasted over 40 venues. The 1900 **Colonial Theatre** at 106 Boylston is the oldest survivor, followed by the 1910 Shubert, the 1914 Wilbur, and the 1925 Metropolitan (now the Wang Center for the Performing Arts), all on Tremont Street. *Wang Center, 268 Tremont Street; 617-350-6000.*

■ SOUTH END

Before it runs into Massachusetts Avenue, Tremont Street bisects the 500-acre South End, the nation's largest National Historic District. This neighborhood of fine 19th-century row houses, tiny parks, and expansive avenues has housed each immigrant group, from the Irish to the more recent Puerto Ricans. Gentrification is slow but detectable, particularly in Union Park near the Boston Center for the Arts. The BCA's fanciful Cyclorama, opened in 1884 for the exhibition of the 400-foot *Battle of Gettysburg* painting, has served many uses. South End native John L. Sullivan, the "Last of the Bare-Fisted Sluggers" fought here in the mid-1890s, and it was here that Albert Champion invented the spark plug in 1907.

■ NORTH END

It is not just the Central Artery (and current "Big Dig") that cuts the North End off from downtown Boston. It's the state of mind. This village of narrow, winding 17th-century streets and minute squares is antique, Italian—and blessedly unself-conscious. Its summer religious festivals are for the residents not the tourists, although everybody is welcome. And some of the best food in Boston is served, without frills, in restaurants smaller than your kitchen.

Paul Revere House

Paul Revere's house is Boston's oldest, the only 17th-century structure occupying its original site. Built in 1677, it was bought in 1770 by Revere, who lived here until 1800. The house was a tenement in the 19th century but was saved from demolition in 1907 and became a museum the following year. The exterior is typical of the 17th century, while the interior is restored to reflect that century as well as Revere's life and time. While some of the Revolution's most dramatic episodes are chronicled here, the adjacent Pierce-Hichborn House, built in 1708 and later owned by Revere's cousin, provides a glimpse of everyday life in the 18th century. *19 North Square; 617-523-2338.*

St. Stephens

Hanover Street is dominated by the tower of St. Stephens, built in 1804. The only Bulfinch-designed church still standing in Boston, it is home to Paul Revere's first bell (entrance at 24 Clark Street). The nearby Paul Revere Mall leads to Old North Church.

Old North Church

Built in 1723, Old North Church (officially Christ Church) is Boston's oldest and most famous, known for that April 18 night in 1775 when two lanterns suspended from the steeple warned the Patriots in Charlestown that the British were coming to Concord by boat, not foot. On June 17, British general Thomas Gage watched from

Paul Revere's house in the North End.

the belfry as his officers and men were mowed down by American fire on Bunker Hill. Today's steeple is a 1955 reproduction, both previous versions having been toppled by hurricanes (in 1804 and 1954). *193 Salem Street (at Hull); 617-523-6676.*

Copp's Hill Burial Ground

Dating from 1660, this burial ground is at the corner of Hull and Snowhill Streets. During the Battle of Bunker Hill, the British launched artillery assaults from the cemetery, and Gen. John Burgoyne noted "we threw a parcel of shells, and the whole town was instantly in flames." The interred include ministers Cotton and Samuel Mather, Capt. Thomas Lake ("peridiously [sic] slain by ye Indians in 1676"), and Mr. Prince Hall, Revolutionary soldier and head of the Black Masons. The Great Molasses Flood of 1919 occurred at Copp's Hill Terrace, across from the burial ground, when a 2.5-million-gallon tank burst, and a molasses wave demolished several houses, killing 21 people. *Hull and Snowhill Sts.; 617-635-4505.*

■ CHARLESTOWN

Charlestown was settled in January of 1629 by Salem colonists, most of whom died of starvation and exposure. John Winthrop and his group found the site equally unwelcoming in 1630 and soon decamped to Boston. Virtually leveled by British artillery during the Battle of Bunker Hill, Charlestown was largely rebuilt in the 19th century, and gentrification is currently homogenizing this traditionally working-class area.

Artery and tunnel excavations near City Square recently unearthed what could be the remains of John Winthrop's 1630 Great House; plaques on Town Hill relate key historical events. The Warren Tavern, on the corner of Main and Pleasant Streets, was one of the first structures to be built after the 1775 bombardment.

Perched on Breed's Hill, the **Bunker Hill Monument** commemorates the Revolutionary War battle that, although a defeat, signalled victory for the American colonial forces. "Nothing could be more shocking than the carnage that followed," one British officer later wrote of the waves of assault that ended in hand-to-hand fighting. The victorious British suffered heavy casualties and their besieged position in Boston was further weakened. "I wish this cursed place was burned," General Gage wrote in his report to London. Forty veterans of the battle attended the laying of the obelisk's cornerstone in 1825, and Daniel Webster delivered the oration.

Copp's Hill Burial Ground in the North End dates from 1660.

FREEDOM TRAIL

| 0 | 500 | 1000 | 1500 | 2000 |

Feet

FREEDOM TRAIL

Past and present converge on the Freedom Trail, a 2.5-mile path—marked with red paint and bricks—that links 16 sites relating to the early history of America.

The trail forms a perfect introduction to the central core of Boston, where the city and the nation began. No other city—save perhaps Philadelphia—can boast so many sites directly related to the American Revolution.

Because the trail represents a colonial city embedded in the midst of a vital, modern city, the transit is not always as fastidious as it would be in a sanitized theme-park version. The Freedom Trail is a walk through three and a half centuries of Boston, warts and all.

Sites are listed in order of their location on the Freedom Trail, beginning with the State House on Beacon Hill and heading north.

—This section was written and compiled by Patricia Harris and David Lyon, authors of the Compass American Guide to Boston.

■ BEACON HILL

State House. *p. 46*
Built 1795-98; open weekdays.
Beacon and Park Sts.; 617-727-3676.

■ DOWNTOWN & MARKET DISTRICT

Boston Common. *p. 45*
Bounded by Park, Tremont, Boylston, and Charles Sts.

Park Street Church. *p. 51*
Built in 1809; open Tues.-Sat. summer only, Sunday services year-round.
Tremont and Park Sts.; 617-523-3383.

Granary Burying Ground. *p. 51*
Laid out in 1660; open daily.
Tremont near Park Street Church;
617-635-4505.

King's Chapel. *p. 52*
Built in 1748-1754; call for hours.
58 Tremont St.; 617-227-2155.

King's Chapel Burying Ground. *p. 52*
Oldest part laid out in 1631; open daily.
617-635-4505.

Old Corner Bookstore (Globe Corner Bookstore). *p. 52*
Built in 1712; open daily. 285 Washington St. (at School); 617-523-6658.

Old South Meeting House. *p. 52*
Built in 1729. 310 Washington St. (at Milk); 617-482-6439.

■ DOWNTOWN & MARKET DISTRICT *(cont'd)*

Old State House. *p. 52*
Built in 1713.
206 Washington St.;
617-720-3290.

Boston Massacre Site. *p. 52*
Congress and State Sts.

Faneuil Hall. *pp. 54-55*
Built in 1742.
Dock Square; 617-242-5642.

■ NORTH END & CHARLESTOWN

Paul Revere House. *p. 57*
Built in 1677.
19 North Square; 617-523-2338.

Old North Church. *pp. 57-58*
Built in 1723.
193 Salem St.; 617-523-6676.

Copp's Hill Burial Ground. *p. 58*
Oldest part laid out in 1660.
Hull and Snowhill Sts.;
617-635-4505.

Bunker Hill Monument. *p. 58*
Erected in 1825.
Charlestown; 617-242-5641.

USS *Constitution*. *p. 63*
Launched in 1797.
Charlestown Navy Yard;
617-242-5670.

■ BOSTON WATERFRONT

For many Bostonians, the waterfront *is* Boston. The sea, after all, touches most of the city and even inland neighborhoods are lashed by nor'easters. Today's harbor activity may be more recreational than seafaring, but the record-breaking pollution of the 1980s has apparently been reversed and derelict wharves revitalized. Boston continues to reclaim its shore.

The Charlestown Navy Yard, home of the USS *Constitution* and heart of the historic waterfront, was established in 1800 and remained active until 1974.

USS *Constitution*

Nicknamed *"Old Ironsides,"* the USS *Constitution* was the first of America's superfrigates when she was launched in 1797. As late as 1812, the U.S. Navy was derided by British politician George Channing as "a few fir built frigates with bits of bunting at the top." Within a year, however, the USS *Constitution* had sunk the HMS *Guerriere* and the British Admiralty was referring to "a new enemy...unaccustomed to such triumphs and likely to be rendered insolent and confident by them."

Winning 42 battles, losing none, capturing 20 vessels and never being forcefully boarded, the *Constitution* had her final victory in 1815 when she captured two British ships off Madeira. Twice consigned to the breaker's yard but rescued by popular demand and refurbished (less than 10 percent of her timbers are original), the *Constitution* now gets one outing a year, on July 4th, when she is turned around in Boston Harbor. *Tour schedule: 617-242-5601.*

The adjacent USS **Constitution Museum** displays some of the famous hull, nautical equipment, and other artifacts, while the Bunker Hill Pavilion presents a multimedia re-creation of the battle. *Museum: 617-426-1812.*

Leisure, not labor, characterizes Boston's waterfront today. The Boston Harbor Walk (near the Charlestown Bridge) and the North End Waterfront (facing the Navy Yard) are lively promenades with fine views. Only the North End's Commercial Wharf echoes the past, in the businesses of yachtbuilders John G. Alden and Son Co. and the Robert Eldrige White Instrument Co., publisher of *Eldrige's Tide and Pilot Tables.*

The Downtown Waterfront, scarred by the 40-story Harbor Towers and the squat obesity of the Rowes Wharf development, nevertheless does offer the 1710 Long Wharf, the 1840s Custom House, and the New England Aquarium, on Central Wharf.

New England Aquarium

One of Boston's most imaginative—and restful—attractions, the aquarium displays 2,000 species of exotic fish, sharks, sea turtles, and eels in its giant, three-story ocean tank. There are also strutting penguins and exhibits on aquatic environments from the Amazon rain forest to the Antarctic. *On Central Wharf; 617-973-5281.*

An artist draws details of the USS Constitution *at the Charlestown Navy Yard.*

Children's Museum

You know you're there when you see children acting like tugboats, dragging their adults to the giant milk bottle that guards the entrance. The renovated warehouse is a wonder of giant Lego structures, enormous soap bubbles, and interactive exhibits. It also provides the ultimate climbing, sliding, swinging, and dressing-up opportunities. *Museum Wharf, between the Congress Street and North Avenue bridges; 617-426-8855.*

Computer Museum

The neighboring Computer Museum is almost as much fun, featuring rare, early machines and a walk-through computer that is just that. *300 Congress Street; 617-426-2800.*

Boston Tea Party Museum

Found midway across the Congress Street Bridge, this museum offers a replica of the brig *Beaver* and predictable souvenirs.

Fish Pier

Here the waterfront becomes a working port again, landing a third of the Massachusetts lobster catch. The quality of nearby fish restaurants ranges from mediocre to superb.

Harbor Tours

To observe the ocean and waterfront at its blushing best, take a Boston Harbor sunset cruise. *From Rowe's Wharf: Massachusetts Bay Lines; 617-542-8000. From Long Wharf: Boston Harbor Cruises, 617-227-0103; or Schooner Liberty, 617-742-0333.*

■ BACK BAY

Graceful Back Bay and the airy parks that circle it are the expression of a confident, optimistic city. In 1857, Boston embarked on the 30-year project of converting 450 acres of tidal slime into a model of residential planning and civic amenity. To the inhabitants of a cramped 19th-century city, the vision of space and symmetry must have been heady. For a pedestrian enjoying the broad sweep of Commonwealth Avenue today, it still is.

Commonwealth Avenue, Back Bay's seam, is a 240-foot-wide boulevard with central mall, modeled on Baron Haussmann's Parisian boulevards. Marlborough, Beacon, Newbury, and Boylston Streets run parallel to it, while the cross streets occur in alphabetical order, from Arlington to Hereford, beginning at the Public Garden. Statues of Alexander Hamilton, Leif Eriksson, and historian Samuel Eliot Morison punctuate the boulevard along with a handful of closely monitored American elms, while cherubs, gargoyles and other creatures enliven the harmonious facades.

The swan boats in Boston's Public Garden have been pleasing visitors since 1877.

Gibson House Museum

The Gibson House Museum on Beacon Street provides a glimpse of the good life in late-19th-century Boston with various beautiful and downright odd relics from the Gibson family. *137 Beacon Street; 617-267-6338.*

Newbury and Boylston Street Churches

These may be the district's fashionable shopping destinations, but this is Boston, and even on these perfumed streets, theology gives commerce a run for its money. **Arlington Street Church, Emmanuel Church, Church of the Covenant, Trinity Church Rectory,** and **New Old South Church** are all graceful structures. But Trinity Church on the Clarendon side of Copley Square is the district's gem. In an essay on his 1877 creation, architect Henry Hobson Richardson described it as a "free rendering of the French Romanesque," a modest summation of a sublime achievement.

Boston Public Library

More secular inspiration is supplied by the Boston Public Library, facing Trinity Church and completed in 1895 according to the design of Charles Follen McKim. "Free to All," as its inscription declares, this pseudo-Renaissance palazzo (constructed largely by Italian artisans) has an imposing marble entrance hall, massive bronze doors decorated with reliefs by Daniel Chester French, and many suitably ennobling murals. The Italian theme is echoed in the library's charming interior courtyard. *666 Boylston Street; 617-536-5400, ext. 216.*

Along toney Newbury Street, chic boutiques cater to the fashion-minded while cafes and bistros serve the see-and-be-seen crowd.

John Hancock Tower and Prudential Center

The John Hancock Tower, until recently Boston's tallest building, is a 60-story office block built in 1975 that literally reflects its surroundings, thanks to a mirrorlike facade. The huge windows began to fall out even before the building was completed, and the building's sway made visitors sick, but adjustments were made and today the rooftop observatory is worth a visit for its views of Boston and a narrated city history. *200 Clarendon Street; 617-572-6429.*

For a 360-degree perspective, ascend to the Skywalk on the 50th floor of the Prudential Center, a short walk away on Boylston Street; *617-859-0648.*

The John Hancock Tower ensconced in fog.

❖

The intersection of Huntington and Massachusetts Avenues is dominated by the vast **Christian Science Center** that sect founder Mary Baker Eddy referred to as "our prayer in stone" when it began life as a humble church in 1893. Its neighbors are more cultural than spiritual: **Symphony Hall, Boston University Theatre, New England Conservatory of Music,** and **Jordan Hall.**

Kenmore Square, nearby, is dominated by Boston University. **Fenway Park,** on the other hand, turns out students of delayed gratification—Boston Red Sox fans, whose baseball team last won the World Series in 1918, sold Babe Ruth to the New York Yankees in 1920 and have tested their followers by snatching defeat from the mitt of victory ever since. Intimate Fenway Park, approached from Kenmore by Brookline Avenue, is baseball's oldest (1912), and its grass is real; *617-236-6666.*

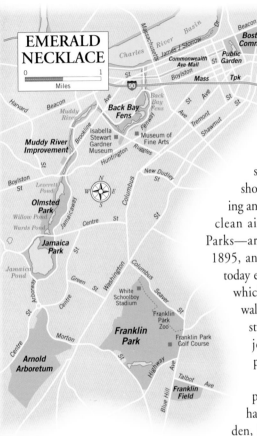

EMERALD NECKLACE

0   1
Miles

■ EMERALD NECKLACE AND THE FENS

The planners of elegant, symmetrical Back Bay envisioned green spaces surrounding it, and during the 1870s the Boston Parks Commission proposed that Frederick Law Olmsted design those spaces. The parks would be not just showpieces but health measures, providing an overcrowded city with green acres and clean air. Olmsted completed the Boston Parks—arguably his finest achievement—in 1895, and the five-mile "Emerald Necklace" today exists as a series of neighborhood parks which can be covered in a leisurely day's walk. Olmsted frowned on anything more strenuous and would have expelled the joggers and athletes who currently pound his turf.

The **Back Bay Fens** area is comprised of North Basin, a marshy bird haven, and South Basin, with its rose garden, baseball diamonds, and cinder track. **Muddy River, the Riverway,** and **Olmsted Park** meander gracefully and offer an interesting selection of native and exotic trees. Beyond Jamaica Pond, with its beaches, is the Frederick Law Olmsted National Historic Site at 99 Warren Street in Brookline, an archive of the landscape designer's work. Further on, at 15 Newton Street, is the Larz Anderson Museum of Transportation, with an automobile collection ranging from the teens through the 1950s.

A joint project of Harvard University and the city of Boston, the **Arnold Arboretum** is the park system's showpiece, with over 15,000 specimens on 265 acres. **Franklin Park,** on the other hand, despite being home to the Franklin Zoo and African Tropical Forest exhibit, is slowly going to seed.

Close to the Back Bay Fens can also be found the Museum of Fine Arts and the Isabella Stewart Gardner Museum.

Museum of Fine Arts

Founded in 1870 but established on its present site in 1909, the MFA is one of the country's largest art museums. It is not just the size (a permanent stock of over one million objects) but the range of its collection that is remarkable. The museum's Asian art holdings, for example, are unrivaled in the Western Hemisphere. Thanks to a 30-year collaboration with Harvard University on archeological digs in Egypt and the Sudan, the museum's Nubian and Old Kingdom collection is surpassed only by that of the Cairo Museum. The MFA also has the world's largest Millet collection in its extensive impressionist and post-impressionist galleries, as well as an impressive cross-section of American paintings, sculpture, furniture, and decorative arts. The American Period Rooms give a superb view of architectural and decorative styles from the 17th through the 19th centuries.

Between The Fenway and Huntington Avenue; parking on Museum Road; Green E line station on Huntington; 617-267-9300.

Henry Roderick Newman's Study of Elms *from the M. and M. Karolik Collection at the Museum of Fine Arts, Boston.*

Isabella Stewart Gardner Museum

Comparisons become irrelevant when you reach the Isabella Stewart Gardner Museum. There is simply nothing like it—anywhere. The exquisite Venetian palazzo at 280 Fenway was completed in 1901 to house Mrs. Gardner's astonishing art collection of nearly 2,500 objects from 30 centuries. She began collecting while traveling in Europe to recover from the death of her only child, and her keen eye was assisted by shrewd advice from Renaissance connoisseur Bernard Berenson, among others. The result is a fine collection of Italian Renaissance works; French, German and Dutch masterpieces; modern paintings that include works by Degas and Matisse; and paintings by Gardner's friends James McNeill Whistler and John Singer Sargent. In 1925, a year after Gardner's death, the house became a museum that, according to her will, cannot be altered in any detail. Consequently, blank spaces recall the 1990 robbery that deprived the museum of 13 works valued at $200 million. *280 The Fenway; 617-566-1401.*

*The Raphael Room (above) and courtyard (right) at the Isabella Stewart Gardner Museum.
(Courtesy Isabella Stewart Gardner Museum, Boston)*

■ CAMBRIDGE

Bordered by the Charles River and bisected by Massachusetts Avenue and Mount Auburn Street, the city of Cambridge is dominated by Harvard University and swayed by each fresh intellectual breeze.

Wilderness surrounded the settlement when Harvard was founded in 1636. "A great many bears are killed at Cambridge and the neighboring towns about this time," student Belknap wrote that year. Elizabeth Horton discovered this in the early days of the settlement when, having been publicly flogged for her Quaker declarations, she was dumped on the town's outskirts "among the wolves, bears, and wild beasts." The wildest creature you will encounter on Cambridge streets today is likely to be a deconstructionist critic who hasn't had his morning latte.

Cambridge was founded in 1630 on the marketplace now known as Harvard Square. Commerce is still the main activity, although the merchandise has changed. Emerging from the Red Line T stop, you will find national and international newspapers at Out of Town News, one of the city's best-stocked news agents. The Harvard Coop (rhymes with "soup"), directly opposite, sells textbooks, souvenir coffee mugs, and T-shirts. The narrow streets radiating at oblique angles from the Square are lined with an eclectic variety of bookstores, boutiques, cafes, and restaurants.

Cambridge Common

The elm-shaded Cambridge Common, bordering Harvard Square to the north and circled today by the ceaseless traffic on Garden Street and Massachusetts Avenue, is surely the city's most pleasing and historic traffic island. Set aside in 1631, it was reduced to its current 16 acres in 1724 and now tolerates baseball games, tai chi, courting couples, and impudent pigeons. Here George Washington took command of the Continental Army on July 3, 1775, supposedly beside an elm that was toppled in 1923, on a spot now marked by a plaque. The **Old Burying Ground** and **Christ Church** opposite the Common (bounded by Farwell Place and Church Street) also have Revolutionary connections.

Brattle Street

Brattle Street is an architectural delight. The 1688 **Hooper-Lee-Nichols House** *(No. 159)* is the oldest in Cambridge, and the 1759 **Henry Wadsworth Longfellow House** is the most famous. The latter was George Washington's residence during the siege of Boston. Longfellow lived here from 1837 until his death in 1882, and his descendants maintained the house until 1974, when the National Park Service acquired it; *105 Brattle Street; 617-876-4491.*

Farther down Brattle is **Radcliffe Yard**, site of the 1879 "Collegiate Institution for Women" that was later assimilated into Harvard University. Radcliffe Yard is now home to the **Schlesinger Library on the History of Women in America.** *3 James Street; 617-495-8647.*

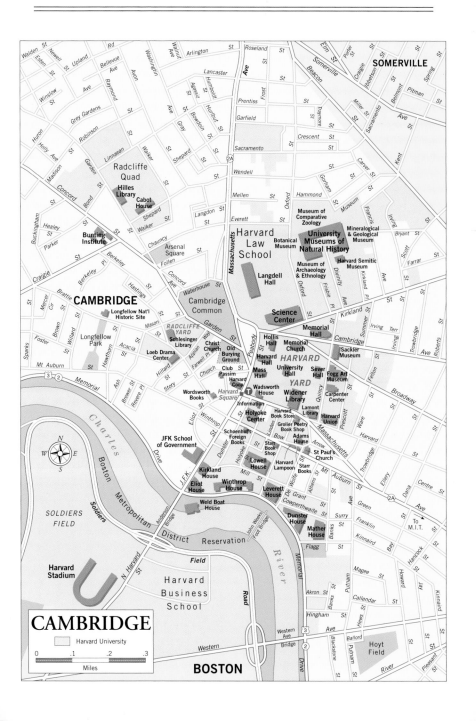

◆ HARVARD UNIVERSITY

Harvard University, which has a student population of about 18,000 in its two colleges and ten schools, owns almost 400 acres of land and 400 buildings in the Cambridge-Boston area. Endowed in 1636 by Charlestown minister John Harvard, the Puritan school imposed a monastic code, limiting tobacco use and forbidding a student to "buy, sell, or exchange anything above the value of a sixpence." Today, however, the institution's accumulated wealth—architectural, archaeological, artistic, literary, historic—makes a brief tour of its campus and museums impossible. Allow several hours, days, or years. *For general information: 617-495-1000.*

Harvard Yard

The calm, shady Yard contains Harvard's historic buildings, Massachusetts Hall (1720) being the oldest. The 1815 University Hall, with its statue of John Harvard, is the demarcation point between the Old Yard, which contains five 18th-century buildings, and the New Yard, whose 18th- and 19th-century buildings include Widener Library, the largest university library in the world and third largest library in the country. It is named for Henry Elkins Widener (class of 1907) whose books were donated, along with funds to house them, when Widener died in 1912 on the *Titanic.* Those without a Harvard library card may view the lobby's historical dioramas and John Singer Sargent murals.

Harvard's three art museums—the Fogg Art Museum, the Busch-Reisinger, and the Sackler Museum—all in Cambridge, together house one of the world's finest university art collections.

Fogg Art Museum

The Fogg displays European and American prints, sculptures, drawings, and paintings from the Middle Ages to the present. The quality and variety of work is even more astonishing given the Fogg's refreshingly modest size. Here medieval pieces, French 19th-century landscapes, pre-Raphaelite creations, and American paintings of the 18th and 19th centuries can be viewed without museum exhaustion setting in. *32 Quincy Street; 617-495-9400.*

Memorial Hall

North of Harvard Yard, to the right of the Science Center, is Memorial Hall, completed in 1878 as a tribute to the 136 Harvard men who died defending the Union in the Civil War. Designed in the Gothic cathedral style and recently restored, it was judged by architectural historian G. E. Kidder Smith to be "a piquant pile...a mammoth ugly duckling, an almost fanatic statement of the taste of its time." But the hefty beauty, enclosing Sanders Theatre in its apse, has always had its admirers.

*An outdoor cafe on Harvard Square, across from Out of Town News. The spire of
Christ Church rises in the background.*

◆ KENDALL SQUARE AND MIT

Kendall Square, east of Harvard on Route 2A, is a center of the biotechnology industry; it is dominated by the area's other great educational institution, the **Massachusetts Institute of Technology,** which has its own small MIT museum and also
houses the Hart Nautical Museum's fine collection of ship models. *Campus entrance:
77 Massachusetts Avenue. Hart Museum: 55 Massachusetts Avenue; 617-253-5942.*

■ LEXINGTON *see map, page 81*

Cozy, sedate Lexington, an affluent suburb of Boston, looks nothing like a battlefield today. But once a year, at dawn on April 19, Lexington re-enacts its most
heroic moment and gives us a chilling glimpse of the 1775 Revolutionary War
battle. Implacable redcoats and agitated militiamen face each other on the town

Green. It all seems entertainingly quaint until Major Pitcairn shouts "Lay down your arms, you damned rebels, and disperse!" The famous first shot is fired and the British soldiers, exhausted and jumpy after a night's marching, fire volley after volley, then level their bayonets to charge the men standing just feet from them. Eighteen Americans fall (eight died) and the effect, even on camcorder-wielding spectators, is palpable.

Present-day Lexington looks much as it did when the British set out from Boston to seize a rebel military supply at Concord and Paul Revere and William Dawes set out to alert the countryside. The houses surrounding the Green are original, as is the late-17th-century **Buckman Tavern**, where the 77 or so Minute Men waited through the night for the Regulars, as the British troops were known. *One Bedford Street, on the Lexington Green; 781-862-5598.*

Samuel Adams and John Hancock were staying at the **Hancock-Clarke House**, now a museum, when Revere and Dawes rode out to warn of the British intentions. *36 Hancock Street; 781-861-0928.*

Minute Man National Historic Park

Route 2A between Lexington and Concord may be straighter and smoother than the original track, but it still follows the line of the 18th-century road and, particularly when walked or bicycled, gives a sense of the terrain on which the 1775 conflict was fought. The Minute Man National Historic Park's North Bridge Visitor Center on Monument Avenue in Concord, reached by traveling west on Route 2A, illustrates the various engagements and preserves the sites; *978-369-6993.*

At Concord's North Bridge, militiamen heading for the town engaged a British detachment, killing some and causing the rest to fall back to Concord center. British officers tried but failed to regroup their pan-icking men at Fiske Hill, and today Battle Road follows the course of the British retreat from Concord. Militiamen, using the stone walls as cover, harried the British along the way, most severely at Bloody Angle, where eight redcoats were killed.

Munroe Tavern

Munroe Tavern, south of Lexington, served briefly as field headquarters for British relief troops and field hospital for the wounded. A bartender was reportedly shot in the back when he ran for the door, and a bullet hole is still visible in the ceiling of the preserved tavern, which was visited by George Washington in 1789. It is now a museum. *1332 Massachusetts Avenue in Lexington; 781-674-9238.*

■ CONCORD

At the time of its settlement in 1635, Concord (then known by its Native American name Musketaquid) was the frontier. The settlers purchased a six-square-mile plantation from the Massachusetts, then sealed the agreement with a peace pipe. The town's name commemorates that friendship.

Today, this charming place is too well bred to beat either its Revolutionary or literary drum too loudly. Ralph Waldo Emerson, Nathaniel Hawthorne, Henry David Thoreau, and Louisa May Alcott lived and wrote here in the birthplace of transcendentalism, but you get the impression that Concord took them in its easy stride. Even the river is sedate, so sedate that Hawthorne said he lived beside it for weeks before working out which way it flowed.

North Bridge, Wright's Tavern, the Hill Burying Ground, Monument Square, and a few lesser sites preserve the Revolutionary part of Concord's history. The literary part is more widely dispersed but is easily accessible from Route 2A.

Old Manse

Rev. William Emerson watched the North Bridge battle from the Old Manse, built in 1770. William's grandson, Ralph Waldo, lived here in 1834 and 1835 and wrote his first book, *Nature,* in a second-floor study.

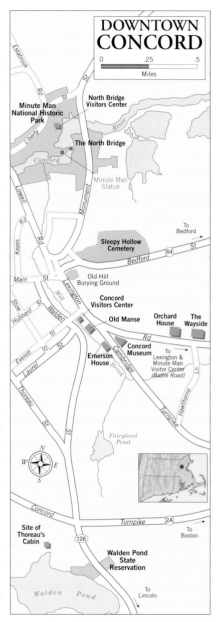

DOWNTOWN
CONCORD

0   .25   .5
Miles

North Bridge, site of the first battle of the Revolutionary War.

Nathaniel and Sophia Hawthorne rented the house for two years, first occupying it on their wedding night in 1842, and Hawthorne wrote *Mosses From an Old Manse* in the second-floor study. The Hawthornes scratched graffiti on a couple of window panes and their first child, Una, was born upstairs. The now-restored house features Emerson and Hawthorne memorabilia. *269 Monument Street; 978-369-3909.*

Orchard House and The Wayside

The Orchard House on Lexington Road is a shrine to the Alcotts, who lived here from 1858 to 1877. Louisa May Alcott wrote her first novel, *Moods,* and her most famous novel, *Little Women,* here, thus keeping the family out of poverty. The Alcotts left the house in 1877, but many family items and manuscripts are displayed here. *399 Lexington Road; 978-369-4118.*

Little Women was based partly on Louisa May Alcott's girlhood memories of the family's other Concord house, The Wayside, where they lived from 1845 to 1848. Nathaniel Hawthorne bought the house in 1852 after the publication of *The Blithedale Romance,* a novel that satirized a utopian community akin to one started by Bronson Alcott. *Adjacent to Orchard House, operated by Minute Man Historic Park; open May–October; 978-369-6975.*

Emerson House

The Ralph Waldo Emerson House was the writer's home from 1835 until his death in 1882. Thoreau, Hawthorne, and the Alcotts visited often; Thoreau is said to have made the dollhouse in the nursery. With the exception of the library's pieces, all of the furnishings are original. *28 Cambridge Turnpike; open seasonally; 978-369-2236.*

Concord Museum

Emerson's library is, in fact, across the busy Concord Turnpike (use walkways when crossing) at the Concord Museum, as is the simple furniture from Thoreau's Walden cabin. The museum houses the largest collection of Thoreau artifacts in the country, but its Revolution-era memorabilia and period rooms are equally impressive. Fifteen rooms and galleries display the decorative tastes of 18th- and 19th-century Concord. *200 Lexington Road; 978-369-9763.*

Walden Pond

Rejecting a society in which "the mass of men lead lives of quiet desperation," Thoreau built himself a cabin by Walden Pond on Emerson's wood lot and lived there from 1845 to 1847. *Walden, or Life in the Woods,* published in 1854, was an account of that experience and its lessons. Were he living at Walden today, Thoreau would hear the soundtrack of that desperation as rush hour traffic roars by on Highway 2. A cairn of stones marks the cabin's original location but the site is now largely dedicated to recreation, not contemplation, and the writer's solitude is literally unimaginable. *Take Highway 126 from Highway 2.*

A swimmer crosses Walden Pond.

NORTH SHORE
CAPE ANN & LOWELL

■ TRAVEL BASICS

North Shore, encompassing Cape Ann and the Merrimack Valley, is an ideal day trip from Boston, but you will want to stay much longer. Salem, the centerpiece, is rich in maritime, architectural, and witch trial history, but small towns like Newburyport and Ipswich are equally impressive. Beautiful Marblehead is a renowned sailing port and architectural jewel, Gloucester still fishes, Rockport still attracts artists, and Essex still perfects its fried clams. When you tire of natural wonders like Crane Beach, experience the 19th-century industrial revolution firsthand at Lowell's artfully restored mills.

Getting Around: A high-speed ferry connects Boston and Salem from July to October. Commuter trains serve Lowell, Ipswich, and Rockport. If you're driving, avoid hectic Route 128. Instead follow Route 127 around Cape Ann and Route 1A northward. Route 495 is a major truck artery but the most direct route to Lowell.

Climate: Boston forecasts generally apply (see page 36) although Cape Ann, regularly pummeled by Atlantic storms, is a breezy retreat when city temperatures rise.

Food & Lodging: For the best in seafood, look beyond the deep fryers of shoreside eateries; lodging is in small inns, B&Bs, and motels, with few large hotels. Massachusetts listings begin on page 328; towns are listed in alphabetical order. Listings map page 327; listing chart page 375.

■ OVERVIEW

Bounded on two sides by the Atlantic Ocean and irrigated by the Merrimack River, the North Shore is often regarded as the poor relation to its southerly cousin, Cape Cod. A glance at the map tells you why. Cape Cod extends a graceful, sandy arm into the Atlantic. The North Shore terminates in the granite knuckle of Cape Ann.

The "other cape" is, however, far from impoverished. Small and decidedly rugged, it is a beautiful, seductive place where the past is not only preserved in grand cities like Salem and Lowell, but can still be evoked on an Ipswich side street or a misty salt marsh. This small triangle, after all, witnessed the death throes of

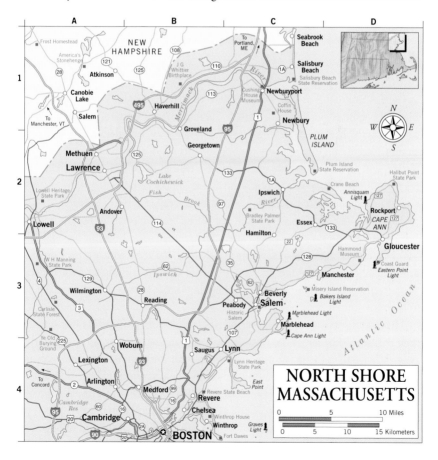

NORTH SHORE
MASSACHUSETTS

0   5   10 Miles

0   5   10   15 Kilometers

Puritan zealotry, the flowering of global maritime trade and the birth of the industrial city. You have to squint at times to bring that past into focus. But a trick of the light or a change in the wind can do it on this wild stretch of coast where the ocean's mood has always meant the difference between a fortune gained or lost, a prosperous life or an early death.

Today, even the fishing villages here follow modern tidal rhythms—the daily ebb and flow of commuter traffic from nearby Boston, flights from neighboring Logan Airport, and the annual inundation of fair-weather visitors. There are, however, quiet times. Bright, bustling summer is flanked by two seasons of glorious suspense—spring, when the human wave has yet to reclaim the beaches, and autumn, when that wave has receded and cold, raw winter is poised to empty the streets of people and refurnish them with snowbanks.

■ HISTORY

In 1623, a group of fishermen and farmers from Dorchester, England came ashore at Cape Ann hoping to fish, trade, and air their religious views. The Dorchester they left behind is better known to us as Thomas Hardy's Casterbridge, a town described by the heroine of *The Mayor of Casterbridge* as "huddled all together and shut in." Cape Ann was certainly the opposite, its windswept shores rewarding the settlers with space—but little else. "No sure fishing place in the Land is fit for planting," John White wrote, "nor is the fishing good where farming is."

The Dorchester enterprise failed within three years. In 1626, however, its last manager, 34-year-old Roger Conant, led 20 followers along the Indian trail to Naumkeag, where they faced the encroaching winter in a cluster of hastily built thatched huts. Naumkeag was renamed Salem in 1629, by which time Conant's group had been placed under the austere rule of Gov. John Endicott, who arrived at Salem flushed from the exertion of chopping down Thomas Morton's maypole at Merrymount.

The Massachusetts wilderness of the time was hardly enticing, as one settler's wife testified. "The air of the country is sharp," she wrote, "the rocks many, the trees innumerable, the grass little, the winter cold, the summer hot, the gnats in summer biting, the wolves at midnight howling." Governor Bradford also warned that "they are too delicate...that cannot enduer the biting of a muskeeto; we would wish shuch to keepe at home till at least they be muskeeto proofe."

More important, however, the fish were biting. Ideal for salting and drying, the codfish caught in these northern waters were soon nourishing not only colonial farmers but much of Europe, and salt cod became a key element in the expanding West Indies trade. By mid-17th century, the area north of Boston, although still the frontier, supported a string of flourishing trading towns and fishing villages, all dependent on the ships built with native white oak and pine. In Salem, Gloucester, Ipswich, and Newbury, shipbuilding was a major industry by 1660. By 1643, ships were ferrying cod and lumber from Salem's port to the West Indies and sailing back to Europe or New England with molasses and rum, trading along the way for manufactured goods.

Increasing interference from the Crown was first ignored then resisted by colonists on the North Shore, who protested the appointment of Governor Andros in 1687 with rallies in Ipswich and neighboring towns. Imperial control was further tightened in 1691, and the following year the witch hysteria in Salem Village briefly threatened to destabilize the entire region. Prosperity would weather not only superstition, but also the impending revolution, a revolution financed largely by Massachusetts ship owners.

The Launching of the Ship "Fame," *by George Ropes, 1802. (Peabody Essex Museum, Salem)*

The launching of the first Gloucester schooner in 1713 galvanized the fishing industry and by 1744 the small town of Marblehead had 90 vessels hauling an annual catch worth £34,000. Later in the century, Massachusetts merchants began charting new international trade routes. In 1784, the *Empress of China* completed her maiden voyage to the Orient, and two years later *Grand Turk,* owned by Salem's Elias Hasket Derby, reached the Chinese port of Canton. The opening of the Indies and China trade was the dawn of the North Shore's golden age, which would last until the early 19th century, with Salem at its center.

Thomas Jefferson's 1807 embargo on shipping to and from England and France during the Napoleonic Wars effectively closed foreign trade to a Massachusetts fleet that was earning about $15.5 million in freight money annually. The War of 1812 dealt North Shore merchants a further blow, and by mid-century the region's trading dominance was lost to Boston's deeper harbor.

Commercial fishing remained healthy, particularly in Gloucester, but Massachusetts was increasingly a manufacturing state. First water and later steam powered the huge new textile mills at Lowell and Lawrence from the 1820s onwards, and in 1848 Salem entered the factory age with the opening of the Naumkeag steam cotton mills.

Indian Encampment at Salem Harbor, painted in the 1920s by John Orne Johnson Frost, is the artist's vision of Salem 300 years earlier. (Shelburne Museum, Shelburne, Vermont)

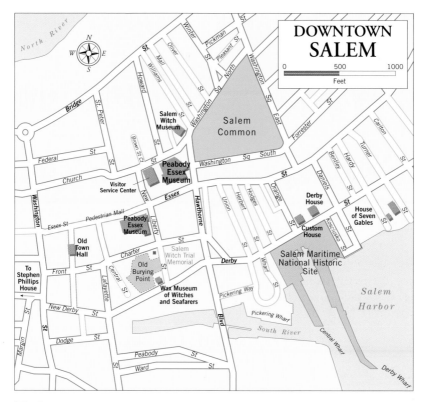

■ SALEM

"To the farthest port of the rich East" is Salem's motto, but its souvenir T-shirts are more likely to read "I did it every witch way in Salem." In a deliciously ironic twist, the Salem witch trials of 1692 have spawned a tourist industry that would confound the Puritan zealots who inspired the phenomenon.

Salem's 18th-century merchants, on the other hand, would instantly recognize the impulse to trade on past infamy. Trade, after all, was their business. It was also the key to Salem's considerable political influence and the source of the city's extraordinary cultural and architectural wealth.

Despite its modest beginnings as Roger Conant's tiny settlement in 1626, Salem has never been a backwater. Each era—maritime, industrial, and commercial—has left its distinct mark on the city, as have the immigrants who continue to arrive. The resulting townscape, while small and eminently walkable, is also somewhat fractured.

One of the most pleasant ways to approach the port is aboard the **high-speed ferry from Boston** that runs from July 1 to October 31, departing Long Wharf six times daily. *(Schedule: 978-741-3442)* Should the relaxing coastal cruise put you in the mood for a **pedicab tour of the city,** be forewarned that delusions of grandeur may set in as your rickshaw is pulled along by an entertaining bicyclist.

Heritage Trail

Salem's 1.7-mile Heritage Trail connects the major historic sites, and entire streets are meticulously preserved. But the spaces in between run the gamut from intriguing shabbiness to phony charm. Most of the phony charm can be found on the **Essex Street Pedestrian Mall.** Farther along toward Salem Common, however, the **Peabody Essex Museum** on East India Square houses genuine riches in its exquisite and informative exhibits.

Peabody Essex Museum

Founded in 1799, this is the oldest continuously operated museum in the country, having started out as a repository for artifacts acquired by Salem's mariners. Its porcelain collection alone is remarkable, but there are also paintings, sculpture, furniture, and textiles from Asia and the Americas. Exhibits related to New England history and to Salem's seafaring tradition provide an invaluable background to any exploration of the city. You may also be delicately fortified for your trip by mussels chablis, Asian-accented swordfish steak, and other treats in the elegant **Peabody Essex Cafe.**

The museum offers tours of three historic houses: the 1684 **John Ward House,** the 1727 **Crowninshield-Bentley House,** and the 1804 **Gardener-Pingree House.** Behind the last of these is a small architectural jewel—the **Derby-Beebe Summer House,** built in 1799 for Elias Hasket Derby. This 12-foot-square piece of elegant whimsy was accurately described by architectural critic Peter Vanderwarker as "a delicate confection in a community of stuffed shirts." *Peabody Essex Museum: 978-745-9500 or 800-745-4054.*

Town Common and Witch Museum

Salem's handsome Common, ringed by elegant houses that bear the stamp of architect Samuel McIntire, is presided over by a statue of Roger Conant. "A moderate and kindly puritan, conciliatory and peaceful," as Samuel Eliot Morison describes him, Conant would have doubtless been horrified by the exhibits in the nearby **Salem Witch Museum,** where a series of dioramas chronicles the events that led to the imprisonment of 150 townspeople and the execution of 20; *978-744-1692* or *800-544-1692.*

Witch-Related Events

Although nearby Danvers, then called Salem Village, was the town contorted by witch hysteria, Salem, the scene of the trials, capitalizes on the 17th-century aberration. Throughout the summer, trials are reenacted in the **Witch Dungeon Museum**

A statue of Roger Conant, Salem's first settler, stands in front of the Salem Witch Museum.

on Lynde Street. *The People vs. Bridget Bishop* is staged in the **Old Town Hall** on the Essex Street Mall, and *Cry Innocent,* a seasonal street theater performance, also embellishes historical truth. Farther down Essex Street is an authentic site—the **Witch House**, home of Magistrate Jonathan Corwin, where the accused were subjected to intimate preliminary examinations in rooms that today seem more cozy than sinister; *310 ½ Essex Street; information for sites above: 978-744-0180.*

Salem Waterfront

The historic waterfront on Derby Street lacks ships today. But on a brisk May morning when a northeast wind corrugates the sea, it is easy to imagine how the air was once perfumed with the exotic spices in a schooner's hold. To develop such visions, visit the **Salem Tea Room** on Pickering Wharf, where the tea is loose, the atmosphere antique, and clairvoyant readings a specialty.

Salem's docks have, however, always concerned themselves with money, not magic. Of the 50 wharves that once ridged Salem Harbor, only the Derby, Central, and Hatch Wharves (dating from 1762 to 1819) remain, their warehouses replaced by a grass walkway and visitor center. Facing the wharves is the 1819 **Custom House** where Salem novelist Nathaniel Hawthorne worked as surveyor of the port of Salem from 1845 until 1849. Fortunately for Hawthorne, Salem's port was declining at

A golden eagle peers off the pediment of the Custom House in Salem.

that time, allowing the writer to fill his notebooks as well as his ledgers during idle work hours. Behind the Custom House, exhibits in The Scale House and Government Bonded Warehouse reveal the variety and value of Salem's 18th-century imports.

Derby House

The neighboring **Derby House** was built for merchant Elias Hasket Derby in 1762, Salem's heyday. Probably America's first millionaire, Derby took over the family business at 44, expanding its European and West Indies trade and profiting immensely from privateering during the Revolutionary War. Derby was also instrumental in opening the East to Salem. His ship *Grand Turk* was the first Salem vessel to reach China, trading its load of ebony, ginseng, gold thread, cloth, and betel nuts for tea, silk, spices, porcelain, and cassia.

Samuel McIntire designed the 1780 **Hawkes House** next door for Derby, who used it as a privateer warehouse during the Revolution. Samuel Hawkes, owner of the Hawkes Wharf, bought and completed the house in 1801. Behind it is the 17th-century **Narbonne-Hale House**, which was the home and workshop of various Salem craftsmen as well as the "Cent Shop" described by Hawthorne in *The House of the Seven Gables*.

House of Seven Gables

A short walk from Derby House, the **House of Seven Gables**, probably built in 1668 but extensively restored in 1910, is a pilgrimage site for those untroubled by the fact that this may not be the house made famous by Hawthorne's 1851 novel. Hawthorne's birthplace, moved to this site, shares a charming harborside garden with the **Retire Beckett House** of 1655 and the **Hooper-Hathaway House** of 1682—an arrangement that would surely have displeased a writer who liked to choose his neighbors. Proceeds from the House of Seven Gables support the charitable services of the House of Seven Gables Settlement, one of many groups established around 1900 to help struggling families. *House of Seven Gables, 54 Turner Street; 978-744-0991.*

Chestnut Street

There is no sign of struggle on Chestnut Street. Arguably Salem's grandest thoroughfare and one of the nation's finest architectural sites, this wide tree-lined street of mostly Federal brick houses was laid out in 1796. Its elegant 19th-century residences, some designed by McIntire, were owned by merchants and sea captains and even today have an air of uninterrupted prosperity. Chestnut Street is particularly lovely in late spring when its exquisite private gardens overrun their brick walls and impudent sparrows play hopscotch on the herringbone brick sidewalks. The **Stephen Phillips Memorial Trust House** is open for tours but you should, above all, dawdle on the street itself to appreciate the remarkable security created by Salem's high-stakes maritime gambling. *34 Chestnut Street; 978-744-0440.*

■ MARBLEHEAD *map page 81, C-3*

Artist John Orne Johnson Frost painted this image of the town of Marblehead, circa 1920. (courtesy Marblehead Historical Society)

Arriving in Marblehead in 1715, the Rev. John Barnard wrote: "Nor could I find twenty families that could stand upon their own legs, and they were generally as rude, swearing, drunken, and fighting a crew as they were poor."

Now the respectable yachting center of the eastern seaboard, Marblehead nonetheless retains a delightfully chaotic demeanor, particularly in its historic district where ancient, narrow streets weave toward the harbor and pre-Revolutionary houses tilt away from each other at impossible angles. Attempting to drive or park in this labyrinth is frustrating and time-consuming, particularly in July and August when other visitors quickly begin to look like the enemy. Far better to relieve yourself of your car in the Front Street public lot or on one of the streets skirting the older part of town and proceed on foot or two wheels. That way you also have an excuse to refresh yourself with lunch or coffee at **The King's Rook** at 12 State Street, a cozy Marblehead cafe housed in a suitably askew 18th-century building.

Fishermen from Devon and Dorset (and later from Cornwall and the Channel Islands) first settled Marble Harbor, as they called it, in 1629. Clinging to a terrace of granite ledges regularly pounded by northeast gales, the town rapidly became a leading fishing, shipbuilding, and trading port. With its fine mansions and thriving businesses, Marblehead became the sixth-largest city in the colonies and a center of Revolutionary and privateering activity. Superstition and wild imaginings also flourished. As you tour the town keep in mind that the "screeching woman of Marblehead" haunted the harbor in the 17th century, and the town's "Mammy Redd" was hanged for turning butter to wool. Moll Pitcher, a famous psychic, was born here in 1743; the wizard Edward Dimond defied gales atop Old Burial Hill; and Marblehead was the model for horror writer H. P. Lovecraft's fictional town of Kingsport.

The charming harbor, into which the old town tumbles, is mesmerizingly peaceful today, especially on a luminous June morning from **Fort Sewall** on Front Street or from **Chandler Hovey Park** on Marblehead Neck, both fine picnic spots.

Pretend you're a local by referring simply to "the Neck" and by merely raising an eyebrow when confronted by mansions like "Carcasonne"—off Ocean Avenue by the viewpoint at Castle Rock. Faking it is tougher during hectic Race Week in July and during the Regatta in August, when individuals who don't know their lanyards from their spinnakers are advised to keep a respectful distance from those who do.

You don't need arcane knowledge or waterproof clothing to appreciate Marblehead's unique buildings (more than 200 date from before the Revolutionary War) and their gardens, both ranging from grand to pocket-sized.

Jeremiah Lee Mansion

The Jeremiah Lee Mansion across from the Marblehead Historical Society on Washington Street shows what 18th-century profits could buy. Completed in 1768, this is one of the finest Georgian houses in the country, with original wallpaper, furniture, and paneling as well as a lovely sunken garden of lavender and boxwood. Lee, a shipping magnate and Revolutionary, was attending a seditious meeting in Arlington when the British passed on their way to Concord in April 1775. He escaped through the fields but died a month later from exposure. *161 Washington Street; 781-631-1768.*

King Hooper Mansion and Abbot Hall

The nearby King Hooper Mansion, built in 1745 for merchant Robert Hooper, now houses the Marblehead Arts Association, while *The Spirit of '76,* America's favorite Revolutionary War painting, hangs in Abbot Hall on elegant Washington Square, where Gen. John Glover assembled his men before marching to Boston. *8 Hooper Street.*

John Singleton Copley's portrait of Jeremiah Lee. (Wadsworth Atheneum, Hartford)

Old Town House

The 1727 Old Town House is one of the most beautiful in New England and one of the most symmetrical in Marblehead: Identical entrances allow the building to face two directions at once. *Washington Street at the top of State Street.*

MASSACHUSETTS
NORTH SHORE

Good Harbor Beach, in the Cape Ann area.

■ ABOUT CAPE ANN TOWNS

You can circumnavigate Cape Ann, the small rugged knob of the North Shore, in an hour's drive along the shore road. But the charming towns of **Essex, Gloucester,** and **Rockport** divert you with fried clams and other temptations. Essex and Gloucester in particular are still seafaring towns with ramshackle appeal. Established by the Story and Burnham families in Essex, shipyards dating from 1668 have launched a variety of vessels over the centuries, from traditional Cape Ann "Chebaccos" and dories to modern schooners and trawlers. The first Essex boat was reportedly built by a Burnham in the 17th century, and today young Harold Burnham builds traditional wooden vessels on the same spot. Along with other local craftsmen, Burnham built the *Thomas E. Lannon* in 1997, the first traditional North Shore fishing schooner to be launched in almost 50 years, which now takes visitors on fishing heritage cruises from Seven Seas Wharf in Gloucester Harbor during the summer. *Lannon tours: 978-281-6634.*

Clams are taken seriously in what food writers Jane and Michael Stern have christened "America's fried-clam belt." And the more venerated they are, the more casually they are served. **Woodman's of Essex** is a perfect example. A not-so-glorified clam shack only minutes from the water, Woodman's has been a New England institution since Cubby Woodman first dropped some clams into a pot of lard at his roadside stand eighty years ago. Serving no-frills chowder, steamers, and fried clams that can silence any food snob, Woodman's reportedly dips its raw clams in evaporated milk before coating them with fresh cornmeal. That suspiciously prosaic explanation cannot, however, account for something that tastes like toasted sunshine. The Essex Clam Fest in September is an ideal opportunity to put Woodman's and its competitors to the test.

■ GLOUCESTER *map page 81, D-3*

In its mid-19th-century heyday, Gloucester had a 350-vessel fleet that once landed almost 10 million pounds of fish in a single day. It still has the credentials to back up its September Seafood Festival. Settled in 1623, this is the oldest fishing port in Massachusetts and one whose occupational hardships have become legendary. Rudyard Kipling's 1897 novel *Captains Courageous* was set aboard the Gloucester fleet, as was *The Perfect Storm,* Sebastian Junger's chilling account of the 1991 gale that annihilated one of its vessels.

A STORM LANDS IN GLOUCESTER

*B*y midafternoon the wind is hitting hurricane force and people are having a hard time walking, standing up, being heard. Moans emanate from the electric lines that only offshore fishermen have ever heard before. Waves inundate Good Harbor Beach and the parking lot in front of the Stop-n-Shop. They rip up entire sections of Atlantic Road. They deposit a fifteen-foot-high tangle of lobster traps and sea muck at the end of Grapevine Road. They fill the swimming pool of a Back Shore mansion with ocean-bottom rubble. They suck beach cobble up their huge faces and sling them inland, smashing windows, peppering lawns. They overrun the sea wall at Brace Cove, spill into Niles Pond, and continue into the woods beyond. For a brief while it is possible to surf across people's lawns. So much salt water gets pumped into Niles Pond that it overflows and cuts Eastern Point in half. Eastern Point is where the rich live, and by nightfall the ocean is two feet deep in some of the nicest living rooms in the state.

—Sebastian Junger, *The Perfect Storm,* 1997

THEY THAT GO
DOWN TO THE SEA
IN SHIPS
1623 — 1923

Gloucester's expansive harbor still shelters a fleet of fishing boats, and on a bone-chilling November day when black-backed gulls hunker down on the quay and sleet pockmarks the water, the heroic mariner's statue on the waterfront seems to be heading the town into the wind, beyond Ten Pound Island, toward fair weather.

Reminders of sacrifice and endurance are everywhere in this port, which was losing 100 fishermen annually at the end of the 19th century. "Full many a gallant ship/ When we were lost/ Weathered the gale" reads the inscription on the carved-wood waves in the beautiful 1870 City Hall. The WPA murals of historic scenes here are as uplifting as the memorial plaques to lost mariners are sobering. On nearby Middle Street, the 18th-century **Sargent-Murray House** displays the wealth generated by such hardship, in particular by the port's fish and molasses trade with Dutch Guiana. "They excell in their parties, their clubs and also in their military parades," wrote Salem's Rev. William of the robust inhabitants at that time. *Sargent-Murray House: 978-281-2432.*

Those instincts are still displayed each June in the three-day **St. Peter's Fiesta**, when parades, boat races, fireworks, competitions, and a blessing of the fleet turns the town into a street party. This is also a good time to sample Gloucester's food,

Scenes from Gloucester: (opposite) the seaman's monument and (above) commercial fishing boats in the town center marina.

much of which has a sublime Portuguese and Italian flavor. You should not wait for the Fiesta, however, to enjoy the remarkable breakfast and lunch in the **Two Sisters restaurant** on Washington Street or the Sicilian pastries and breads in **Caffe Sicilia** on Main Street.

◆ CAPE ANN HISTORICAL MUSEUM

Gloucester resonates with epic achievements, and the wonderful Cape Ann Historical Museum gives visitors a taste of the town's glorious past. *27 Pleasant Street; 978-283-0455.*

Howard Blackburn's *Great Republic*

A modest boat in the museum testifies to Gloucester's most exceptional seafaring story. The sloop *Great Republic* belonged to Howard Blackburn, a dory fisherman who lost all his fingers to frostbite while long-lining off Newfoundland in the late 19th century. Despite his disability, Blackburn completed two solo transatlantic voyages, the first from Gloucester, Massachusetts to Gloucester, England in 1899, and the second from his home town to Lisbon, Portugal, in 1901. The voyage to Lisbon set a new world's record of 39 days.

Edward Hopper's painting Gloucester Harbor, *1912.*
(Whitney Museum of American Art, New York, Josephine N. Hopper Bequest)

Fitz Hugh Lane's painting Ships in Ice off Ten Pound Island, Gloucester, *circa 1850.*
(Museum of Fine Arts, Boston)

Blackburn achieved this remarkable feat in his second 30-foot sloop, *Great Western,* a replica of which is currently being built in Gloucester. To commemorate the Blackburn voyages, a disabled mariner will sail the replica singlehanded from Gloucester to Gloucester in 1999 and from Gloucester to Lisbon in 2001.

Alfred Johnson's *Centennial*

Another local fisherman, Alfred Johnson, was the first man to sail the Atlantic solo in 1876, and his boat, *Centennial,* is also displayed at the museum. Joshua Slocum started his 1895 solo circumnavigation of the globe from Gloucester, as did Philip Weld, a legend of the modern Observer Single-Handed Transatlantic Races.

Marine Paintings

The historical association flaunts Gloucester's artistic pedigree as well, in its collection of marine paintings. So popular was this coast with 19th- and early-20th-century artists that one of them, John Sloan, once wrote to Van Wyck Brooks that "there was an artist's shadow beside every cow in Gloucester, and the cows themselves were dying from eating paint rags." The rain-washed, clear light that inspired Milton Avery, Childe Hassam, Maxfield Parrish, Edward Hopper, Cape Ann native Fitz Hugh Lane, and others is just as striking today, and the skeleton of Gloucester's streets remains virtually unchanged from Hopper's day.

◆ HARBOR SITES NEAR GLOUCESTER

Just outside town overlooking Smith's Cove, **Rocky Neck Art Colony** is the nation's oldest working art colony, with more than 30 artists in residence. From Gloucester's East Main Street, the loop out there and back unrolls like one long canvas of magnificent seascapes. Beyond the Neck, with its galleries and waterside restaurants, Eastern Point Boulevard skirts Niles Beach and proceeds past impressive mansions that command even more impressive views. **Beauport,** an eccentric monument to one man's obsession, was built and furnished here between 1907 and 1934 by Henry Davis Sleeper, an interior designer whose fine antique collection is artfully arranged in period rooms. If you find the glorious interior maze exhausting, you can refresh yourself with tea overlooking Gloucester Harbor.

Past Eastern Point is the rocky outline of Back Shore and the elegant sweep of Good Harbor Beach. The largest summer crowds, however, favor Cape Ann's biggest beach, **Wingaersheek**—back toward Highway 128—a sandy expanse with dunes, salt marshes, and plentiful parking. A mile away, the **Cape Ann Camp Site** provides 300 shaded tent and trailer sites overlooking the Annisquam River, while the smaller Camp Annisquam offers saltwater fishing and a small tidal beach.

Larger thrills are provided by the numerous whale-watching cruises sailing chiefly out of Salem, Gloucester, and Newburyport. Experienced boaters are even encouraged to approach the whales in kayaks launched at sea. Less energetic mariners may ship out aboard the *Thomas E. Lannon* for Gloucester's **Seven Seas Wharf** for cod jigging, lobster bakes, and sunset cruises.

■ ROCKPORT *map page 81, D-2*

After robust Gloucester, Rockport, at the tip of Cape Ann, seems prettily demure. Perhaps it is the fact that this has been a "dry" town (no alcohol can legally be sold here) since seamstress and herbal healer Hannah Jumper preached abstinence almost a century ago. Or perhaps it is the abundance of gift stores and art galleries. Reproduced in painting after painting, Rockport seems to be permanently admiring itself. And who could blame it? On a cloudless June morning, even the herring gulls screeching and wheeling above the harbor seem to be choreographed players in a picture-perfect scene. Tidy lobster boats rock contentedly beside snooty yachts, and the quay is littered with still-life arrangements of fishing nets, old rope, and lobster pots.

Motif No. 1

It is hardly surprising, then, that Rockport's most famous site is a fisherman's shack at the breakwater on Bearskin Neck—a short walk from downtown's Dock Square. Known as Motif No. 1 and a favorite subject for generations of painters, the shack is annually venerated in May, on the Saturday before Memorial Day, when local artists paint it and sell their work—often still wet—to onlookers.

Lifting your head from the canvas, you will notice that Bearskin Neck offers its own stunning views of the Atlantic and that the humble **Portside Chowder House** offers some of the best chowder and shellfish in town. The fact that it doesn't have a phone, doesn't take credit cards, and doesn't serve dinner should be taken as a recommendation.

Pigeon Cove

The Portside Chowder House is not the only holdout in a town teetering on the edge of cuteness. Pigeon Cove, north of Dock Square, is preserved as a lobstering and fishing harbor.

Yankee Clipper Inn

Those wishing to live, however briefly, in old Rockport style will appreciate the Yankee Clipper Inn, which has been managed by one family for half a century. Perched on a dramatic promontory, it comprises a 1920s art deco mansion, an 1840 Bulfinch Greek Revival house, a shingled captain's quarters, and a modern quarterdeck, which is only steps from the shore.

Katherine Anne Porter was sufficiently inspired to stay here to finish her only novel, *Ship of Fools*, published in 1962. Those wishing to indulge in some benign snooping may also avail themselves of Rockport's annual Kitchen Tour in early May, when many noteworthy private houses open their doors. *Yankee Clipper Inn: 96 Granite Street; 978-546-3407.*

Halibut Point State Park *map page 81, D-2*

For natural curiosities, there is Halibut Point State Park, where you can find a secluded spot between massive rocks even on the most hectic summer weekend. Rockport was protected and sustained by granite since its founding in 1690, and in the mid-19th century the town's quarries—still visible at Halibut Point—were the primary source of its prosperity. Today bathers plunge into some of the quarries (access is limited) while waders prefer to stand heron-like on the rocks, supervising the ankle-licking waves, exploring the many crab pools, or waiting for inquisitive seals to pop up only feet from the shore.

Hardy individuals visiting the same spot in winter encounter nature at her moodiest, sullenly hurling gray waves about under leaden skies or shrieking at gale-force pitch.

Then Rockport's **Twin Lights**—the only surviving double lighthouses in the world —seem a great deal more than picturesque, and the pleasing town, battened down for the assault, reveals its granite backbone.

■ IPSWICH *map page 81, C-2*

Ipswich, north of Cape Ann, was an isolated frontier settlement when John Winthrop Jr. and a dozen other pioneers founded the town in 1633. Winthrop's wife and baby daughter died here the following year, and when Governor Winthrop visited his son, he reportedly had to walk the 30-mile Indian trail from Boston. Today, he would have his pick of mounts for the return journey, as Ipswich is an affluent center of equestrian activity, and Winthrop Road, in particular, has more horses than the governor could shake a stick at.

Winthrop Jr. was a broad-minded man of science, and under his influence this outpost quickly became a 17th-century intellectual and cultural center. Home to Anne Bradstreet, America's first woman poet, and to satirist Nathaniel Ward in the 1630s and '40s, modern Ipswich is also the setting for many of John Updike's novels. And it is one of New England's most beautiful towns, with more 17th-century houses preserved and occupied than anywhere else in the country.

Theodore Wendel's Bridge at Ipswich, *circa 1905. (Museum of Fine Arts, Boston)*

Heard House and Whipple House

The 1725 John Heard House at the corner of the Green is a fine local museum, but the John Whipple House, facing the Common, is the most dramatic of the town's restorations. Built in 1640, it was hailed in 1890 by its savior, Rev. Thomas Franklin Waters, as "a link that binds us to the remote Past and to a solemn and earnest manner of living, quite in contrast with much in our modern life." Despite Waters's benediction and the building's dominant presence, the Whipple House, with its lovely 17th-century garden and graceful proportions, is more beguiling than solemn —a reminder that Puritanism was not all severity. *Heard House: 978-356-2811.*

Old Burying Ground

The many poignant gravestone inscriptions in the Old Burying Ground on High Street, Ipswich's main thoroughfare, reinforce that impression. "Warm from his lips the heavn'ly doctrine fell," the 1775 testimony to Rev. Nathaniel Rogers begins, with imagery befitting a love poem.

High and East Street Houses

Anne Bradstreet's secular poetry scandalized her neighbors on High Street when she lived at No. 33, and she acknowledged "I am obnoxious to each carping tongue/ Who say my hand a needle better fits."

Gracious 17th- and early-18th-century houses line High and East Streets in particular, but even the town's side streets evoke its uninterrupted prosperity and architectural creativity.

A great American elm at the corner of East Street is also a reminder of how such towns looked when these giants shaded every thoroughfare.

◆ IPSWICH RIVER AND PARKLAND *map page 81, C-2*

Today the Ipswich River is stocked with trout, and much of its watershed is protected in three adjacent conservation areas between Ipswich and neighboring Topsfield off the Topsfield Road: the **Willowdale State Forest, Bradley Palmer State Park,** and the **Ipswich River Wildlife Sanctuary.** One of the North Shore's best kept secrets, the 2,800-acre wildlife sanctuary was once the private estate of amateur horticulturist Thomas Proctor, who favored plantings that would encourage birds and wildlife throughout the year. *Sanctuary : 978-887-9264.*

Proctor's legacy is a riverside parkland that is most exuberant in early spring when the Ipswich is in full flow, its creeks roaring, its riverbanks daubed with wildflowers and the air shimmering with butterflies. Ten miles of nature trails border eight miles of river here, and you can also canoe the gentle waterway, putting in at Foote Bros. canoe rental by the Willowdale Dam. *Foote Bros. canoes: 978-356-9771.*

Children particularly approve of Proctor's most outlandish construction, **the Rockery.** A gigantic rock garden constructed out of glacial boulders, its caves and

CHOWDER HEADS

*T*here is a terrible pink mixture (with tomatoes in it, and herbs) called Manhattan Clam Chowder, that is only a vegetable soup, and not to be confused with New England Clam Chowder, nor spoken of in the same breath. Tomatoes and clams have no more affinity than ice cream and horse radish. It is sacrilege to wed bivalves with bay leaves, and only a degraded cook would do such a thing.

Representative Cleveland Sleeper of Maine recently introduced a bill in the State legislature, to make it illegal as well as a culinary offense to introduce tomatoes to clam chowder. And immediately a chowder battle ensued—with high-class chef's asserting that a tomato and clam should never meet, and the low maestros of Manhatten advocating their unholy union.

Anyone who wants tomato soup can have it; but Manhattan Clam Chowder is a kind of thin minestrone, or dish water, and fit only for foreigners.

—Eleanor Early, *New England Sampler*, 1940

tunnels are ideal for hide and seek. Whatever your age, you will be impressed by **Wolf Hollow** outside Ipswich, where Joni and Paul Soffron have studied American timber wolves in natural enclosures for six years and invite you to do the same. *144 Essex Street, on Route 1A outside Ipswich: 978-356-0216.*

♦ CRANE ESTATE *map page 81, C-2*

Outlying Ipswich is a dreamy place of marshes and estuaries, which can be viewed in splendor from the Crane Estate. The Great House, built between 1910 and 1928 for plumbing magnate Richard T. Crane Jr., sits on 165 landscaped acres. Far more impressive than the mansion is the Grande Allee—a green ribbon that stretches from an Italianate pavilion to the sea below.

Castle Hill, on which the Crane estate stands, is a 2,000-acre reserve of meadow, beach, and wetland extending into Essex. Land smudges into water here, and on a misty day the 1725 **Choate House** on Hog Island seems more ship than house. Home to over 180 species of birds and other wildlife, Hog Island became more famous as a setting for the 1996 film *The Crucible*. A Crane Islands tour via boat and hay wagon takes in the "Proctor House," which was built for the film, as well as spectacular ocean views. *Castle Hill and the Crane Estate: 978-356-4351.*

In spring and summer, **Crane Beach**, below Castle Hill, is an idyllic, pastel arrangement of low-lying dunes, azure sea, and bleached sky, and you can see why Native Americans of the Agawam tribe were attracted to the tidal creeks and plentiful shellfish. In winter, however, when the shore is concussed by relentless surf, Crane lives up to its designation as a barrier beach, shielding Essex Bay and its estuaries from the Atlantic's ferocity. Sea ducks ride the waves on even the stormiest days, however, and a winter walk along the mile-long interpretive beach trail leading to a peaceful woodland may raise a snowy owl, red fox, or some other tough off-season resident.

■ NEWBURY *map page 81, C-1*

Route 1A, an old highway, meanders along the coastline between Newbury and Newburyport, dictating a leisurely pace. A Newbury pace, you might say. This sleepy town, settled in 1635, comprises an Upper Green and Lower Green with a duck pond in the middle for excitement. The **Coffin House**, north of the town center, was occupied by the Coffin family from about 1653 until 1929, and its restored features show how New England life evolved over three centuries.

Off Route 1A between Newbury and Newburyport, the **Spencer-Peirce-Little Farm**—with its stone and brick manor at the end of a maple-lined avenue—is one of the most atmospheric 17th-century sites in the country. The estate has been continuously farmed for 350 years, and when the Draft Horse Plow Match—a New England–wide competition—is held in these flat, dreamy fields each April, the clank of harnesses and the presence of docile equine giants reinforces the sense of a place suspended in time.

Visitors to the house are taken step by step through its history, from the 1940s dining room through the 19th and 18th centuries to the the whitewashed 1690 family chamber. The attic walls even have their original graffiti, including a painstaking sketch of a sailing ship. *Spencer-Peirce-Little Farm: follow signs from Route 1A; 978-462-2634.*

■ NEWBURYPORT *map page 81, C-1*

Originally an offshoot of its sleepy neighbor, Newburyport capitalized on its position at the mouth of the Merrimack River to become an important shipbuilding
and trading center in the 18th and early 19th centuries. Specializing in the West
Indian and European markets, the town also developed rum and whiskey distil-
leries as well as goldsmithing, textile, and printing industries. The many editions
of Nathaniel Bowditch's *Navigator* (the seaman's bible) and Captain Furlong's
American Coast Pilot were printed here.

The society created by such enterprises was considered one of the most sophisticated in post-colonial America, far ahead of Salem in manner and style. Lavish
balls and liveried servants were the order of the day in 1809 when the town had
just 8,000 inhabitants but a merchant's cellar typically held 1,200 gallons of wine.

The decline of the Federalist party in the early 19th century punctured Newburyport's political power; Jefferson's 1807 embargo on all foreign commerce
wounded its shipping; and an 1811 fire destroyed 15 acres in the city center. Shipbuilding was revived, however, in the clipper era, when Donald McKay made his
reputation here between 1841 and 1843 with the construction of three speedy
packet vessels.

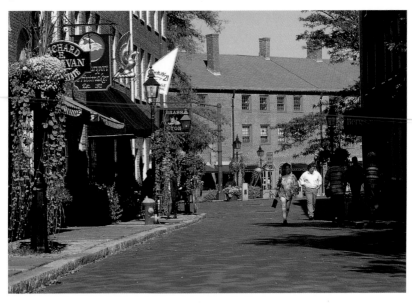

Inn Street is now a pedestrian walkway on Market Square, in downtown Newburyport.

Martin Johnson Heade's Newburyport Marshes: Passing Storm, *circa 1865.*
(Bowdoin College Museum of Art, Brunswick, Maine)

Market Square Historic District

Newburyport's historic district has pre-served many commercial waterfront build-ings, in particular the 1835 Custom House, which is now a maritime museum. (*Custom House: 25 Water Street; 978-462-8681*). Practically every street demands attention, however, not simply for the unparalleled examples of Georgian, Federal, Greek Re-vival, and Victorian residential architecture, but for the sense those streets give of New-buryport's vigorous heyday.

One theory suggests that ship carpenters designed and built Newburyport's man-sions, and the originality of the ornamenta-tion seems to support the view. Quirkiness of a more modest kind survives in the wa-terfront's early-18th-century dwellings and downtown in **Fowle's Soda Shop.** With its art deco facade and unaltered interior, the latter is frequented by alienated youth and respectable matrons alike who share an ap-preciation for the house-roasted coffee and

impressive selection of international news-papers.

Brown Square

Conscience as well as commerce had its say in Newburyport when abolitionist William Lloyd Garrison exposed a merchant who was taking slaves as freight from Baltimore to New Orleans in 1829. Today, Garrison's statue dominates Brown Square, which is also the site of the **Garrison Inn,** a hand-some redbrick mansion built in 1809 for rum merchant Moses Brown; *978-499-8500.*

Plum Island

Plum Island—with its sandy beaches, ex-tensive marshes, and wildlife sanctuary—is Newburyport's main outlying attraction, recently named by the Nature Conservancy as one of the best birding spots in North America and rated by *National Geographic* as one of the top 10 beaches in the country.

■ AMESBURY

Upriver from Newburyport, practically on the New Hampshire border, is the modest town of Amesbury, settled in 1654. The contrast with Newburyport is immediately evident and, on Amesbury's part, quite deliberate.

Although never comparable to Newburyport, Amesbury was an important shipbuilding center until the steam revolution of the 1850s. Impressive 18th-century shipwrights' houses line the beautiful sweep of Point Shore Road on the Merrimack's banks, where America's oldest dory shop, the **Lowell Boat Yard,** built in 1793 by Simeon Lowell, still builds dories, skiffs, and other small vessels. *978-388-0162.*

Amesbury's once teeming riverfront is a beautiful, soothing place today, and it is easy to see why Robert Frost spent his summers here at 5 Evans Place. Part of the Merrimack River Loop bike route, this quiet, shady riverside road winds from Amesbury to the neighboring town of Merrimac, offering grassy banks at regular intervals for picnicking or stone-skimming.

It is on Main Street, however, that Amesbury shows it is not Newburyport. Instead of stripping itself down to a Federal core that was never particularly glorious and attempting to attract upscale antique and speciality stores, the town preserved local businesses like Fuller's Menswear, which has been in the same family for four generations. In doing so, Amesbury was assisted by the National Main Street Center, a branch of the National Trust for Historic Preservation, which selected Amesbury precisely because it was so average.

The decision to be a real rather than a tourist town produced small, delightful surprises. The **Bartlett Museum** on Main Street, for example, displays an idiosyncratic collection of Native American artifacts, natural science exhibits, and carriages. Main Street is an eccentric mix of storefronts and pleasing curves; the Millyard is a complex of restored mill buildings housing offices and stores, while steep, winding dead-ends like Union Street reveal the town's curious angles and roof pitches.

Perhaps Amesbury has always seen itself as more substantial, less frivolous than its southern neighbors. The **Rocky Hill Meetinghouse,** at the intersection of Elm Street and Rocky Hill Road, certainly supports that view. Built in 1785, literally on a rocky hill, the large, austere building is an outstanding example of New England meetinghouse architecture. Little used, it has remained unchanged. The only fanciful detail is the crude marbleizing on its interior columns.

Plain Amesbury attracted more than one poet, however. John Greenleaf Whittier lived here from 1836 until his death in 1892. He is buried at Union Cemetery, and **The Garden Room** at his home on Friend Street remains as it was when the poet and abolitionist wrote his inspiring and lucrative works here. Like most New England outposts, the town also has its share of witch and ghost lore. Susanna Martin, better known as Goody Martin, was a famous Amesbury witch hanged in Salem in 1693. Legend insists that the loom of Goody Whitcher's, another local witch, kept weaving long after she met a less gruesome end.

■ LOWELL *map page 81, A-2*

The looms at Lowell also run unattended these days—for demonstration purposes only. They are fueled not by the powers of darkness but by the Merrimack River and by the determination of this purpose-built mill city to preserve its industrial heritage. "Many workers…wanted the good and the bad of the past preserved, rather than flattened and denied," the late Congressman Paul Tsongas explained in 1978, promoting the restoration of the city's historical sites.

In the 1820s, a group of Boston investors led by Francis Cabot Lowell found the ideal location for a modern mill city at Pawtucket Falls on the Merrimack. Cabot had memorized the latest power-loom mechanisms while on a tour of English mills. He had also been appalled by the squalid working conditions and demoralized workers. Determined to create a factory city free of such evils, the Boston Associates built dormitories for the workers and provided educational, athletic, and religious activities.

This paternalistic enterprise depended from the outset on Southern cotton and aided the expansion of slavery through what Senator Charles Sumner called the "unholy union…between the lords of the lash and the lords of the loom." Unperturbed by such criticism, new companies sprang up in Lowell between 1826 and 1840, and by 1846 the mills were producing almost one million yards of cloth a week. Lowell's population kept pace, growing from about 2,500 in 1826 to 33,000 in 1850, when 10 mills employed over 10,000 people.

New England farm girls, valued by the employers for their apparent virtue and tractability, were the earliest labor source for Lowell's "bale to bolt" cotton mills. Many were drawn to the promised attractions of town, but more were driven by economic burdens at home. "The whip which brings us to Lowell is necessity," Sarah G. Bradley wrote in 1848.

The "El Dorado on the Merrimack" certainly attracted distinguished visitors and lecturers. Emerson, Thoreau, Frederick Douglas and Edgar Allan Poe were among those who addressed the workers. But the mill girls had to find the time—and energy—to attend. The workday began at 4:50 A.M. and ended at 7 P.M. Curfew was 10 P.M. The average pay in the 1830s was $3.50 for a six-day week. "Up before the day at the clang of the bell and…into the mill…just as though we were so many living machines," one worker wrote.

The mill girls were soon writing and editing two factory publications: the *Lowell Offering,* which idealized factory life and the *Voice of Industry,* which criticized it. Disillusionment grew as production was accelerated to keep pace in a newly competitive market. "Romantic young women came…with rose-coloured pictures in their minds of labor turned pastime," Lucy Larcom recalled in 1881, "which were soon doomed to be sadly blurred by disappointment."

By the mid-1840s industrial accidents were increasing worker discontent. "Distant parents," Barilla A. Taylor wrote in July 1844, "Ann Graham, if you know her, has got her hand tore off…in the card room. I heard she has got to have it

taken off above her elbow." Labor protest erupted as early as 1834 in response to wage reductions and continued through subsequent decades. But Lowell's women workers still earned less in 1860 than they had in 1836, despite increases in productivity. First Irish immigrants in the 1840s, then French-Canadians, Poles, Portuguese, Russians, Greeks, Syrians, and others replaced the New England women on the factory floor. By the end of the 19th century, Lowell was a city of distinct immigrant enclaves, each as squalid as the English slums that had originally shocked Francis Cabot Lowell.

The Lowell Offering *was a literary magazine written by female mill workers in Lowell, Massachusetts. (Library of Congress)*

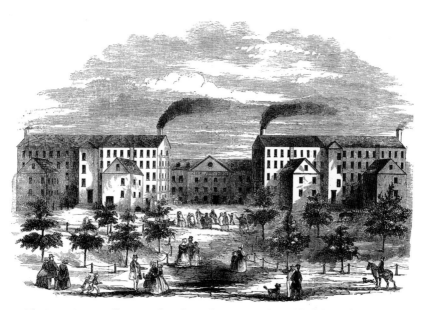

The Boott Cotton Mills in Lowell, as depicted in a Harper's Weekly *lithograph, circa 1880.*

A general strike in 1912 won a 10 percent wage increase, but mill owners were already moving their operations to the cheaper South. The mills closed in the 1920s and '30s, and some were subsequently demolished. Others, however, were restored in the 1970s and '80s as part of Lowell National Historic Park.

◆ LOWELL NATIONAL HISTORIC PARK *map page 81, A-2*

Market Mills, the park's gateway on Market Street, houses the visitor center where exhibits and an introductory slide show present industrial Lowell's major themes. The canal system was the key to Lowell's success, and a tour of the remaining waterways in the city takes in an 1820s industrial canyon, a series of gatehouses, a turbine exhibit, and several canal locks.

The **Boott Cotton Mills Museum** is housed in an elegant complex of 1830s mill buildings and features a working weave room as well as exhibits on every aspect of textile production and working life. A superb slide show and several video presentations put Lowell in its historical context, while exhibits on Wang Laboratories and other Lowell enterprises explain the city's revitalization.

Displays in the adjacent 1850s boardinghouse reveal the everyday life of the closely supervised mill girls. "I object to the constant hurry of everything," one of them wrote, "We have only thirty minutes to go from work, partake of food and return to the noise and clatter of machinery." *Lowell Visitor Center: 978-970-5000.*

A paved area in the nearby park commemorates Jack Kerouac, born of French-Canadian parents in the Centralville area in 1922. Lowell natives are largely bemused by the interest in the city's most famous writer, and one diner waitress recalls him only as someone who "didn't look after his family." It is the ultimate condemnation in this close-knit city.

Lowell's other museums include the American Textile History Museum at 491 Dutton Street, the New England Quilt Museum at 18 Shattuck Street, and the Whistler House Museum of Art, birthplace of James Abbott McNeill Whistler, whose father was Chief Engineer of the Locks & Canals Company in the 1820s.

The city vibrates in July when its hosts the nation's largest and most popular free folk festival, where salsa meets polka and everything in between. You may even hear Lenny Gomulka singing the official state polka of Massachusetts—"Say Hello to Someone in New England."

(above) The gravesite of Lowell native Jack Kerouac draws visitors from all over the world.

(opposite) The Boott Cotton Mill National Historic Site with Lowell Canal in the background.

CAPE COD, ISLANDS, & SOUTH SHORE

■ HIGHLIGHTS

■ TRAVEL BASICS

Cape Cod retains its mesmerizing beauty on its 50-mile-long national seashore and enchanting Wellfleet ponds. Martha's Vineyard and Nantucket Islands, thronged in summer, reveal their extraordinary charms best in spring and autumn when whales are equally content to be admired and schooners to be sailed.

Getting Around: Traveling on Cape Cod, expect heavy, often stalled traffic in peak season and holiday weekends, particularly in ferry ports like Woods Hole and Hyannis. Route 6A from Sandwich to the Outer Cape is pretty and the 25-mile Cape Cod Rail Trail bike route invigorating. Year round and weather permitting, car ferries serve Martha's Vineyard (508-477-8600) and Nantucket (508-778-2600).

Climate: Summer temperatures are in the 80s and 90s, with cooling breezes. Spring and autumn days range from the pleasant 50s to 70s, and nights are cool. Hard freezes and heavy snowfall are rare, but the islands and even parts of Cape Cod can be cut off by winter storms.

Food & Lodging: Historic sea captain's homes are now B&Bs, and motels line every beach. Seafood is king at both family-style food halls and chic cafes and restaurants with New American menus. Genuinely fine oysters and chowder can still be found alongside more exotic culinary imports. Listings for Massachusetts begin on page 328; towns are listed in alphabetical order. Listings map on page 327; listings chart page 375.

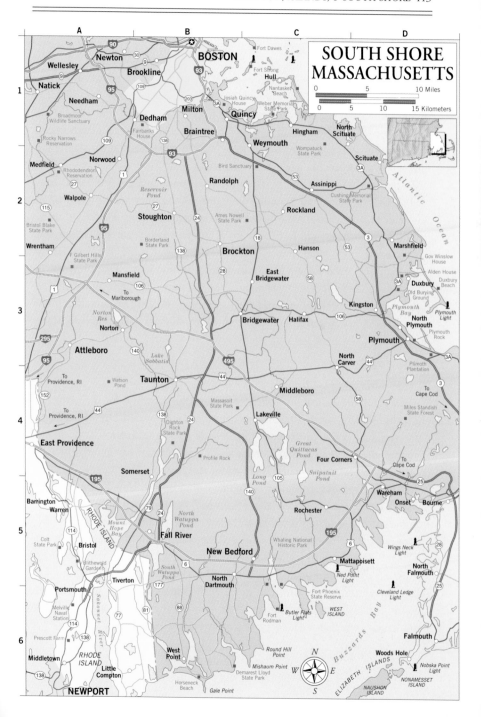

SOUTH SHORE MASSACHUSETTS

0   5   10 Miles

0   5   10   15 Kilometers

A

Wellesley
Newton
90
30
9
Natick
Needham
Broadmoor
Wildlife Sanctuary
9
95
Brookline
109
Medfield
Norwood
Rocky Narrows
Reservation
Dedham
Fairbanks
House
109
Rhododendron
Reservation
27
138
Walpole
115
Reservoir
Pond
27
95
Stoughton
Bristol Blake
State Park
Wrentham
Borderland
State Park
138
F. Gilbert Hills
State Park
1
Mansfield
106
To
Marlborough
Norton
Res
Norton
Attleboro
140
Lake
Sabbatia
295
95
Watson
Pond
Taunton
152
To
Providence, RI
To
Providence, RI
44
138
Dighton
Rock
State Park
24
East Providence
Profile Rock
195
Somerset
Barrington
Warren
114
Mount
Hope
Bay
79
24
North
Watuppa
Pond
Colt
State Park
Bristol
Blithewold
Gardens
Fall River
South
Watuppa
Pond
6
Portsmouth
Tiverton
177
North
Dartmouth
Melville
Naval
Station
114
81
88
77
Prescott Farm
RHODE
ISLAND
138
West
Point
Middletown
138
Little
Compton
NEWPORT

B

⊕
BOSTON
93
Milton
203
Braintree
138
93
Randolph
24
Ames Nowell
State Park
28
Brockton
Bridgewater
Halifax
495
44
Middleboro
Lakeville
Massasoit
State Park
Great
Quittacas
Pond
Four Corners
Long
Pond
105
Snipatuit
Pond
140
Rochester
195
New Bedford
Round Hill
Point
Mishaum Point
Demarest Lloyd
State Park
Horseneck
Beach
Gale Point

C

Fort Dawes
Fort Strong
Hull
Nantasket
Beach
Josiah Quincy
House
Weber Memorial
State Park
3A
Quincy
Hingham
Weymouth
Wompatuck
State Park
Bird Sanctuary
53
Assinippi
Cushing Memorial
State Park
Rockland
18
Hanson
53
East
Bridgewater
58
Kingston
106
North
Carver
44
58
To
Cape Cod
Whaling National
Historic Park
Mattapoisett
Ned Point
Light
Fort Phoenix
State Reserve
WEST
ISLAND
Fort
Rodman
Butler Flats
Light

D

North
Scituate
Scituate
3A
Atlantic Ocean
3
Marshfield
Gov Winslow
House
Alden House
3A
Duxbury
Duxbury
Beach
Old Burying
Ground
Plymouth
Bay
Plymouth
Light
North
Plymouth
Plymouth Rock
Plymouth
Plimoth
Plantation
3A
Miles Standish
State Forest
To
Cape Cod
3
25
Wareham
Onset
Bourne
Wings Neck
Light
28
North
Falmouth
25
Cleveland Ledge
Light
Buzzards
Bay
Falmouth
Woods Hole
Nobska Point
Light
ELIZABETH ISLANDS
NAUSHON
ISLAND
NONAMESSET
ISLAND

1

2

3

4

5

6

N
W   E
S

■ OVERVIEW

Like the best escape routes, the journey south from Boston to one of the world's most spectacular coasts is a form of surrender. As you venture from the solid deck of the South Shore out onto the bowsprit of Cape Cod then cast yourself adrift on the sandy rafts of Nantucket or Martha's Vineyard, you submit to a landscape of shifting sands and milky light, where roses grow in the dunes and the setting sun lingers on the horizon like a reluctantly departing guest.

To most visitors, it is simply the beach—an excuse to wear adult-sized baby clothes, walk barefoot, and eat with your hands. But this bewitching place has always hidden more than it has revealed. Its dunes conceal piping plovers, its waters harbor singing whales, and its fishermen's shanties accommodate summering software tycoons.

"A man may stand there and put all America behind him," Thoreau wrote of Cape Cod in 1849. Visit the most popular spots at peak times and you will find all America not only behind but ahead of you, creating an inland sea of traffic. But if you follow Thoreau's lead and travel out of season, you will reach a similarly ecstatic conclusion.

■ HISTORY

We can thank the Wisconsin Stage Glacier for Cape Cod and for the islands in particular. Moving south 25,000 years ago, the glacier paused, depositing boulders, sand, and debris to form the fragile hook and its satellites. The deep, enchanting ponds dotting the interior are also a glacial legacy, having originated as enormous ice blocks that melted as the glacier retreated.

In 1602, Capt. Bartholomew Gosnold, sailing up the New England coast, named Cape Cod for "the great store of cod-fish" he observed in its waters. Landing on a nearby island, Gosnold and his fellow explorer John Brereton were so impressed by "the incredible store of vines and the beautie and delicacie of this sweet soil" that Gosnold named it after his daughter, calling it Martha's Vineyard.

Gosnold also noticed that he was not the first white visitor. Encountering some Native Americans, he was surprised to see them "apparelled with a waistcoat and breeches of black serge, made after our sea-fashion" and to see that they understood "much more than we for want of language could comprehend."

◆ PILGRIMS AT PROVINCETOWN

The *Mayflower* Pilgrims, coming ashore first in Provincetown in November 1620, were equally amazed when they discovered a skeleton with blond hair in a Wampanoag grave. The coast had indeed been visited before either Gosnold or the *Mayflower* set sail, chiefly by Portuguese, Spanish, Basque, French, and Italian explorers content to chart its waters and shoreline.

The Pilgrims, however, were the ones who stayed. "There was the greatest store of fowl that ever we saw," they wrote, "and excellent black earth." This is surely a rosy recollection. Provincetown was mostly sand, and after a month of vicious weather, the Pilgrims decamped to the cleared Indian cornfields across the bay at Plymouth, where they survived with the assistance of the Native Americans.

Theirs remained a borderline existence. By 1630, the Plymouth Colony numbered just 300 whereas the Massachusetts Bay Colony, established in 1628, had over 2,000 inhabitants. Within a decade, however, the Plymouth settlers had founded communities along the South Shore at Duxbury, Marshfield, Hingham, and as far north as Quincy. Their first permanent toehold on Cape Cod was at present-day Bourne, quickly followed by Sandwich, then, in 1639, by Barnstable and Yarmouth.

The first Thanksgiving at Plymouth, painted by Jennie A. Brownscombe in 1914.
(Courtesy of the Pilgrim Hall Museum, Plymouth)

◆ SHIPBUILDING, COD FISHING, WHALING

The increasingly populous South Shore was from the late 17th century set on a prosperous course that would make it a major shipbuilding, whaling and, eventually, industrial center. Cape Cod and the islands would remain largely poor and isolated by comparison. There were, of course, exceptionally good times: Nantucket's century-long reign as the globe's whaling metropolis and the rise of towns like Barnstable, which grew rich on the China and fur trade.

In hard times, Cape Codders and islanders alike depended on nature's generosity: fish, shellfish, cranberries, sea salt, the salvage from a wrecked schooner, the detritus blown in on a gale. Like their farming cousins inland contesting with rock, these resilient seafarers cultivated thrift and endurance, waiting out repeated adversity as they waited out recurring storms.

*This painted etching depicts a South Sea whale hunt by New England whalers in
the early 19th century. (Private collection)*

By 1835, Cape Cod's fishing fleet was double the size of Cape Ann's and whaling was creating unimaginable fortunes. At its peak in 1843, Nantucket had 88 whalers, a population of almost 10,000, and was exporting more refined oil and spermaceti candles than any American port, while sea captains like Daniel Fisher on Martha's Vineyard made fortunes supplying lighthouses with highly prized whale oil.

By 1850, however, inadequate harbors, antique fishing methods and the lack of rail transportation condemned Cape Cod in particular to steady decline. The Cape's population of 35,000 was, at that time, 95 percent native born and wholly dependent on the

Codfish is split and washed on a New England wharf in this 1912 vintage photograph. (Courtesy of Joseph Garland)

sea, although some prescient individuals, following the lead of Capt. Zebina Small of Harwich, had begun to sell their ships and set out cranberry bogs.

This was the insular world Thoreau entered when he first walked the coastline in 1849 and wrote what is surely the finest evocation of a mysterious, haunting seascape inhabited by eccentric, resourceful people. "He looked as if he sometimes saw a doughnut, but never descended to comfort," he wrote of an old beachcomber, "too grave to laugh, too tough to cry; as indifferent as a clam....He may have been one of the Pilgrims...who has kept on the back side of the Cape, and let the centuries go by."

Shoe manufacturing played a major role in Brockton, where in 1952 President Truman made a visit to a factory while campaigning for Governor Stevenson. The familiar face of John Kennedy peers over his shoulder. (Underwood Photo Archives, San Francisco)

■ ABOUT THE SOUTH SHORE

With the exception of Fall River's factory outlet stores, the South Shore's chief attractions—Plimoth Plantation and the New Bedford Whaling Museum—evoke a past markedly different from its suburban present. And once you escape the contorted south-east expressway, Boston's frequently stalled roller-coaster, you will be tempted to keep moving until you reach those sites. Whizzing past salt marshes and bypassing historic districts has its guilty appeal, especially when there are plenty more down the road. Some stops, however, are worth making.

■ PLYMOUTH

Plymouth makes the most of its status as New England's earliest European settlement. British speciality stores abound and even the laundromat is called Ye Olde Pilgrim Washing Well. Despite this pride, many of the town's earliest, humble dwellings have disappeared.

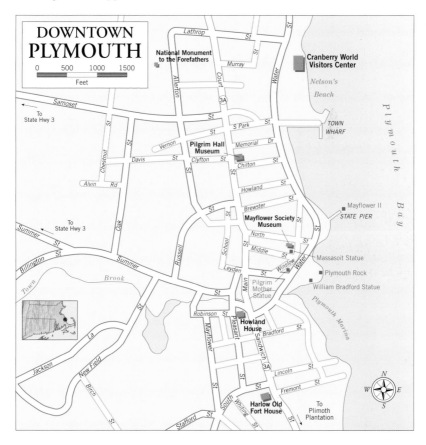

DOWNTOWN
PLYMOUTH

0   500   1000   1500
Feet

Plymouth Rock

To the uninitiated, the sight of vacationing Americans staring into a pit (a centuries-long accumulation of sand has left the rock lying at the bottom of a hole), taking pictures of—even throwing pennies at—an unresponsive, corralled rock is comical. But in a multimedia age, this veneration of the nation's doorstep is also touching. Plymouth Rock is uncontestably old. Formed some 690 million years ago, this granite boulder received its current credentials in the 17th century as the site of the first Pilgrim footfall. Accidentally halved in 1774 and subsequently hacked at by early tourists, it was repaired and enshrined in 1921.

Coles Hill, across the street from Plymouth Rock, is the burial site of settlers who were felled daily by disease and exposure during that first bitter winter of 1620. A nearby statue commemorates **Massasoit**, the Wampanoag chief who helped the remaining Pilgrims to survive.

Mayflower II

If the rock is the teeming waterfront's still point, the *Mayflower II* is its eye-opener. Boarding the tiny, flamboyant ship, you will be astonished that 104 people, with their worldly goods and livestock, survived on board for 66 tempestuous days. Even the replica has proved itself: Built in England in 1955, it sailed the Atlantic to Plymouth two years later. *508-746-1622.*

Cranberry World Visitor Center

Also on the waterfront, the Cranberry World Visitor Center describes the history, cultivation, and uses of the berry now harvested most intensively to the south by the Ocean Spray company at Wareham. *225 Water Street; 508-747-2350.*

Burial Hill

Burial Hill on School Street saw the first Pilgrim constructions—a meetinghouse, fort, and watchtower—and its 17th-century cemetery includes the grave of Governor Bradford.

Mayflower Society Museum

The Mayflower Society Museum, built in 1754, is run by the General Society of Mayflower Descendants, and its nine period rooms present a graceful if decidedly selective evocation of the past. *4 Winslow Street; 508-746-2590.*

Pilgrim Hall Museum

In the center of town, the Pilgrim Hall Museum houses the largest collection of Pilgrim artifacts, including Myles Standish's swords and Governor Bradford's Bible, as well as special exhibitions. The painting of the first Thanksgiving by Jennie A. Brownscombe which appears on page 115 is also in their collection. *75 Court Street; 508-746-1620.*

(opposite) The symbol of the Mayflower *appears on the stern of* Mayflower II, *the replica of the original ship.*

◆ PLIMOTH PLANTATION *map, page 113, D-3*

Nothing in Plymouth proper prepares you for the extraordinary 17th-century immersion at Plimoth Plantation, just south of town off Route 3A. On paper, this living history experience sounds theme-parkish and hokey. In fact, it is mind-altering, even unsettling.

A dusty track descends from the Visitor Center and Carriage House Crafts Center, past corn planted in the hummocked, Native American manner, into the stockaded 1627 village. Everything here—the primitive wooden houses, agricultural and domestic implements, clothing, crops, animals, costumes, and speech—has been meticulously researched and reproduced. The livestock has even been "back-bred" for authenticity.

Questions you always wanted to ask about the *Mayflower* voyage, the early struggles, theological debates, Native American reactions, and practically any other drama, will be answered here by the people who lived through the events. Or so it seems. When you wander past Myles Standish's house and a green-stockinged Pilgrim greets you with "Good day, Mistress" the instinct to laugh him off quickly evaporates. These costumed interpreters, each living the historically accurate life of his/her assigned character from 9:00 A.M. to 5:00 P.M. daily, are too convincing to

Costumed interpreters replicate the life of the Pilgrims at the Plimoth Plantation.

This columned structure houses Plymouth Rock, believed to be the original landing site of the Pilgrims in 1620.

be dismissed. Appearing neither rehearsed nor programmed, they are consummate actors who effortlessly draw you into their world.

Spend even an hour here, visiting women in their gardens, men building Governor Bradford's house, or the Wampanoags at their homesite outside the stockade, and you will enter not only this life, but this mentality. Afterwards, getting back into a car seems positively surreal.

The daily life of Plimoth Plantation also includes reenactments of events such as the Pawtuxet Strawberry Thanksgiving in June, the 1621 First Thanksgiving in October, colonial musters, and the arrival of Dutch messengers from New Netherlands (New York).

There are regular lectures and workshops on everything from rare livestock breeds to 17th-century scandal, and the center's bookshop is a superb 17th-century resource. The Irreconcilable Differences exhibition in the Nye Barn is an informative, subtle examination of the Plymouth Colony. *Just south of Plymouth; take Exit 4 off Highway 3 and follow signs; 508-746-1622.*

■ NEW BEDFORD *map, page 113, C-5*

New Bedford, being a modern port disfigured by a modern highway, cannot entirely immerse its visitors in the maritime past. Considering its handicaps, however, it does a remarkable job. A vibrant whaling port for over a century, New Bedford in its prime had a fleet of 400 whalers and a single-minded merchant class. "They hug an oil-cask like a brother," Emerson quipped.

Herman Melville's Ishmael set sail from here, and Melville himself shipped out of New Bedford in January 1841 aboard the *Acushnet,* jumping ship in the Marquesa Islands and returning three years later. He knew well the Seaman's Bethel on Johnnycake Hill and made it the setting for the sermon episode in *Moby Dick.* "The world's a ship on its passage out," Ishmael mused here, "…and the pulpit is its prow." Contemplating that prow-shaped pulpit today, it is delightful to realize that Melville's image sprang from such solid inspiration.

BOUNTIFUL NEW BEDFORD

*I*n New Bedford, fathers, they say, give whales for dowers to their daughters, and portion off their nieces with a few porpoises a-piece. You must go to New Bedford to see a brilliant wedding; for, they say, they have reservoirs of oil in every house, and every night recklessly burn their lengths in spermaceti candles.

In summer time, the town is sweet to see; full of fine maples—long avenues of green and gold. And in August, high in air, the beautiful and bountiful horse-chestnuts, candelabra-wise, proffer the passer-by their tapering upright cones of congregated blossoms. So omnipotent is art; which in many a district in New Bedford has superinduced bright terraces of flowers upon the barren refuse rocks thrown aside at creation's final day.

And the women of New Bedford, they bloom like their own red roses. But roses only bloom in summer; whereas the fine carnation of their cheeks is perennial as sunlight in the seventh heavens. Elsewhere match that bloom of theirs, ye cannot, save in Salem, where they tell me the young girls breathe such musk, their sailor sweethearts smell them miles off shore, as though they were drawing nigh the odorous Moluccas of the Puritanic sands.

—Herman Melville, *Moby Dick,* 1851

The New Bedford Whaling Museum houses a half-scale model of the whaling bark Lagoda *among many other displays of sea-faring interest. (courtesy of the New Bedford Whaling Museum)*

CAPE COD, ISLANDS
SOUTH SHORE

New Bedford Whaling Museum

The city's Whaling Museum is the largest devoted to the story of American whaling, and in addition to its extensive scrimshaw, nautical equipment, marine painting, and documentary collections, it houses a half-scale replica of a fully rigged whaling ship, the *Lagoda,* and an enormous panorama depicting a whaling voyage. The 89-foot-long *Lagoda* is the world's largest ship model, and along with the museum's numerous ship's logs and mariner's journals, it vividly recalls New Bedford's golden age.

The museum is not all whaling. The world's first solo circumnavigation, completed in 1898, is also commemorated here, most movingly in the reconstruction of the *Spray's* tiny, neat cabin. In 1894, Joshua Slocum was offered the ship, then rotting in a field across the harbor in Fairhaven. Slocum rebuilt her, departed Boston a year later and performed the three-year feat which he later chronicled in *Sailing Alone around the World.* Located at *18 Johnny Cake Hill; 508-997-0046.*

Historic Schooners

Alongside its modern trawlers, New Bedford still hosts elegant, historic vessels, particularly over the July 4th weekend when schooners like the *Ernestina,* an 1894 fishing vessel and arctic explorer, dock here.

County Street Architecture

Architectural evidence of New Bedford's previous wealth can be found on County Street, overlooking the waterfront, site of the magnificent **Rotch-Jones-Duff House and Garden Museum,** built in the 1830s for a whaling merchant. *396 County Street; 508-997-1401.*

Refuge

In the pre–Civil War years, the city was an important station on the Underground Railroad, which smuggled runaway slaves to Canada, and abolitionist Frederick Douglass himself hid here for a time after escaping from Maryland. Conrad Aiken also found solace here with his aunt after the murder-suicide of his parents in Georgia. He later referred to the city in his autobiography, *Ushant,* and his novel *Blue Voyage.*

■ CAPE COD

Bridges are punctuation marks between departure and arrival, often between work and play. Cross the Cape Cod Canal—the world's largest sea-level canal—on either the Sagamore or the Bourne Bridge, and the monochrome highway beneath you suddenly becomes a watery ribbon decorated with canoes, puffing work boats, and elegant schooners.

◆ BOURNE

Arriving in Bourne's small town center, beside Buzzard's Bay, you see what tourism looked like here 50 years ago. A string of pleasingly ramshackle businesses lines the street—Ma's Breakfast and Lunch, for example—and in the fine Chamber of Commerce Visitors Center the only attempt at slick marketing is a highly informative video on cranberry growing. *Bourne Visitor Center: 508-759-6000.*

Here you may also receive your first exposure to the Cape Cod accent as the information woman repeats the word "Aahdfex" until you realize that she is referring to artifacts. Adding to your confusion and delight is the discovery that the menu at Leo's restaurant up the road has a distinct Portuguese accent.

Bourne is an old hand at cross-cultural experiences. This was, after all, the site of the **Aptucxet Trading Post,** established in 1627 by settlers from Plymouth who bartered with Wampanoags who had arrived on the Cape some 3,500 years earlier. A reproduction of the trading post, bordered by 17th-century herb and wildflower gardens stands at *24 Aptucxet Road; 508-759-9487.*

◆ FALMOUTH AND WOODS HOLE

Finicky eaters will feel out of place in **Betsy's Diner,** a Falmouth institution where the food is hearty, the portions large, and the service brisk. To walk off your indulgence, explore **Falmouth Green** at the center of town, which was declared a common in 1749 and is surrounded by fine 18th- and 19th-century houses. A refuge for Quakers in the 17th century, Falmouth refused to surrender two cannons to the British in 1814 and was lightly bombarded for its impertinence.

Woods Hole is the jumping-off point for Martha's Vineyard (see pages 143-151), and from June to October the town may appear to be just one long queue for the ferry. You can escape the crowds by dawdling on the **Shining Sea Bike Path,** which runs from Falmouth to Woods Hole, or by visiting the renowned **Woods Hole Oceanographic Institute,** established in 1930, where marine mysteries are revealed. *86 Water Street; 508-457-2000.*

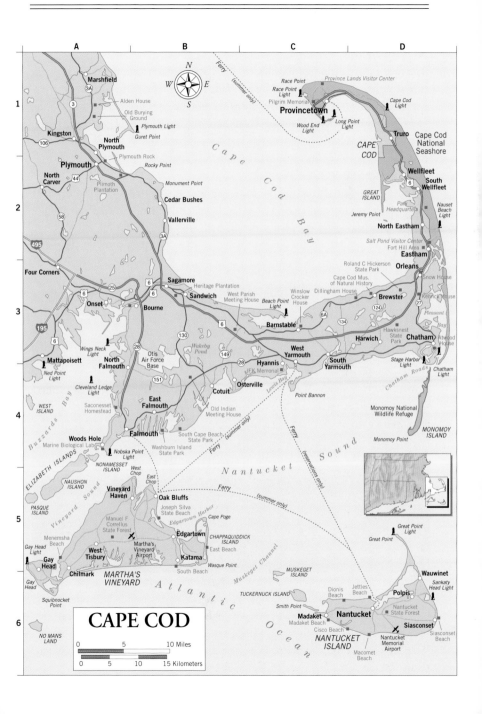

CAPE COD

◆ SANDWICH

The road from Sagamore to Sandwich, the Cape's oldest town, meanders between tidy shingled cottages bordered by rose-laden picket fences and shaded by overhanging locust trees. Sandwich's major attraction, on the outskirts of town at Pine and Grove Streets, is the **Heritage Plantation** with its 76 acres of gardens, a reproduction of the round Shaker barn at Hancock Village, collections of antique cars from 1899 to 1937, firearms, Native American artifacts, and historical illustrations. *2 Grove Street; 508-888-3300.*

But Sandwich itself, settled in 1627, is the real charmer. The town's earliest buildings were clustered around Shawme Pond, which was harnessed for milling by the colonists. Today the pond contents itself with being beautiful, although the Dexter Mill, which ran for almost three centuries, still puts some of the water through its paces.

Boys jump from the boardwalk at Town Neck Beach in Sandwich.

A 1912 carousel at work at the Heritage Plantation in Sandwich.

Hoxie House

Overlooking Shawme Pond, the Hoxie House, built in the 1630s, is Sandwich's—and perhaps the Cape's—oldest house. It is also one of the oddest. An extreme saltbox with a steep back roof and a few tiny windows placed apparently at random, it resembles a child's drawing with its out-of-scale apertures and crazy lines. The fine restoration makes a tour worthwhile, but it is also delightful to sit on the bench outside the back door, leaning against the sun-warmed walls, listening to the occasional creak and groan of the timbers. *18 Water Street; 508-888-1173.*

Dunbar Tea Shop

The Dunbar Tea Shop, across the street from the Hoxie House, is the best place to snap out of such reveries and to slip into others. Tea fanciers will lose their minds here, particularly when they discover that the sensitive beverage is free to express itself in a loose not a shamefully bagged state. Surrendering their place in the lunchtime queue, zealots will dart from shelf to shelf, examining the huge selection of teapots for spout angle, filtering capability, and heat retention before prostrating themselves in front of the fine selection of teas from Ceylon, South Africa, and elsewhere. *One Water Street; 508-833-2485.*

Sandwich Glass Museum

The Sandwich Glass Museum, down the hill on Main Street, is a calming antidote. Glassmaking became the town's chief industry in 1825, when the Boston and Sandwich Glass Company introduced the delicately tinted objects that are tastefully displayed today alongside a diorama of the factory as it looked in 1850. Students from the Massachusetts Institute of Technology built the diorama in 1940.

The factory closed in 1888 after a labor dispute, causing the town's economy to decline. *129 Main Street; 508-888-0251.*

Whimsy

A more whimsical heritage is displayed at the **Yesteryears Doll Museum** on Main and River Streets, where antique dolls, vintage toys, and miniatures may be viewed.

Adult children may further indulge their nostalgia by visiting the **home of Thornton W. Burgess**, the naturalist and author best known for *Peter Rabbit and the Briar Patch,* on Water Street.

A leisurely ramble down practically any of Sandwich's side streets reveals a wealth of the small and mid-size Victorian houses that Edward Hopper found so pleasing.

Leaving Sandwich, follow Route 6A, part of which traces the route of the Old Kings Highway and snakes through the woods once it reaches the Outer Cape. As you head toward Barnstable, the road crosses misty salt marshes ringed with pale pink roses and vibrating with birdsong.

The salt hay from these marshes was one key to Barnstable's success. The other was the town's commodious harbor. For "the Barnstable boy," Thoreau noted in 1849, "…it is but a bound from the mother's lap to the masthead….He can hand, reef and steer by the time he flies a kite."

◆ BARNSTABLE *map, page 127, C-3*

The whole town of Barnstable, which includes the territories of Cotuit, Santuit, Osterville, Centerville, and Hyannis, was purchased from the Wampanoags for two breeches, four coats, three axes, three kettles, a broad hoe, a day's ploughing, one house, and 20 English pounds. It proved to be a bargain.

From its agricultural beginnings in 1639, Barnstable grew on trade and fishing to become the Cape's wealthiest port in 1850. Today, like every other Cape town, it is a tourist destination, but unlike most of its neighbors, it has not become one long "antiques and collectibles" strip. In an unpretentious coffee shop like Village Landing, locals banter with the waitresses, and the miniature walnut tarts are inexpensive and delicate enough to encourage greed. Even James Otis, Barnstable's most esteemed 18th-century patriot, staring across from his pedestal on the courthouse lawn, seems tempted.

Donald G. Trayser Memorial Museum
This museum, occupying the town's 1856 Custom House on Cobb's Hill, is where you may really lose yourself, especially on a thundery, humid June day when the building is a cool retreat.

You encounter the first distraction before you enter the museum. On the edge of the parking area, what appears to be a garden shed is actually one of the most unusual and haunting buildings in the country: it is the **Old Jail,** thought to have been built between 1690 and 1700, and the small, dark space you enter today immediately convinces you of its antiquity. Although a 1973 fire erased much prisoner graffiti, one remarkable example remains. On a cell wall, under the ghostly carving of a ship, are the words "N. Bartlett 13 October 1698 A.D. He Went Out." No other clues to sailor Bartlett's life exist but, caught in flight, his voice fills the darkness. Reemerging into the daylight, you would not be surprised to catch a glimpse of him, making for the harbor.

Exhibits in the museum itself are superbly arranged and delightfully non-interactive. There are no electronic buttons to push in the post office that occupies one corner of the ground floor, no China trade videos running in the dining room and parlor of sea captains Daniel C. Bacon and Thomas Harris.

The voices, however, are here. "Thursday, all officers sick in bed," Capt. Allen Knowles wrote in his log on December 29, 1856, when his crew had overindulged themselves on shore leave in Acapulco. "Monday, all mates sick yet," he continued, "Thursday, mates sick. Friday, all mates sick and off duty. Fine time for me." Knowles's irritation was excusable. Earlier that year, he had endured "the longest and hardest passage...ever...around Cape Horn," 145 days. *Open seasonally; 508-362-2092.*

◄○►

If you choose to head east from Barnstable, you'll enter the seemingly endless kitsch alley around Dennis and Brewster. At its most commercialized, the Cape will be anything the restless visitor wants it to be. It will use whaling lore to sell beer, Melville quotes to sell T-shirts, and pirate tales to sell ice cream. Even a venerable institution like the Brewster General Store seems torn between being a souvenir stall, a video-cum-bookstore, and a coffee shop.

◆ HYANNIS AREA *map, page 127, C-3*

It is hard to avoid being drawn into the vortex of Hyannis—the Cape's tourist hub, a major ferry port, and site of the **John F. Kennedy Museum.** *397 Main Street; 508-790-3077.*

Unlike feverish Hyannis, which has largely obliterated its original allure, Oster-ville and Cotuit (to the southwest) retain the quaintness that first attracted tycoons and intellectuals. Known as "little Harvard," Cotuit became the summer retreat not only of academics but of psychologists like Erik Erikson. And when you stew in Hyannis traffic on a summer weekend, you may find Erikson's diagnosis of "identity crisis" particularly apt.

Northwest of Cotuit on Route 130, Mashpee has significant Native American sites. And Harwich Port, on the coast between Hyannis and Chatham, has a beautiful historic district.

◆ CHATHAM *map page 127, D-3*

Surrounded by water on three sides, Chatham is sedate in the middle and wild around the edges. Main Street is pretty, the Old Atwood House museum on Stage Harbor Road is enlightening, and the Railroad Museum on Depot Road is charming. The daily catch in the Chatham Squire tavern on Main Street is also likely to be a fresh catch. Chatham's dramas, however, center on North Beach, which was split in half by a fierce storm in 1987, and Chatham Light, which was toppled in the 1870s. The current lighthouse on Shore Road dates to 1877.

The shoreline near North Chatham.

◆ MONOMOY NATIONAL WILDLIFE REFUGE *map, page 127, D-4*

Having survived the sprawl of Hyannis, you'll want to keep the world at bay by rushing directly to the Monomoy National Wildlife Refuge, comprising two islands off Chatham. One of the northeast's most spectacular birding areas, its marshes, ponds, beaches, and dwarf forests attract clouds of migrating shorebirds, including golden plovers and godwits, from July to September. Peregrine falcons pass through during the autumn, seals congregate during the winter, and the vast nesting colonies also include those of the common tern, the oystercatcher, and the short-eared owl.

The Cape Cod Museum of Natural History and the Wellfleet Bay Wildlife Sanctuary provide **day trips to Monomoy's twin islands.** *Tour information: 508-945-0594.*

◆ ABOUT CAPE COD NATIONAL SEASHORE AND THE OUTER CAPE

Heading north from Chatham, Route 28 skirts Pleasant Bay. Ahead of you, when you reach Eastham, lies the Outer Cape, the narrowest and, historically, poorest stretch separating Massachusetts Bay from the Atlantic Ocean. "The country looked so barren," Thoreau observed, "that I several times refrained from asking the inhabitants for a string or a piece of wrapping-paper, for fear I should rob them…." Another writer, Henry Beston, was so captivated when he came to Eastham in 1927 that he built a Walden-like shack on the beach and lived there for a year, chronicling his experiences in his supremely evocative book *The Outermost House.* This thin spindle of land, veering north from Orleans, is also the site of the peninsula's greatest natural treasure—the 50 mile-long **Cape Cod National Seashore.** Established in 1961, largely through the efforts of President John F. Kennedy, the 27,000-acre federal preserve seems to absorb its five million annual visitors without diluting its wildness.

At the **Fort Hill Area** off US 6 in Eastham, you will catch the seashore in one of its deceptively calm moments. Once you have recovered from the view across to Nauset Harbor and Coast Guard Beach, you follow a shell-strewn trail through watery fields into sandy groves of dwarfish red maples. Intoxicated by honeysuckle vapors, you are also bombarded with mockingbird arpeggios, cardinal whistles, and catbird squeaks, the combination of which sounds like heaven trying to get through on the shortwave. Bluebirds, indigo buntings, and other birds now rare on the Cape also favor this spot. *Map page 127, D-2*

OCTOBER ROAR

*A*way from the beach, the various sounds of the surf melt into one great thundering symphonic roar. Autumnal nights in Eastham village are full of this ocean sound. The 'summer people' have gone, the village rests and prepares for winter, lamps shine from kitchen windows, and from across the moors, the great levels of the marsh, and the bulwark of the dunes resounds the long wintry roaring of the sea. Listen to it a while, and it will seem but one remote and formidable sound; listen still longer and you will discern in it a symphony of breaker thunderings, and endless, distant, elemental cannonade. There is beauty in it, and ancient terror. I heard it last as I walked through the village on a starry October night; there was no wind, the leafless trees were still, all the village was abed, and the whole sombre world was awesome with the sound.

—Henry Beston, *The Outermost House,* 1949

Dune shacks on Cape Cod were inhabited by many famous artists and writers.

Attitudes have clearly changed since 1692, when the town of Eastham ruled that no man could marry until he had killed six blackbirds or three crows. "The blackbirds, however, still molest the corn," Thoreau reported, "From which I concluded, that either many men were not married, or many blackbirds were." The Eastham windmill, used to grind that contested corn, is the Cape's oldest, having been built in Plymouth in 1680 and later moved to its location on US 6.

Near the Fort Hill parking area, the elegant **Captain Edward Penniman House,** built in 1867 with a fine octagonal cupola, recalls another Eastham story. Born here in 1831, Edward Penniman ran away to sea at the age of eleven. By the age of 21 he was harpooning in the New Bedford fleet; at 29 he was commanding his own whaler, eventually amassing a considerable fortune. *Open seasonally; 508-255-3421.*

◆ SALT POND *map, page 127, D-2*

Myles Standish surely never imagined such advancement when he came ashore nearby at what is now called First Encounter Beach for his first, jittery, meeting with the Wampanoags. A mile north of the Fort Hill area, the Salt Pond Visitor Center is the starting point for a delightful bike trail that takes you soaring through the dunes to Coast Guard Beach, dodging terns as you go. *Salt Pond Visitor Center: 508-255-3421.*

◆ WELLFLEET *map page 127, D-2*

The Pilgrims soon discovered what the Native Americans had known for centuries—that oysters thrive here. Wellfleet was known for the shellfish as early as 1606, when they so impressed Champlain that he named the harbor Oyster Port. Second only to Gloucester as a cod and mackerel port in 1850, Wellfleet was New England's oyster capital from 1830 to 1870. The town also introduced America to the banana when Wellfleet Captain Lorenzo Dow Baker returned from the West Indies with some of the strange fruit in the late 19th century. Rapturously received, it was the seed of the United Fruit Company, established in 1899.

Finding a good banana in Wellfleet today is easy, but finding good shellfish requires a little more work—and luck. Perhaps mimicking the bivalves they serve, oyster and clam shacks seem to open and shut down with mysterious regularity, and only a local can point you in the right direction.

Locals do exist, despite the fact that Wellfleet and its neighbors, Truro and Provincetown, have long been fashionable summer destinations for artists and writers. The sleepy center of Wellfleet seems unaltered by the presence in past years of critics like Edmund Wilson, novelists like Mary McCarthy, and flocks of sun-worshipping psychoanalysts. The clock in the 1850 Congregational Church still strikes "ship's time" every half hour, and Newcomb Hollow beach (where Thoreau was once accommodated by a garrulous Wellfleet oysterman) has been significantly altered only by the ocean. Even the canoe tours of Wellfleet's ponds, organized by the Audubon Society, seem pleasantly antiquated.

Sitting beside **Horse Leech Pond,** in the middle of the sandy woods on a spring evening, you see why restless minds alighted here. It is not simply that "meditation and water are wedded for ever," as Melville observed. It is the mist in the air, the honeysuckle that seems to grow out of the water, and the hypnotic bellowing of reverberating bullfrogs. You know that sharp things lurk just out of sight—snapping turtles, pickerel, sharks, and salesmen—but this part of the Cape, more than any other, lulls the visitor with its dreamy softness, even on its ocean side, where tremendous gales regularly devour the dunes. Having spent a morning on any Wellfleet beach, equipped with a book and a companion, you may find that you have ignored both and instead spent the hours mesmerized by the Atlantic endlessly unfurling and refurling its long bolts of gray-blue silk.

Edward Hopper painted the gas station in Truro in 1940. (Museum of Modern Art, New York)

◆ TRURO *map, page 127, D-1*

Edward Hopper captured this softness and luminosity, even in his painting of a local gas station. The pumps are gone, but the shanty of a store remains practically unaltered on US 6 outside Truro, selling a few Hopper postcards but otherwise ignoring the association.

Guglielmo Marconi did not dream away his hours here. Instead, he erected radio towers on the beach in 1901 and transmitted the first message across the Atlantic on January 18, 1903, from the site now dedicated to his achievement in South Wellfleet.

Marconi's invention came too late for the 57 fishermen lost in a storm off Truro in 1841 and for hundreds of others lost in the Cape's most treacherous waters. They had to rely on the 1802 *Shipwrecked Seaman's Manual,* which warned: "This highland approaches the ocean with steep and lofty banks, which it is extremely difficult to climb, especially in a storm." Conquering that, the sailor might take shelter in one of the "humane houses" that once dotted this coast. Cape Cod's first lighthouse, 1797 **Highland Light**, stands on Lighthouse Road. At the nearby **Museum of the Truro Historical Society** on Highland Road, you may examine domestic items and more haunting salvaged ones; *508-487-3397.*

Writers also washed up in Truro. During the 1920s, Eugene O'Neill spent his summers in the converted Coast Guard station at Peaked Hill Bar, which was

CAPE COD, ISLANDS
SOUTH SHORE

From the beach, the lighthouse at Truro appears to peek over sand dunes.

subsequently claimed by a 1930 storm. The shack the playwright inhabited at Race Point outside Provincetown suffered a similar fate. Fifteen years later, Mary McCarthy, recalling her 1945 summer here with Dwight MacDonald, James Agee, and others, wrote: "I remember our beach picnics at night around a fire and our discussions of Tolstoy and Dostoevsky."

Thoreau—being Thoreau—visited Truro before it became fashionable. The town's harbors began to silt up in the early 18th century and, arriving here in 1849, the writer found it and neighboring Provincetown practically empty. "Nearly all who come out must walk on the four planks I have mentioned," Thoreau wrote, referring to Provincetown's gangplank sidewalks, "so that you are pretty sure to meet all the inhabitants…who come out in the course of a day, provided you keep out yourself."

◆ PROVINCETOWN *map page 127, C-1*

Today, many Provincetown residents are out in every sense of the word. The site of the first Pilgrim landing and once a busy fishing and trading port, the town is now more popularly known as an "alternative lifestyle" playground, where exhibitionism and sensitivity walk—often literally—hand in hand.

Between June and October, you may find yourself gridlocked on Commercial Street, coveting a parking spot already being claimed by two duelling cars and trying not to stare at the wave of human extravagance passing on either side. Even in the off-season, Provincetown seems to be all clever restaurants, pastel guest houses, and art galleries. But there are still fishing boats in the harbor and the town is still heavily Portuguese, as you will discover if you catch the Blessing of the Fleet weekend festival in mid to late June, when Portuguese flags and food stalls are everywhere. If you miss that feast, you can still sample the fine soup and seafood specials at Tip-for-Tops'n on Bradford Street.

Provincetown—historically known as Helltown—has always been wayward. For almost a century after the Pilgrim's departure, fishermen here drank and gambled with visiting Wampanoags, prompting respectable Truro to refuse jurisdiction over its scandalous neighbor until 1727. Wrecking was a common occupation, as was its unlawful cousin "mooncussing" (so-called because the revealing moon was the illegal wrecker's enemy). Ships were even lured to their doom with false lights. In the shadow of the dunes, smuggling and rum running also thrived.

Fishing boats docked at the end of MacMillan Wharf, with flags for the annual Blessing of the Fleet.

Provincetown Art Museum

This fishy place was transformed by the establishment of the Cape Cod School of Art in 1899 and the discovery of the area's clear light by painters like Hans Hoffmann, Robert Motherwell, and Ford Maddox Ford's brother-in-law, Jack Tworkov. The Provincetown Art Association and Museum, founded in 1914, now displays a fine permanent collection as well as new works by local artists. *460 Commercial Street; 508-487-1750.*

Pilgrim Monument

The best view in town is from the **Pilgrim Monument** on High Pole Road, a 250-foot granite tower erected in 1907 and modeled after the Torre del Mangia in Siena, Italy. From here you can see dramatic Race Point Beach, calm Herring Cove, and remote Long Point, as well as the ridge of the Outer Cape. The superb museum at the base of the tower displays whaling equipment, ship models, a *Mayflower* diorama, and items from the pirate ship *Whydah*, which sank off Wellfleet in 1717 and was resurrected in 1985. *Expedition Whydah Sea Lab: MacMillan Wharf; 508-487-8899.*

Stellwagen Bank

Even from Pilgrim Monument, you won't see Stellwagen Bank, the underwater marine sanctuary north of Provincetown. Take a whale-watch cruise from MacMillan Wharf, however, and you may observe the humpbacks, fin whales, and endangered northern right whales that favor this feeding ground. *Cape Cod Cruises: 508-747-2400.*

A woman prepares fried dough, a specialty at the Portuguese Bakery.

Sunset behind the Pilgrim Monument in Provincetown.

■ MARTHA'S VINEYARD *map page 127, A-5, B-5*

Getting there: Ferries for Martha's Vineyard leave from Woods Hole, all year, several trips daily. Auto reservations required. 508-477-8600. From Hyannis, all year service. Auto reservations required ($70–90); 508-477-8600.

Despite being the closest island to the mainland, within easy reach of day-trippers, Martha's Vineyard is more than just a floating buffet of tourist attractions. The island's eccentric history—crowded with religious zealots, Native Americans, writers, and dilettantes—has created a distinct sense of island identity while the intensely varied landscape and architecture preserve a sense of real, not just photogenic, life.

All of which is best appreciated in the early spring or late autumn, when the crowds have thinned and the island seems welcoming, not besieged. From 1956 until their deaths, Lillian Hellman and her consort, Dashiell Hammett, found privacy here despite, as Hellman described them, "the army of young who fornicate ...during the nice summer evenings." In the 1970s, Thornton Wilder also retreated to the island to finish *Theophilus North*.

The golden rule of the maverick visitor—travel out of season—is particularly applicable here. One statistic says it all: the baseline population of Martha's Vineyard is 11,000 but it swells to 90,000 in July and August. It is not just a matter of breathing space. Hours spent in a ferry line, even in a picturesque port, are not usually the happiest. Yet, the island should be approached by water. The everyday shore should gradually recede, not shrink abruptly, allowing you to relish the sight of your working life being reduced to a thin, distant line as the opposite shore of pleasure materializes out of sea fog. From the ferry, the 100 square miles of Martha's Vineyard appears first as a lump, then a sand-fringed lump. As you approach it, the lump grows colors, textures, and buildings, each raised into view like a drawing in a pop-up book.

◆ VINEYARD HAVEN

Vineyard Haven's harbor, of course, grows wooden ships, some of the loveliest on the eastern seaboard. You glide past the schooner *Shenandoah* and her neighbor *Alabama,* both of which take schoolchildren and other visitors sailing to the nearby Elizabeth Islands and beyond. You may also spot the *When and If,* General Patton's schooner, her name reflecting the soldier's wry intention to sail when and if he made it back from World War II. The Vineyard tradition of shipbuilding endures at the nearby Gannon and Benjamin Marine Railway, a few minutes from the ferry dock.

Your first instinct may be to sample the **Black Dog Bakery's** pastries and coffee, on offer near the ferry terminal, and then leave Vineyard Haven for an island exploration. But the town deserves more than a backward glance. An important port throughout the 18th and 19th centuries, this was a vital refuge for British ships during the Revolution.

Old Schoolhouse Museum on Colonial Lane and Main Street stands where young Polly Daggett and two friends destroyed the town's Liberty pole to thwart the British captain who wanted it for a spar. The museum displays scrimshaw and other whaling mementoes and also recalls the 1778 raid by the British who were, according to one witness, "so Curious in searching as to Disturb the ashes of the Dead." Their livestock and produce plundered, the islanders were saved from starvation only by a northeast blizzard that drove a school of sea bass into Lagoon Pond where they froze and could be harvested throughout the winter.

Such deprivation is unimaginable today on Vineyard Haven's Main Street, where even the thrift store is full of designer clothes—some of the island's best bargains, especially at the summer's end. Frenzied souvenir selling is largely concentrated on the waterfront; back roads like Williams Street are perfect for quiet strolls.

Unless you want to make noise and look foolish, avoid renting a moped; you'll see bike rental shops near the harbor. The island has three excellent bike trails and numerous tiny roads that make silent exploration pleasurable.

◆ OAK BLUFFS

On the way to Oak Bluffs from Vineyard Haven, lobster fanciers should visit the **State Lobster Hatchery and Research Station,** reportedly the world's oldest, where prospective meals may be viewed in their infancy. "Man needs to know but little more than a lobster in order to catch him," Thoreau concluded, and an insight into crustacean intelligence may force you to agree.

Vineyard Haven and nearby Oak Bluffs are contrasting neighbors. Vineyard Haven is a "dry" town (it does not sell alcohol) and Oak Bluffs a distinctly wet one (it sells it at every turn). Vineyard Haven has elegant, wooden boats in its harbor, while Oak Bluffs attracts the oversize, plastic variety with crews that often include matching Rottweilers. With its gaudy colors and ramshackle gentility, Oak Bluffs

A visitor learns how to band lobster claws—with the help of a professional.

offers an irrepressible, unapologetic welcome to the visitor. If you're looking for restraint, it seems to say, go to Edgartown.

Yet restraint, ironically, was the making of Oak Bluffs. In 1835, a Methodist minister thought the site perfect for a summer campground, and soon thousands of fervent believers were living in tents then eventually in small cottages built beside the Methodist Tabernacle at Wesleyan Grove.

The result today is a uniquely charming maze of about one thousand houses, jammed into an improbably small space, each one bristling with intricate fretwork on roof, wall, porch, and doorway and competing with its neighbor for outrageous colors and candystriping. Nineteenth-century Methodism was clearly not a monochrome affair.

Spend long enough exploring this tiny enclave and you'll feel that you have wandered into an overstuffed Victorian parlor where the streets are actually mantelpieces crammed with the treasures of a lifelong collector. The prospect is further enhanced every August on Illumination Night, when thousands of oriental lanterns are strung through the village, a tradition that dates back to 1869. The Cottage Museum at One Trinity Park provides a view of life inside one of these architectural confections and services are still held in the 1879 Trinity Park Tabernacle; *508-693-7784.*

Oak Bluffs has long been known as the affordable or rough end of the island, depending on your interpretation, and the **Ocean View bar and restaurant** on Chatman Avenue (at the edge of town toward Vineyard Haven) is perhaps the best place to sample its unpretentious appeal. The bar is lively, the seafood is straightforward, and at least one game is always on at least one television.

◆ EDGARTOWN

The road from Oak Bluffs to Edgartown skirts Sengekontocket Pond, which is surrounded by the 350-acre **Felix Neck Wildlife Sanctuary**. Cleverly planned trails snake through this dreamy saltwater estuary leading you through marshes, fields, and diminutive woodland to Waterfowl Pond, a favorite meeting point for migratory and nesting water birds. This is also an osprey nesting site. Seventy-five pairs were recorded in 1995, and visitors are encouraged—by the Audubon Society, not the birds—to observe their predatory and domestic habits.

Like Oak Bluffs, Edgartown was established on a religious impulse. But there the resemblance with its exuberant neighbor ends, for Edgartown is the island's aristocrat. Founded in 1642 by Thomas Mayhew—who established missions for the conversion of the island's 3,000 or so Wampanoags—the port grew rich on Arctic whaling, and today displays evidence of that wealth in its elegant 18th- and 19th-century architecture.

The loftiest example is the austere **Old Whaling Church,** built in 1843, whose soaring white columns make it seem like a ship under sail, magnificently oblivious to the commercial detritus bobbing in its wake on Main Street. High-end gift shops, galleries, and restaurants line this thoroughfare and waterfront. But the streets behind this strip are quiet, residential, and glorious, particularly on a still autumn evening when shadows dye the sloping lawns a deeper green and the white clapboards appear to be etched not affixed.

◆ CHAPPAQUIDDICK ISLAND

It takes about half a minute to reach Chappaquiddick Island from Edgartown by ferry and when you arrive, there is nothing to buy. Relieved of that chore and armed with a picnic, you can instead lose yourself for hours in either of its nature reserves. The 500-acre **Cape Poge Wildlife Refuge,** at the far end of the island, is a mesmerizing arrangement of sand, water, hummock, and marsh, teeming with hawks, terns, plover, ducks, and songbirds. At the opposite end of Chappaquiddick, the Wasque Reservation catches nature in one of its melodramatic moments as Wasque Bluffs sweep up out of Katama Bay in a flourish of grassland and wildflowers.

◆ WEST TISBURY AND GAY HEAD

After all that drama, the road from Edgartown to West Tisbury seems disappointingly functional, but quieter beauty lurks nearby at the **Long Point Wildlife Refuge.** This 633-acre preserve encompasses Long Cove, an exquisite saltwater inlet; Tisbury Great Pond, which shimmers whatever the season; and many other ponds that are home to otters and muskrats as well as ospreys, harriers, swans, and water fowl.

Less ambitious ducks bob contentedly on the charming little town pond in West Tisbury, a perfect rest stop for bicyclists who wish to donate their excess crumbs to the web-footed supplicants. You may think twice, however, if you have paid the inflated sandwich rates farther up the road at Alley's General Store, an island institution that at least does not charge for a seat on its front porch. Real value can be found at the farmer's market outside the Agricultural Hall every Saturday from 9 A.M. to noon.

Winding from West Tisbury to Gay Head, **South Road** is one of the loveliest on the island, particularly for bicycling. It swoops and twists between small stretches of woodland, wildflower meadows, and sheep pastures, affording tantalizing views of glinting ponds and creating such a sense of rural calm that the tumult of nearby Lucy Vincent Beach seems shocking when you emerge from the dunes on to its breathtaking Atlantic-pummeled shore. Here you may enjoy the peculiar spectacle of naked people rolling in the cliff's clay for healing purposes as fully clothed fishermen cast into the surf nearby for bluefish and striped bass. This beach, like many on the island, is most accessible out of season when residency restrictions are waived.

Following South Road through **Chilmark**, you might stop at the Chilmark Store to stock up on emergency rations or, better still, at Chilmark Chocolates to stock up on emergency handmade treats, before pushing on to Gay Head at the island's westernmost tip. The undulations become a little steeper outside Chilmark, but it is the view not the gradient that forces you to stop when South Road cuts between Menemsha Pond and Squibnocket Pond. On your right, a lobster boat rocks on the glassy water and on your left, a blue heron hunches in the reeds, seemingly hypnotizing his prey.

Wampanoag Indians at Gay Head in the late 19th century. (courtesy Devin-Adair Publishers)

The lighthouse at Gay Head Cliffs. (photo by Markham Johnson)

The multicolored cliffs at **Gay Head,** rising 150 feet out of the ocean, are most impressive when viewed from the water, particularly at sunset when their layers become positively gaudy. But even the view from the lookout point near the parking area is rewarding. For a closer inspection, find Maushop Beach on Maushop Trail Road, where a short walk brings you underneath the strange protuberances. Surely the ancient glacier's most outrageous handiwork, the cliffs contain 70-million-year-old glacial deposits in which the fossils of early marine creatures and even horses are preserved.

The souvenir stalls lining the route to the lookout also seem an oddly antique part of the island's tourist machine. But then Gay Head has always been apart. In 1711, the Society for Propagating the Gospel—oblivious, no doubt, to the irony of the transaction—bought the lands here for the sole use of the original inhabitants, the Wampanoags. Today, the tribe owns the National Historic Landmark on which some of its members live.

◆ MENEMSHA

Lighthouse Road skirts Lobsterville Beach and returns to the small fishing village of Menemsha, where the nets and lobster pots on the dock are in use, not for sale. Despite having an unofficial anthem written for it by Carly Simon and being used as the location for the movie *Jaws,* Menemsha is still a place where people would rather watch the water than the celebrities. And everybody's favorite special effect is still the flamboyant sunset, attended nightly by adoring fans. You may join them on the beach or enjoy the drive-in performance from your car. Instead of popcorn, you can snack on the fine crab cakes and fish cakes from either **Poole's** or **Larsen's** fish markets, behind you on the dock, long-established local businesses and the island's best fish sources.

North Road passes **Menemsha Hills Reservation,** where the view from Prospect Hill is more than worth the easy ascent along marked trails. You can see everything from here—the delicate chain of the Elizabeth Islands, Cuttyhunk to the north and Nomans Land across Vineyard Sound, Menemsha and Squibnocket Ponds, and Gay Head. Descend through the scrub and you arrive at one of the island's most secluded public beaches, where you may recline, seal-like, on a glacial boulder.

(photo by Markham Johnson)

During spring and autumn, the chief hazards on the way back to Vineyard Haven are flocks of wild turkeys and the occasional deer. Follow the stately turkey's example and veer repeatedly off the asphalt onto lovely intermediary tracks like Teawaddle Lane and Music Street, leading into West Tisbury, or Lambert's Cove Road, closer to Vineyard Haven. This being an island, after all, it is impossible to get lost, and the detours hold not only delightful views but surprises like the 17th-century Indian cemetery on Christiantown Road. Your return to Vineyard Haven may be further delayed by a visit to Chicama Vineyards on State Road, where seasonal tours and tastings can easily soak up an hour; *508-693 0309.*

Wauwinet village on the north end of Nantucket Island.

■ NANTUCKET *map, page 127, D-6*

Getting there: The island of Nantucket is reached by ferry from Woods Hole or Hyannis; call 508-778-2600 for schedules, auto reservations, and prices.

In *Moby Dick,* Herman Melville described Nantucket as "a mere hillock, an elbow of sand; all beach, without a background." Even today, approached by high-speed ferry, the small sandbar seems more an act of faith than a destination. Roaring along for an hour through dense sea fog, you begin to doubt the existence of a place known to Native Americans as Canopache, or The Place of Peace, and re-named Nanticut, or The Far Away Land. Both sound about as real as Brigadoon.

Then suddenly the engines' hum drops an octave, the fog lifts, and there it is, a fragile blob 14.5 miles long and just 3.5 miles wide that is part Manhattan-chic, part California-aesthetic, and—miraculously—part Nantucket.

Your foggy doubts give way to a disorienting first impression: the ferry seems to have docked in a shopping mall. Tourists stroll from one gray-shingled specialty store to the next along a cobblestone thoroughfare that you expect to terminate in a food court. Sleek young women wearing Ralph Lauren carry demure "lightship baskets" that were first made by whaling men but are manufactured and sold today by artists, often for thousands of dollars. No wonder Russell Baker said that if you listen closely on a summer's night you will hear "the sound of the island eating money."

Your head ringing with Melville, it would be understandable if, like Ishmael, you immediately headed seaward, fleeing corruption. But it would also be a pity. Despite the relentless merchandising, Nantucket town is still one of the nation's loveliest—and oddest—jewels.

To orient yourself in the island's extraordinary past, visit the **Whaling Museum** and the **Peter Foulger Museum,** both on at 15 Broad Street near the dock, and the splendid **Nantucket Atheneum** *(One India Street; 508-228-1110).* Formerly a spermaceti candle factory, the Whaling Museum displays various maritime artifacts including the skeleton of a 43-foot finback whale, while the 1847 Atheneum (also the island's public library) houses special collections on Nantucket history and 19th-century life. *(Foulger: 508-228-1655. Whaling Museum: 508-228-1736.)*

(above) A stone marker from 1841 marks the edge of Nantucket town.

(opposite) A lamppost stands in the center of a Nantucket town street intersection.

Here you will find the Nantucket girl's song (from the journal of Eliza Brock, born in 1810) testifying to the liberating side of the brutal whaling existence. "Then I'll haste to wed a sailor, and send him off to sea," Eliza writes, "For a life of independence, is the pleasant life for me." Men often set sail with similar eagerness, for, as historian Samuel Morison observes, "Not even Cotton Mather could extend the long arm of Puritan elder into cabin and forecastle."

Nantucket itself was chosen by its first settlers precisely because it seemed beyond Puritan reach. Fleeing theological severity on the mainland, Quakers from Amesbury and Salisbury emigrated to Nantucket in June of 1661, accompanied by Peter Foulger of Martha's Vineyard. At that time, the island's Native American population was around 3,000, a number it would take the English settlers another hundred years to reach.

Accomplished at whaling close to shore, Nantucket's Native Americans made up 75 percent of the crews when the settlers began to hunt right whales from small boats in 1690. By the mid-18th century, however, when the lucrative sperm whale was being hunted for fortune, not for food, over 60 percent of the Wampanoag population, living near Miacomet Pond, had been killed by a mysterious shipborne illness. They are buried in a sacred site near the corner of Miacomet and Surfside Roads.

By 1775, Nantucket's products accounted for one-third of New England's exports to England, and the island's African-Americans were among those who benefitted from the newfound prosperity. The first Africans had arrived on the island as slaves, but slavery was outlawed here in 1773, a decade ahead of the rest of Massachusetts, and Absalom Boston was one of those who went to sea, eventually becoming a master of his own whaling vessel with an all-black crew. Today, the African Meeting House at Five Corners, dating from about 1827, preserves this history. For information on it and other African-American sites, trace the Black Heritage Trail; *508-228 4058.*

Follow Polpis Road to the **Nantucket Life Saving Museum** at Folger's Marsh, which reminds us that the sea has always been colorblind, swallowing black and white mariners alike. *508-228-1885.*

♦ NANTUCKET HOUSES GREAT AND SMALL

By 1840, many humble Nantucket Quakers had become millionaires. To appreciate that economic curve, you should first visit the **Coffin House** (follow signs for the "island's oldest house") on Sunset Hill near the outskirts of town, and then return along Center Street and Main Street to explore one of the town's grandest mansions.

Built in 1686 for newlyweds Jethro and Mary Gardner Coffin, the Jethro Coffin House (not to be confused with the Jared Coffin House inn and restaurant) is a plain evocation of the farming community's early existence. The 1845 **Hadwen House** at 96 Main Street, on the other hand, displays the affluence of the whaling era in its magnificent furnishings and elegant gardens. Across the street, **Three Bricks** is a trio of identical houses built by Joseph Starbuck for his sons in the 1830s.

One such mansion on an isolated island in the Atlantic would be surprising, but streets of them on Nantucket seem positively fanciful—as if Chestnut Street in Salem had been set down 18 miles offshore. Walking down leafy Main Street, the island's architectural showpiece, past elaborate entrances bearing silver escutcheons that read "Starbuck" or "Coffin" or "Macy," you conclude that these merchants were so entirely creatures of the sea and of this island that they saw nothing odd in constructing urban palaces on a sandbar.

This independent mentality and skewed perspective produced salty wit. Benjamin Franklin's mother being a Folger of Nantucket, for example, a quip of the time had it that "Ben's keel was laid in Nantucket, but the old lady went to Boston to launch him."

Robert Benchley's humor, though more urban—"Why don't you slip out of those wet clothes and into a dry martini?"—may have been colored by his years here in the 1930s. His son, Nathaniel, and his grandson Peter, author of *Jaws,* also lived on Nantucket.

William Hadwen's house was just a year old when fire destroyed one-third of the town and the entire waterfront, foreshadowing even greater desolation in the 1870s when Nantucket's whaling supremacy was lost first to New Bedford then to petroleum, and the population dwindled from a peak of 10,000 to just 3,000. Despite early attempts to attract summer visitors to its 80 miles of beach, a century of poverty followed, ensuring, ironically, the preservation of many historic buildings.

In 1955, a group of Nantucket enthusiasts headed by Green Stamps heir Pete Beinecke created the nation's first historic district in the town, preventing change or demolition and eventually dictating the style of future development by purchasing land and imposing a gray-shingle orthodoxy that some find charming, others cloying. "The island has become the built embodiment of a fantasy," Jane Holz Kay writes in *Preserving New England,* "Nantucket as the Platonic ideal of a New England whaling village, Nantucket peopled by a new race, an alien—and, to

some, disturbing—culture dedicated to pleasure."

In its quiet moments, however, the island defies judgment and categorization as it always has. Crowded during the summer, Nantucket town is loveliest in early spring, late autumn, or even winter, when footsteps echo on the narrow, cobblestoned streets and winding lanes that tumble drunkenly down to the water. Squint a little on a gray February afternoon and spiky bare tree limbs turn into the spars and rigging of a whaler just in from the Pacific. Keep your eyes wide open on a May morning on the beach at Madaket and you will still be fooled by isolated funnels of sea mist hovering in the distance, mimicking whale spume.

When you leave Nantucket town, you enter a dreamscape best experienced on a bicycle or on foot. In spring, whichever direction you take, you push your way through the heavy scent of Russian olive and wild roses as red-winged blackbirds cheer you on from the marshes and red-tailed hawks hanging overhead seem to monitor your progress. It is easy to feel heroic. The island is, after all, tiny, relatively flat, and equipped with five bike paths, the most arduous of which, terminating at Siasconset, is mercifully unchallenging. Walkers can also cheat by taking one of the municipal shuttle buses, taxis, or tour buses, then setting out on foot to explore the peaceful, sandy expanse of Great Point Reservation, for example.

◆ NATURAL AREAS

Almost one-third of Nantucket's 32,000 acres is protected as conservation land, and the 1,400-acre **Coskata-Coatue, Great Point Wildlife Refuge System** is one of its jewels. On the map, Coatue and Great Point form the wishbone that protrudes from Nantucket Harbor and is almost swallowed by the Atlantic Ocean on one side and Nantucket Sound on the other before being regurgitated as a terminating dot to the north, crowned by Great Point Lighthouse.

This 18-mile shoreline is a textbook barrier beach, protecting the harbor at one end and an extraordinary bird population at the other. Crossing the haulover at Wauwinet—so-called because fishermen once hauled their boats over the narrow sand bridge here rather than battling their way around Great Point—you enter a wind-blasted spit of land, apparently held in place by tufts of spindly beach grass. Here the ocean is constantly busy. Like a compulsive housekeeper rearranging the furniture, it ceaselessly picks up sand from one shore and dumps it on the other only to start all over again. Winter storms make particularly drastic alterations, wiping out as much as 20 feet of shoreline with one blow and threatening, with

(opposite) Great Point Lighthouse at the northern tip of Nantucket.

the cooperation of the tide, to wipe out the entire peninsula.

On a warm May afternoon, however, everything at Great Point seems calm and permanent. Snowy egrets stand immaculate and immobile at the edge of shallow ponds, black-breasted plovers strut between the dunes, pleased with their avant-garde plumage, and a harrier delivers lunch to his mate in mid-air. At land's end, presided over by Great Point Lighthouse, you stare at seals who stare unflinchingly back until the silence becomes awkward and they dip their black heads politely under the water, barely causing a ripple.

Great Point borders the grounds of the Wauwinet Inn, which sits on a narrow ridge separating Nantucket Sound from the ocean. Originally an inexpensive hotel patronized by fishermen and adventurous pioneer tourists, its situation remains glorious even if its menu, decor, and rates have changed beyond recognition. If you get the right room, you can lie in bed and simply watch the window fill up with navy-blue ocean and paler blue sky. Only a herring gull flying through the frame disturbs the composition. Faced with the bill, of course, you may recall Melville's observation that "The act of paying is perhaps the most uncomfortable infliction that the two orchard thieves entailed upon us."

The front porch of the Wauwinet Inn.

Eastman Johnson's Cranberry Harvest, Island of Nantucket, *1880.*
(Timkin Museum of Art, the Putnam Foundation, San Diego)

◆ SIASCONSET

Just south of Wauwinet is the small, enchanting village of Siasconset (pronounced Sconset.) A cluster of fishermen's shanties interwoven with narrow, grassy lanes, pretty Siasconset is blessedly relieved by its eccentricity. Rambling from the comically misnamed Broadway to the overgrown intimacy of Front Street, you enter a twisting lane that passes between ancient gray-shingled cottages, each different, each askew, facing each other, not the sea, as if for reassurance. "Sea views are only for urban folk who never experience its menace," Jane Austen once remarked, "The true sailor prefers to be land-locked than face the ocean."

Today's residents are largely "summer people," recreational mariners, but the houses cannot tell the difference. They look, as they always did, like ship's cabins riding the waves of roses and honeysuckle that flood their tiny gardens. The view from nearby Sankaty Head Light, tracking the sea in one direction and barren heath in the other, makes Siasconset's coziness seem not only beguiling but miraculous.

Returning to Nantucket town on Milestone Road, you pass the Middle Moors, a desolate sweep of former sheep pasture that is particularly lovely in autumn, when the heath's vegetation throbs with color. Milestone Bog to the southeast was the world's largest natural cranberry bog, covering 234 acres, until it was bisected by ditches in 1959. Cranberries are still grown here and in mid-October the spectacular harvest may be viewed during the annual Cranberry Harvest Weekend.

The island that Melville described admiringly as an "ant-hill in the sea" teems with different life today. But nature may still have the last word. According to current predictions, Nantucket, like the whales that made it famous, may sink beneath the waves in less than 600 years.

INTERIOR
MASSACHUSETTS

■ TRAVEL BASICS

Central and western Massachusetts, encompassing the upper Connecticut River Valley and the Berkshire Hills, is quiet and surprisingly rural compared to the coast. A couple of hours west of Boston, suburbs give way entirely to forest, dairy farms, apple orchards, and sleepy New England villages. There is real wilderness surrounding the Quabbin Reservoir, superb collections in the many art museums, and summer music festivals like Tanglewood to enhance bucolic pleasures. We begin in this chapter with the small, historic town of Deerfield; map page 162. *D-2*

Getting Around: Driving from Boston, follow Highway 2 West or the busier Massachusetts Turnpike until you reach lovely meandering roads like Routes 202, 122, 47, and 7. The central region's backroads are ideal for bicycling. Rail and bus service from Boston beyond the suburbs is limited.

Climate: Summer temperatures often rise to the 90s during July and August with high humidity, while winter numbers can drop as low as 25 below zero at night and single digits in daytime. Autumn is the most predictably moderate season, with 70-degree temperatures during the day and 30s and 40s at night.

Food & Lodging: Historic inns and unpretentious diners tend to be real not franchised and Yankee pot roast still gives vegetarian cuisine a run for its money. Here you will find more traditional New England meals, often with a twist, at fine country inns, where guest rooms may be furnished with antiques. Massachusetts listings begin page 328; towns are listed in alphabetical order. Listings map page 327; listings chart 375.

■ OVERVIEW

"A hideous and desolate wilderness, full of wild beasts and wild men," is how William Bradford saw Massachusetts in 1620 and how many coastal residents view the inland part of their state today. To most Bostonians in particular, interior Massachusetts means outlet shopping, ski resorts, maple syrup, and fall foliage. That's it. You go to the Berkshires for culture and the Pioneer Valley for college. Everything else is backwoods—skinny people with few teeth who stare at passing cars.

The stereotype is laughable but the urbanites are right about one thing. Much of central and western Massachusetts is a backwater, possessing subtle rather than spectacular charms. Aside from the alpine drama of the Berkshire Hills and the steeper reaches of the Connecticut River, this is an intimate place that draws you into its valleys and hillsides instead of keeping you at an awestruck distance. On an October morning, for instance, when mist hangs on a distant hillside and a sudden breeze showers you with incandescent leaves, you feel you have witnessed one of nature's private moments, not a public display.

Fall in the southern Berkshires.

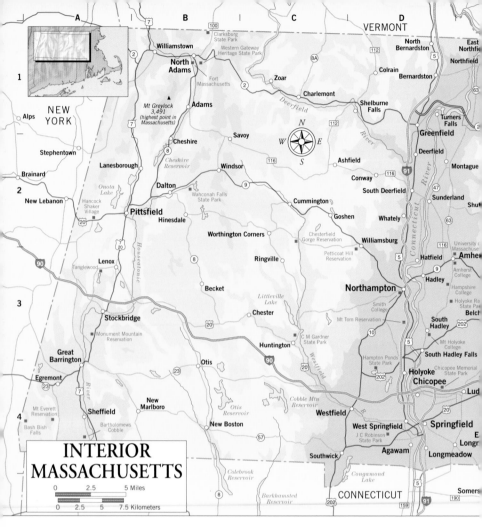

INTERIOR
MASSACHUSETTS

Become ecstatic, however, and you risk embarrassing the residents of this self-effacing place. A real Yankee will never bellow, "What do you think of our meetinghouse?" When pressed, he might agree that it's "not half bad" or even "pretty good." This was, after all, the home of Calvin Coolidge, America's most laconic President, and the birthplace of Emily Dickinson, its most reclusive poet.

It was also home to two of the nation's chief icon makers. Here Daniel Chester French created America's best-known sculpture of Abraham Lincoln, and Norman Rockwell painted his sentimental version of small-town America. The surprise today is that Rockwell's icons are living realities. The town common, the church spire, the tidy farm, the covered bridge, the stone walls, and the dour old Yankee

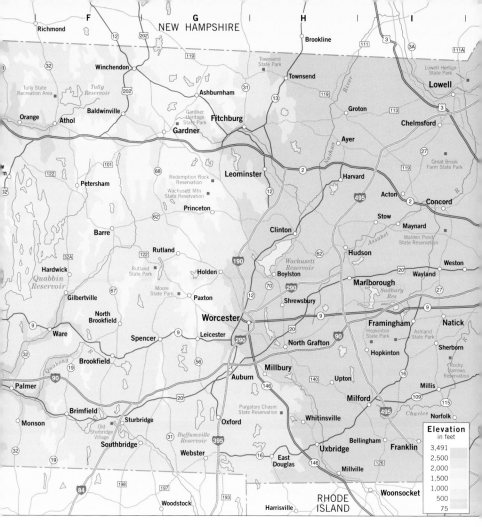

have survived the encroachment of "Colonial Outlet Villages" and "Antique Condominiums." Not everywhere, of course. But the rule of thumb is fairly simple. Like the "Family Style" restaurants that invariably turn out to be impersonal feedlots, if it advertises itself as "authentic," it probably isn't.

■ HISTORY

The shady Common, the covered bridge, the stone wall, the sturdy barn—it is no coincidence that the most familiar rural Massachusetts landmarks were designed to enclose and protect. Winter is one reason. When it is a balmy 20 degrees in

Boston, it can be minus 30 out here with a rapier wind freezing the tears on your cheek and turning your breath to ice. Henry Adams wrote in 1907 of "a cold that froze the blood and a heat that boiled it. Winter and summer…marked two modes of life and thought, balanced like lobes of the brain." But winter was not the only enemy. Interior Massachusetts was, after all, the frontier. And whereas canoes on the Connecticut River today mean recreation, for long after the region was settled by white men, they augured imminent attack.

◆ EXPANSION INTO INDIAN LANDS

Inland explorations began in the 1620s, but the encroachment was slow and perilous. Springfield was settled in 1636, Northampton in 1654, Deerfield in 1669. Even after the border warfare known as Pontiac's Rebellion in 1763, life in these and scores of other outposts remained precarious. When Newburyport merchants were laying down cases of wine in their cellars, farmers inland worked their fields, armed and edgy. City dwellers just 70 miles away read of frontier massacres with their morning tea. Increase Mather's account of King Philip's War, for instance, was with a Boston printer just 12 days after Metacom's death in 1676.

Native Americans—chiefly the Penacooks in the north, the Nipmucks in the eastern interior, the Pocumtucs in the Connecticut Valley, and the Mohicans in the Housatonic Valley—had long-established hunting, fishing, and farming grounds as well as seasonal camps throughout the region. And the near extermination of the Pequots in the war of 1636 had convinced many that attack was the only response to white settlement. Subsequent conflicts—notably King Philip's War and the lengthy French and Indian Wars—would devastate the frontier and decimate its settler population.

The villages that gradually took root in this hostile environment were small and self-sufficient, clustered around a common that still forms the center of beautiful towns like Royalston, Templeton, and many others. "The trees possess a domestic character," Hawthorne once wrote of a typical common, "They have lost the wild nature of their forest kindred, and have grown humanized by receiving the care of man as well as by contributing to his wants." Sugar maples, in particular, continue to provide not only shade but sap that is boiled down into maple syrup. In early March, when snow still coats their branches, tin buckets decorate their trunks like the votive offerings of a tree cult, a reminder of a time when sweetness was a true luxury.

THE SHAKER "DANCE": RUMORS ABROAD

*T*hese people are called Shakers from their peculiar form of adoration, which consists of a dance, performed by the men and women of all ages, who arrange themselves for that purpose in opposite parties: the men first divest themselves of their hats and coats, which they gravely hang against the wall before they begin; and tying a ribbon round their shirt-sleeves, as though they were going to be bled. They accompany themselves with a droning, humming noise, and dance until they are quite exhausted, alternately advancing and retiring in a preposterous sort of trot. The effect is said to be unspeakably absurd: and if I may judge from a print of this ceremony which I have in my possession; and which I am informed by those who have visited the chapel is perfectly accurate; it must be infinitely grotesque.

—Charles Dickens, *American Notes,* 1842

◆ SELF-SUFFICIENT SETTLERS

Self-governing and self-sufficient, these isolated communities supplied the Revolutionary forces with provisions, ammunition, and men, then rebelled in 1786 against the mortgage foreclosures and tax bills imposed by their new government. Today, Route 202 is named after Daniel Shays, the agrarian rebellion's leader, and traces of his somewhat haphazard campaign pepper the state, from the hills near Worcester to the final defeat of his cause near Great Barrington. You can even hear populist objections similar to Shays's hurled about at the annual town meetings that still constitute local government in much of the area.

From the outset, frontier dwellers feared not only the dangers but the temptations of the wilderness, temptations to which some captives succumbed by choosing to remain with their Indian captors. It is hardly surprising that this harsh place kindled America's first religious revival—the Great Awakening of the 1730s and '40s, sparked by the preaching of Jonathan Edwards in Northampton—and produced many utopian communities, the most successful being the Shakers who flourished in the 1840s.

Even visionaries tire of growing rocks, however, and by the mid-19th century, the rich farmlands of the Western Reserve had enticed many Massachusetts farmers and emptied the countryside. But their cellar holes and collapsed chimneys still punctuate the forest. Each fresh snowfall dusts the bare woodland for the farmer's fingerprints and finds them, in the cart tracks and stone walls that pattern the land.

◆ HILL TOWNS: REALITIES AND ROMANTICISM

By the late 19th century, hill towns connected by telephone and engaged in small manufacturing were nonetheless set on their backwater course. Shelburne Falls and Ashfield had less than a thousand inhabitants in 1900 and today retain their outpost atmosphere. The fertile Connecticut River Valley, by contrast, expanded its agriculture, manufacturing, and immigrant labor force. In the mid-1880s Northampton had a population of over 16,000, Holyoke over 40,000, and Springfield over 50,000.

Untaxed industrialists built summer "cottages" in the Berkshires—mansions that evoked a very different Europe from the one their workers had left behind—while 19th-century writers and artists found their romantic impulses perfectly complemented by the heroic landscape and dramatic climate. Here Melville met Hawthorne, Thoreau attempted conversation with tight-lipped Yankees, and Edith Wharton nursed her repeatedly broken heart.

◆ COLLEGES AND COMMUNES

Education also flourished. Williams College was founded in 1790; Amherst College in 1821; Mount Holyoke, the first American institution of higher education for women, in 1837; the Worcester Polytechnic in 1865; and Smith College in 1871. Today the Five Colleges in the Pioneer Valley—Amherst, Mount Holyoke, Smith, Hampshire, and the University of Massachusetts at Amherst—have a nationwide reputation not only for academic excellence but also for progressive politics.

Fuzzier idealism spawned the "back to the land" movement of the 1960s counterculture, a modern utopian experiment that endures in some rural communes today and, more profitably, in spin-offs like the Kripalu Institute, a yoga-based spa in Lenox. The resulting collisions are often surprising. Tree goddesses move in next to dairy farmers and before you know it the general store stocks healing crystals.

Each new arrival here, from 17th-century settlers to 20th-century urban refugees, has regarded their conquest as virgin land. Yet, as Jane Holz Kay points out, "There is no natural landscape [here]…the evidence of the human hand is everywhere." Even the region's biggest wilderness, the 85,000 acres surrounding the Quabbin Reservoir, was created in the 1930s for thirsty Boston. But natural beauty is not a zero-sum game. And when you sit drinking cappuccino in a gristmill turned bookstore, overlooking the rapids of the Sawmill River, facing a shelf of texts on Zen Buddhism, you realize that layers of human presence only add to the fascination of this backwater.

■ DEERFIELD *map page 162, D-2*

"Not long before the break of day, the enemy came in like a flood upon us," the Rev. John Williams wrote in *The Redeemed Captive,* his account of the 1704 Deerfield Massacre. Today, the doorway of the 1698 John Sheldon House, with its gaping tomahawk hole, is graphic evidence of the attack's ferocity and a chief exhibit in the town's **Memorial Hall Museum.** The Indian House, a 1929 reproduction of the town's oldest dwelling, also gives a sense of the besieged lives of the early settlers. *8 Memorial Street; 413-774-3768.*

Historic Deerfield has, however, long been a peaceful, even staid place, with its mile-long street of restored 18th- and 19th-century houses, many of them museums, set in the river valley's farmland. On fall evenings the tree-lined thoroughfare is particularly soothing, and even a visitor uninterested in the town's architecture will linger on the porch of the **Deerfield Inn** to watch the shadows devouring the clapboards. Walkers can also explore the Blake Meadow Walk to the Deerfield

The Dwight House, which stands in Deerfield, was built in 1730.

A classic example of a Connecticut River Valley doorway, this at the Ashley House, built in 1732.

River or hike the nearby Pocumtuck Ridge, named after the valley's first inhabitants.

In the gray light of a bone-chilling February morning, however, it is easy to imagine that terrifying moment. Under French command, on February 29, 1704, 350 Indians attacked, killing 49 people and marching 112 prisoners 300 miles to Canada, 20 of whom died on the way. John Williams's account of the attack quickly became a best-seller, but his lifelong effort to persuade his daughter Eunice to return from her captors failed, as John Demos recounts in his 1994 book, *The Unredeemed Captive.*

In the **Old Burying Ground** you will find Lt. Mehuman Hinsdell, who died in 1736, aged 63, "the first male child born in this place and was twice captivated by the Indian salvages." The nearby **Deerfield Academy,** a preparatory school, was founded in 1797, and **Hall Tavern,** across the street, houses the town's information center. On paper, **Historic Deerfield** sounds like a colonial theme park, with its museum store and its 14 meticulously restored houses displaying 20,000 artifacts dating from 1650 to 1850. But the town's enticements are restrained and tasteful and, except on holiday weekends, a tour of this small historic district is more of a stroll than an endurance test.

Tours of the individual houses are, however, uneven and relatively expensive. To maximize your chances of an informed guide, purchase an "All of Deerfield" ticket ($12), which covers the Memorial Hall Museum and all 14 houses and is valid for one week.

■ CONNECTICUT RIVER VALLEY RAMBLES *map page 162, D-1, D-2*

In this part of the Connecticut River Valley, the detours are as appealing as the destinations. So from Deerfield, head south on Route 5 and turn left before the Cheapside Bridge onto meandering River Road. This leads to Sunderland, home of the biggest sycamore east of the Mississippi; the tree sits meekly on Route 47, one of the prettiest roads in the area. Crossing the Sunderland Bridge, follow Route 47 northward through gentle hills, fuzzy with new leaves in spring and multicolored in fall, to the charming town of Montague.

◆ MONTAGUE

The Book Mill, found at the edge of town along the river, started life as a grist-mill, became a second-hand bookstore, and is now better known as the site of a restaurant and of the Book Mill coffee shop, which overlooks the rapids. The

romantic setting is marred only by occasional troops of helmeted, spandex-clad cyclists who, having raced along the adjacent Meadow Road oblivious to its mockingbirds and hay-scented air, refresh themselves with literary criticism and tofu snacks. *Book Mill: open daily for breakfast and lunch; 413-367-9206.*

◆ TURNER'S FALLS

Tofu never took hold in Turner's Falls, a few miles north of Montague. Site of the first dam on the Connecticut River, this mill town was built on a series of terraces rising 100 feet above the water, and as late as 1913 these impressive waters were the final destination of enormous log

The Book Mill on the river in Montague.

(following pages) The long shadows of late afternoon set off golden fall foliage and verdant farms along the Connecticut River.

The Watermill Lumber Company in North Leverett, south of Turner's Falls.

drives. The town may be distinctly unfashionable, even decayed in places today, but its dramatic setting, 19th-century mill houses, and attractive main thoroughfare are not its only advantages. **The Shea Theatre,** at 71 Avenue A (the town's main street), is one of the finest small performance venues in the area and the **Shady Glen** at the bridge is one of the best diners, serving banana cream pie that would tempt even the seriously spandexed. Waddle across the road from the Shady Glen to the **Fish Ladder** at First Street in late spring and you may see salmon conquering the current to reach their spawning grounds upriver.

East of Turner's Falls, Highway 2 crosses the Connecticut River at the magnificent **French King Bridge.** Here the granite walls of French King Gorge force the normally sedate Connecticut into one of its wildest and most beautiful contortions, and the view from the bridge's 140-foot height is spectacular. Between the adjacent town of Miller's Falls and the New York border, the 63-mile stretch of Highway 2 follows a trail used by the Mohawk Indians during the French and Indian Wars. Opened in 1914 and known as the **Mohawk Trail,** the highway connects beauty spots and recalls a time when motoring was a hobby, not a chore. The small jog of 2A between Turner's Falls and Greenfield follows the Connecticut River along banks that were favorite Native American fishing encampments.

◆ GREENFIELD AREA

Greenfield, once a thriving manufacturing center and site of the first cutlery factory in America, retains hints of its former beauty in its wide Federal Street, in the heroic 1930s reliefs decorating the Sweeney Ford Garage on Main Street, and in the steep residential streets that wind up to Mountain Road and Poet's Seat, a favorite spot for viewing July 4th fireworks.

Near Greenfield Municipal Park, off Plain Road, twisting **Eunice Williams Drive**—named not for John Williams's captured daughter, but for his wife of the same name *(see page 168)*—leads to a covered bridge over the Green River. The Green River Road, which winds north to Vermont, is an unspoiled, verdant delight.

Driving west on the Mohawk Trail (Highway 2) from Greenfield, you encounter tourism at its most antique. Peeling totem poles and pockmarked wooden Mohawk braves stand beside faded tepees and trading-post gift shops. Signs invite you to "See Live Deer Free," and tiny pink motel cabins proclaim their vacancies.

A tourist shop along the Mohawk Trail offers gifts and "live" entertainment.

The effect is oddly comforting, like discovering a forgotten childhood toy at the bottom of the wardrobe.

Before the turnoff for Shelburne Falls another detour beckons. The **Shelburne-Colrain Road** climbs north through woodland, apple orchards, and farmyards to a plateau that commands a romantic view—ideal for picnics or for a pancake breakfast at **Davenport's,** a working dairy farm whose seasonal opening is regarded by many as the official beginning of spring. *269 Mohawk Trail (Highway 2).*

Back on Highway 2, the turn to **Shelburne Falls** drops you into a green bowl of trees or a white bowl of ice, depending on the season. Famous for its **Bridge of Flowers**—an old trolley bridge that is now a delightful walkway—and for glacial potholes, this pretty town, along with Buckland across the river, has also become a crafts center, as numerous glass, ceramics, and "holistic healing" stores testify.

■ CHARLEMONT AREA *map page 162, C-1*

Charlemont seems a remote musical venue, but this lovely town's annual Mohawk Trail Concerts attract the nation's most celebrated classical musicians and composers, and the journey here, alongside the Deerfield River, is part of the evening's

The Bridge of Flowers in Shelburne Falls.

A view over the Berkshires from Mount Greylock.

pleasure. Highway 2 follows the Deerfield for much of its length, and the waters at Charlemont and Zoar are particularly popular with canoeists and white-water rafters.

Outside Charlemont, just before the Indian Bridge and the heroic *Hail to the Sunrise* statue of a Mohawk, the **road marked Rowe and Zoar** is a scenic delight. Turning left after a couple of miles at the first intersection, you follow the Deerfield's course between steep hills—swallows skimming the road ahead—until you reach the gloomy entrance to the Hoosac Tunnel, open only to train traffic.

Retracing your route, take Whitcomb Hill Road (to the right), which climbs valiantly to Whitcomb Summit and a view that embraces the highest points of Massachusetts, New Hampshire, Vermont, and New York.

■ MOUNT GREYLOCK AREA *map page 162, B-1*

The descent to North Adams is precipitous, and the former mill city bursts into view like a surprise party, flanked by Mount Greylock on one side and the Hoosac Mountains on the other.

Highway 2 passes through a picturesque Victorian graveyard as it exits the town in the direction of Williamstown. The 3,491-foot mass of Mount Greylock on the left, however, defies even the most indifferent alpinist to pass by. Henry David Thoreau couldn't resist Southern New England's highest point in 1839. "I made my way steadily upward in a straight line through a dense undergrowth of mountain laurel," he wrote, "until the trees began to have a scraggy and infernal look, as if contending with frost goblins, and at length I reached the summit, just as the sun was setting."

Thoreau's wild route is untraceable today, and he would surely deride the idea of following one of the mountain's 40 maintained trails. But an ascent by car is challenging enough for most visitors. As the road winds upwards through forest and mountain meadows, the maples, hemlocks, and ash trees seem to cower on the hillsides, holding their ground against ferocious gales that batter this giant all winter. But Greylock has its tranquil seasons. In May and June, painted triliums, yellow violets, and many other wildflowers cover the slopes. The elusive blackpoll warbler nests here, and the forest is particularly rich in thrushes who endlessly test its acoustics with their liquid riffs. Coyotes, black bears, and bobcats are increasingly numerous though rarely glimpsed. The 11,000-acre **Mount Greylock State Reservation** surrounds the mountain and encompasses five other major peaks and a beautiful stretch of the Appalachian Trail.

"I soon cooked my supper of rice, having already whittled a wooden spoon to eat it with," Thoreau wrote. Replete from his feast, he then settled down on the ground. "But as it grew colder towards midnight, I at length encased myself completely in boards, managing even to put a board on top of me, with a large stone on it...and so slept comfortably." Today, **Bascom Lodge**, built by the Civilian Conservation Corps in the 1930s and maintained by the Appalachian Mountain Club, provides a more conventional form of bed and board for weary hikers. Thoreau would be appalled.

■ WILLIAMSTOWN *map page 162 B-1*

Back at ground level, Highway 2 leads to Williamstown, a renowned college town and cultural center where even the trailer park on the outskirts, the Bay Colony Mobile Home, has massive white lions flanking its entrance. The town largely consists of the 450-acre **Williams College campus** with its exquisite 19th-century buildings and art museum. The Williamstown Theatre Festival runs from June through August, but the internationally renowned **Sterling and Francine Clark Art Institute** is the town's main attraction. Situated on a gentle, manicured rise at the edge of town, this small museum is particularly known for its extensive Renoir collection and its French impressionist and American paintings, including works by Homer, Sargent, Cassatt, and Remington.

"Do not mention the opening of the Institute to anyone," its founder Robert Sterling Clark wrote to a friend in 1955, "as you will treat me to a cloud of newspapermen to the detriment of my health." One of the heirs to the Singer sewing machine fortune, Clark was an art collector and racehorse owner who opened his collection to the public in 1955, the year after his chestnut colt, Never Say Die, won the Epsom Derby. Relying on their own taste rather than expert advice, Clark and his French wife, Francine Clary, accumulated distinctly "Clarkian" works. Their taste is recognizably florid, but there are some delicate surprises in these airy galleries: the Italian Renaissance and 16th-century Dutch portraits, for instance; Van Gogh's 1886 *Terrace in the Luxembourg Gardens*, which looks like a Renoir; the Renoir landscapes that look like Turners. Turner himself is superbly represented by *Rockets and Blue Lights to Warn Steamboats Off Shoal Water.* The museum is located at *22 South Street; 413-458-9545.*

There are also earthier pleasures. You can picnic on the beautiful grounds or take a half-hour walk up **Stone Hill,** an 18th-century road traveled by George Washington in 1790, for fine views of Williamstown and the surrounding hills of the Taconic Ridge.

Heading south from Williamstown along Route 43 on a spring evening is like driving or—better still—bicycling through one of the Clark Institute's French landscape paintings. Lush, tree-ringed fields border the curving road and cattle wade in the Green River. Soon, however, the mohawked slopes of the Brodie Mountain and Jiminy Peak ski resorts remind you that you are in the heart of a modern recreation area.

■ LITERARY LIGHTS

It seems a peculiarly landlocked place for Herman Melville to have finished *Moby Dick.* To him, however, the Taconic mountains were the sea. "I look out of my window in the morning when I rise as I would out of a porthole of a ship in the Atlantic," he wrote of the view from **Arrowhead,** his 18th-century farmhouse south of Pittsfield. Here Melville also wrote *Pierre* and *The Confidence Man.* The market's reaction to *Moby Dick* was lukewarm, and he was forced to sell Arrowhead to his brother in 1863. His death in 1891 was largely ignored, but today Arrowhead is a partially restored museum; *780 Holmes Road off US 7; 413-442-1793.*

Twenty miles east of Pittsfield on Route 9 is **Cummington**, site of the region's most beautiful and evocative literary site—the **William Cullen Bryant Homestead.** Born here in 1794, the poet spent his boyhood and old age on this lovely hill, where, even on the most stifling midsummer days, breezes rustle the maples that he planted. The bewitching **Rivulet Walk,** below the house, winds through old-growth forest, and the view of the Westfield Valley and Hampshire Hills invites reveries. *207 Bryant Road, signs on Route 9; 413-634-2244.*

As you head south from Pittsfield, the return to reality on US 7 is softened a little by coffee and sweet compensation at the **Old Creamery** grocery store.

■ HANCOCK SHAKER VILLAGE *map page 162, A-2*

Unlike many other utopian groups, the United Society of Believers in Christ's Second Appearing, as the Shakers called themselves, embraced profitable innovation. This celibate sect was, after all, one of the nation's most successful separatist

In a residential building (above) is a meeting room where Shakers could speak with members of the opposite sex. A Shaker apothecary (opposite) with bowls for mixing medicinal remedies.

An exterior and interior view of the round stone barn built by the Shakers in 1826.

communities, accumulating thousands of acres of farmland, pioneering mail-order seed catalogues, and inventing numerous agricultural and domestic appliances.

The mystics also knew good land when they saw it. **Hancock Shaker Village,** a museum since the last Shakers left in 1960, is set on 1,200 acres of rich, river-bottom pasture and lush forest. The village preserves 20 Shaker buildings, including a round stone barn built in 1826, the massive Brick Dwelling from 1830, and a modest privy, as well as a working farm and herb garden.

Established in 1790, Hancock at its peak in the 1830s housed 300 celibate, pacifist Shakers who professed equality but separation of the sexes, held property in common, confessed their sins to each other, and revived themselves with the ecstatic, trembling worship that gave them their popular name. Founded by dissenting English Quakers who reached America in 1774, led by Mother Ann Lee, they eventually numbered over 6,000 in 19 communities throughout New York, New England, Kentucky, and Ohio. *Hancock Shaker Village is located west of Pittsfield, at the junction of Routes 20 and 41; 413-443-0188.*

■ LENOX *map page 162, A-3*

Highway 41 heading south from the Shaker Village brings you to Lenox Road, which passes **Tanglewood,** the summer home of the Boston Symphony Orchestra and perhaps the country's most bucolic concert venue. Nathaniel Hawthorne rented a small farmhouse on the estate from the Tappan family in 1850 and—with characteristic humor—complained about the beauty of the surroundings. "I often find myself gazing at Monument Mountain," he wrote, "…instead of at the infernal sheet of paper under my hand." He did, however, complete *The House of the Seven Gables* and *A Wonder Book for Boys and Girls* here. *Tanglewood: 413-637-5165 or 800-274-8499.*

From 1880 to 1900, during America's self-styled Gilded Age, the new rich—Vanderbilts, Carnegies, and Westinghouses—discovered Lenox and transformed it, building immense summer "cottages" with names like Blantyre and Cranwell that stand today as monuments to Europhilia. The original owners of Bellfontaine would never have called their estate Canyon Ranch. They might, however, have enjoyed the pampering that the modern spa offers on the site of their old mansion.

Seiji Ozawa conducts the Boston Symphony Orchestra at Tanglewood.

MASSACHUSETTS
INTERIOR

Lenox remains a fashionable retreat for New Yorkers in particular, who inhabit some of the 19th-century mansions as inn guests today. The quiet, leafy town center consequently has an abundance of boutiques, coffee shops, and restaurants serving an urban rather than an agricultural market. Scented candles perfume the air in places, and psychotherapists advertise their services on tasteful shingle signs.

Housed in the elegant 1803 **Lenox Academy,** the historical society displays a sled similar to the one that figured in the pivotal accident scene of Edith Wharton's novel *Ethan Frome.* Wharton wrote the desolate story at **The Mount,** the Italian palazzo-style mansion south of Lenox, where she lived from 1902 to 1911. Its somewhat tragic air is perfect for the Shakespeare dramas staged here throughout the summer. *Shakespeare and Company; 413-637-1199 or 413-637-3353.*

■ STOCKBRIDGE *map page 162, A-3*

"In Lenox you are estimated, in Stockbridge you are esteemed," a Stockbridge aristocrat once informed a Lenox parvenu. Ironically, "old money" Stockbridge was immortalized for most Americans in 1967 by Norman Rockwell, the country's most plebian artist, when he depicted its Main Street at Christmas. And on the first Sunday in December, when the town stages a live re-creation of Rockwell's painting, even the obliging late afternoon sky seems to turn just the right shade of pink.

Rockwell's Stockbridge Main Street at Christmas. *(Norman Rockwell Museum at Stockbridge)*

Red Lion Inn

The magic moments might continue when you repair to the Red Lion Inn after the festivities. Opened in 1773, destroyed by fire and rebuilt in 1896, this rambling establishment, crammed with antiques and oddball memorabilia, has had the good sense to disregard fashion. The smell of roast beef rather than potpourri greets you when you wander in off the enormous porch, and the waiters are busy serving not reciting ludicrous specials. *30 Main Street; 413-298-5545.*

The Red Lion has also seen action. When 100 of Shays's rebels looted Stockbridge in 1787, they occupied the inn while the sheriff hid in a wardrobe. After a night of plotting and revelry, they marched the next morning to their defeat at Great Barrington. The guest list has also included Presidents Cleveland, McKinley, Coolidge, and both Roosevelts; Hawthorne, Longfellow, John Wayne, and Bob Dylan, all of whom, no doubt, the Red Lion took in its generous stride.

Mission House

The restored Mission House on Main Street was built in 1739 for Rev. John Sargeant, the first missionary to the Mukhekanews or Stockbridge Indians, who is buried alongside his Christianized flock in the adjacent Village Cemetery. Provided with six square miles of town land and elected to town office, the Mukhekanews served as scouts during the Revolutionary War, when their chief was killed in action. But this counted for little in subsequent transactions with the double-dealing settlers. The disillusioned tribe migrated to New York in 1785 and finally to Wisconsin. The Mission House itself is interesting, but its small garden of period plants is glorious. *19 Main Street; 413-298-3239.*

Merwin House and Naumkeag

Two other houses illustrate Stockbridge's development from missionary outpost to playground. The Merwin House, a Federal jewel built around 1825, reveals the cultural and decorative tastes of the town's 19th century aristocrats, while Naumkeag, a 23- room mansion and formal estate on outlying Prospect Hill Road reflects the Choate family's appetite for novelty. Completed in 1886 for New York lawyer Joseph Hodges Choate, Naumkeag houses an extensive Chinese porcelain collection, a 16th-century Flemish tapestry, and its gardens, laid out by Fletcher Steele, feature a birch-lined stairway that you might call art deco oriental. *Merwin, 14 Main Street; 413-298-4703; Naumkeag, Prospect Hill Road; 413-298-3239.*

Norman Rockwell Museum

Just outside Stockbridge on Route 183, the Norman Rockwell Museum occupies one of the most beautiful hillsides in the area. Sitting outside Rockwell's small studio on a spring afternoon, watching the Housatonic River execute a graceful bend, you suspect that the wall of birdsong is a recorded broadcast until you notice the red-winged blackbirds, mockingbirds, thrushes, and warblers darting between the trees. Picnickers are welcome and it seems a shame to go inside. But it is worth it.

The elegant museum houses the world's largest collection of Rockwell paintings as well as temporary exhibitions and instructive programs. Rockwell spent 25 years in Stockbridge until his death in 1978, and his studio and contents were moved here from South Street in 1986. *413-298-4100.*

Interior of Baldwin's Vanilla Shop in Stockbridge, a town fixture for over 100 years.

The summer studio of Daniel Chester French, who sculpted the statue of Abraham Lincoln at the Lincoln Memorial in Washington, D.C., can be found in Chesterwood, on Route 183.

South of Stockbridge, Route 183 plays tag with the Housatonic River and skirts Monument Mountain, where David Dudley Jr. introduced Nathaniel Hawthorne to Herman Melville in August 1850 during a hike. Not to be upstaged by this literary conjunction, nature staged a violent thunderstorm and the group was forced to hunker down and drink champagne. Lightning snapped, verses flew, and Melville teetered on a ledge, demonstrating how mariners haul in their sheets. Just as well Thoreau wasn't there.

■ GREAT BARRINGTON AREA *map page 162, A-4*

Nature is still an exhibitionist here, staging pyrotechnic extravaganzas in summer thunderstorms and rolling out shameless views of farmland and forested hillside. The pretty town of Great Barrington is the site of two historical defeats. In 1676, during King Philip's War, a band of Narragansetts was decimated here by English troops. And in 1787, Shays's Rebellion ended here with two fatalities on each side when the Sheffield militia defeated the hundred rebels who had spent the preceding night in Stockbridge. W.E.B. Du Bois, the black writer, educator, and civil rights pioneer, was born here in 1868.

Today, the town's rural character has largely been defeated by metropolitan fashion. New York City is just two hours away and that proximity has spawned a glut of sushi bars, gourmet coffee bars, and craft and antique stores. This is Berkshire shopping at its most intense and Berkshire life at its most diluted. There are cultural compensations. **The Aston Magna Festival,** for instance, is the oldest American summer festival of baroque, classical, and early romantic music.

South of Sheffield, on Cooper Hill Road off Route 7A, is **Bartholomew's Cobble,** a nature preserve, bordering two miles of the Housatonic River, that shyly reveals its treasures to the attentive walker. There are 53 species of fern, 500 different wildflowers, and 240 recorded species of birds in these fields and riverbanks. But the allure is not a matter of statistics. On a summer morning, the stillness and beauty settles in on you as you walk past yellow poplars and giant cottonwoods rarely found in this region. Even the turkey vulture above you, patrolling the sky, seems benevolent.

Bash Bish Falls, the most dramatic waterfall in southern New England, is within the Mount Washington reservation to the west, where it is visible from the New York side of the state line. But a return journey to the Connecticut River Valley through the central Berkshires is a quieter affair of accidental discoveries rather than special effects. Emulate the Housatonic at its laziest and meander through the lovely **Tyringham Valley,** then continue on back roads through hill towns that host unlikely events such as the Jacob's Pillow summer dance festival in Becket. Route 20, also known as Jacob's Ladder, spirals downward toward the civilization of the Springfield area, trailing its springtime perfume of wild azalea.

Fall colors in the Berkshires.

■ SPRINGFIELD *map page 162, D-4*

Springfield has superb art, science, and historical museums in its **Museum Quad-rangle** area, accessible from the State Street exit off Route 91; *413-734-8551.* A short walk to the north, the Springfield Armory was sited here by George Washington. Two centuries of its output are on display in the Main Arsenal building at the Springfield Technical Community College, which houses the world's largest collection of small arms; *413-734-8551.* The city is also home to the **Basketball Hall of Fame,** as Dr. James Naismith is credited with inventing the game at Springfield's YMCA in 1891. *West Columbus Avenue at Union Street; 413-781-6500.* And, you can visit the **Indian Motorcycle Museum,** housed in one of the company's former buildings. *33 Hendee Street; 413-737-2624.*

■ MOUNT HOLYOKE COLLEGE *map page 162, D-3*

On a September day, the drive from Springfield and Holyoke to South Hadley along Route 116 is golden, and the Tudor-style campus of **Mount Holyoke College** at the town center seems more a construction of leaf-filtered light than red brick. Established in 1837 as Mount Holyoke Female Seminary, the college retains a cloistered air, although student tastes have changed considerably as the

The campus of Mount Holyoke College in South Hadley. (above)

A view of downtown Springfield. (opposite)

Thomas Cole's painting View from Mount Holyoke, Northampton, Massachusetts, after a Thunderstorm—The Oxbow, *1836. (Metropolitan Museum of Art, New York, gift of Mrs. Russell Sage, 1908; 08.228. Photo © Metropolitan Museum of Art.)*

fashionable stores and restaurants abutting the campus testify. **The Art Museum** displays a wide range of European, American, Asian, Egyptian, and Classical art as well as Medieval and Renaissance paintings and sculpture. Its visiting exhibitions are particularly imaginative. *On campus; 413-538-2245.*

Mount Holyoke itself, the northernmost spur of the Metacomet Range, is an unusual traprock formation, forced into its east-west orientation some 200 million years ago. Autumn inflames these slopes, and on September nights, the sunset seems to soak up its color from the trees below. The view from the **Summit House** of the Connecticut River's oxbow winding through the valley is mesmerizing, as are the wheeling motions of hawks riding the thermal updrafts during their autumn migration.

■ HADLEY AREA *map page 162, D-3*

Despite the encroachment of strip malls and traffic, **Hadley,** to the north on Route 47, retains the character of a prosperous farming town.

Route 47, a soothing green road, should be followed for its own sake, and the short loop from Hadley to Sunderland then back to Northampton gives a sense of how the valley looked in its agricultural prime. On one side of the road, the sedate Connecticut River tolerates the dragonflies tickling its surface. On the other, tobacco barns dot the fields, their slatted walls open for ventilation.

Just north of Hadley on Route 47, the **Porter Phelps Huntington Museum,** on the bank of the river, is a 1752 house containing family possessions that span ten generations in this valley. Regarded by many as the best-preserved colonial house in New England, it serves a genteel afternoon tea with musical accompaniment on the porch during the summer and stages livelier concerts in its charming garden. *Open seasonally; 1300 River Drive; 413-584-4699.*

Cross the Sunderland bridge and turn south on River Drive to **Whately,** where altitude and beauty conspire to immobilize even the most harried travelers. Farther south and bordering the river, **Hatfield** is equally seductive. It was not, however, always this peaceful. The town was repeatedly targeted during King Philip's War, and following a ferocious attack in 1677, Benjamin Waite and Stephen Jennings paddled from here to Quebec—some 300 miles through hostile territory—to rescue their captive wives and children by paying a ransom of £200.

A collection of wood planes from the Farm Museum in Hadley; 413-584-8279.

■ NORTHAMPTON

map page 162, D-3

The soporific dawdle along Route 47 hardly prepares you for the sights and sounds of **Northampton,** an elegant college town where the taste for body piercing and gender-bending is immediately evident. **Smith College** for women was established here in 1875, and the campus where Sylvia Plath walked and *Who's Afraid of Virginia Woolf* was filmed is a tree-shaded delight on a midsummer day.

The Smith College Museum of Art on is one of the area's finest, with a superb collection of works by Pablo Picasso and his contemporaries; *on Elm Street; 413-585-2760.*

Lyman Plant House is a short walk away and a miracle in early spring when snow and ice sterilize the outside world and the annual bulb show assaults you with riotous colors and the dimly remembered smell of hyacinths. Its Victorian greenhouses overlook Paradise Pond. *Located on campus; 413-585-2740.*

Those assuming that the thoughts of Calvin Coolidge, America's notoriously taciturn President, would fill a postcard will be surprised by the extensive collection in the Calvin Coolidge Memorial Room at the beautiful **Forbes Library**. Coolidge lived in Northampton after retiring from politics, and the man that emerges from these documents and photographs is more complex than the image. The President's mechanical bucking horse also conjures up unlikely images. *20 West Street; 413-587-1011.*

On a humble side street here in 1983, the Teenage Mutant Ninja Turtles were born, and today the **Words and Pictures Museum** on Main Street houses the 7,000-piece comic-illustration collection of their co-creator, Kevin Eastman. Dedicated to "fine sequential art of the renaissance years of the '70s, '80s, and '90s," the galleries in this tiny museum are ingeniously designed without being Disney-esque. The original work of artists and comic illustrators like Simon Bisley, Jack Kirby, Frank Miller, and John Severin is displayed, and the museum's whimsical little cafe sustains the cartoon mood. *140 Main Street; 413-586-8545.*

❖

One of the most relaxing travel routes from Northampton to Amherst is the **Norwottuck Rail Trail,** an 8.5-mile bicycle bath that vaults the Connecticut River and slips through corn fields from its starting point at Elwell State Park on Damon Road in Northampton to Station Road in Amherst.

If you're driving, take Route 9 out of Northampton, but leave it at the first opportunity, turn back onto Route 47 (Middle Street) at Hadley, and follow Rocky Hill Road to Amherst.

■ AMHERST *map page 162, D-3*

If you approach the homely college town of Amherst from the east, the high-rise dormitories of the University of Massachusetts materialize like surreal battlements on the outskirts but disappear as you approach the picturesque center. Across from the Common on Amity Street, the Jones Library and the Strong House Museum are fine starting points for any exploration.

Jones Library

Robert Frost taught at Amherst College for 18 years (until 1938), and the elegant Jones Library houses a large collection of items relating to the poet's life and work. The Emily Dickinson collection includes original manuscripts, letters, and illustrations. Massachusetts local history comes vividly to life in the correspondence, journals, and ephemera that comprise the Boltwood Collection, which includes the 18th-century letters of British general Lord Jeffrey Amherst and various Civil War diaries that evoke the voices as well as the events of history; *43 Amity Street; 413-256-4090.*

Strong House

The 1774 Strong House displays 18th- and 19th-century rooms, dedicating one to Mabel Loomis Todd, the late-19th-century neighbor of Emily Dickinson and the first editor of her poems. Loomis's steamy affair with Emily's brother William Austin is not commemorated here but was documented in the diaries kept by the couple and later in Polly Longsworth's 1984 book *Austin and Mabel; 67 Amity Street; 413-256-0678.*

Emily Dickinson Homestead

When Emily Dickinson limited her perambulations to her "father's fields," the reclusive poet was referring to 14 acres of meadow, not the hillock on which the Dickinson Homestead now stands. The house and gardens at 280 Main Street are modest, and most of Dickinson's possessions are at Harvard, yet a tour of the rooms is strangely moving, perhaps because it is so intimate. Dickinson lived here most of her life, and when you see the tiny white dress in her bedroom or the afternoon shadows bisecting her garden, her words materialize: "The soul selects her own society...There's a certain slant of light." The Amtrak Vermonter rumbles across Main Street in the afternoon and you hear, "I like to see it lap the miles/ And lick the valleys up." The Evergreens, next door, once the home of Emily's brother William Austin, is currently undergoing restoration. Emily Dickinson is buried a short distance away in West Cemetery, where her simple tombstone reads "Called Back." *Dickinson Homestead: One East Pleasant Street; 413-542-8161.*

Amherst College
and Common Area

Founded in 1821 to educate men for the ministry and now one of the country's leading establishments, Amherst College borders the Common, and its **Mead Art Museum** and **Pratt Museum of Natural History** provide an edifying excuse for a stroll through the beautiful campus. Amherst has the highest student population in the Five College area and consequently the area's best pizza, at **Antonio's** on North Pleasant Street. **Pasta E Basta,** around the corner, is also an inexpensive, clattery delight. *Both museums are on the main quad. Mead Museum: 413-542-2335. Pratt Museum: 413-542-2165.*

◆ HAMPSHIRE COLLEGE *map page 162, E-3*

Hampshire College has long had a reputation as a school on the thin wedge of the counter-cultural edge. While this may be less true than it used to be, the college still boasts a vibrant artistic and intellectual culture.

The college's green, rolling campus seems far removed from Eastern Europe, but the **National Yiddish Book Center** is housed here in buildings designed to resemble a 19th-century shtetl. The only such institute in the nation, the center preserves a vanished culture and a fragile tradition in a remarkable collection of volumes and exhibits. *Three miles south of Amherst on Route 116; 413-256-4900.*

Driving east and uphill from Amherst, you leave the valley and enter sleepy hill country. Here back roads are often dirt roads and the only concession to tourism may be the creaky postcard rack outside the general store. Wandering should be your aim, as you bear in mind Thoreau's advice. "What's the hurry?" he wrote, "If a person lost would conclude that after all he is not lost…but standing in his own old shoes…how much anxiety and danger would vanish."

The National Yiddish Book Center. Located at Hampshire College, it is the nation's first—and the world's largest—repository for Yiddish language books.

Pine trees line the edge of the Quabbin Reservoir.

■ PELHAM–QUABBIN AREA *map page 162, E-2*

There have always been rebels in these hills. Daniel Shays, leader of the region's 1786 agrarian revolt, lived in **Pelham**, and the historical society, housed in the former church next to the severe 1742 meetinghouse, recalls his exploits. This rocky territory was also fertile ground for domestic scandals, one of which is commemorated in **Knights Cemetery,** south of Pelham off Route 202. The tombstone inscription for Warren Gibbs, aged 36 when he died by arsenic poison in 1860, begins "Think my friends when this you see/ How my wife hate dealt by me/ She in some oysters did prepare/ Some poison for my lot and share…"

Don't be misled by the oysters. The living was never easy on this begrudging land, and the stone walls bordering roads and enclosing even the smallest pasture testify to the perseverance of farmers who endured until the promise of black soil lured them westward in the 1830s. Forest reclaimed the abandoned fields. But the area's greatest modern transformation occurred in the 1930s when the creation of

MASSACHUSETTS
INTERIOR

the **Quabbin Reservoir** produced an 85,000-acre wilderness. Much of the pleasantly undulating Route 202 runs through this forested preserve, and at the peak of the fall foliage season, the view from the lookout point just north of Pelham—and all along the highway—is spectacular as maples and ashe turn into color bombs detonated by the slanting sunlight.

Those seeking more human inspiration may find it on the tombstone of Ephriam Pratt, who died in nearby Shutesbury in 1804, at the age of 117. "He swung a scythe 101 consecutive years," we learn, "and mounted a horse without assistance at the age of 110." As you traverse these roads you begin to see how old Ephriam did it. He just looked around him—at a landscape that was too beautiful to leave. Even vicious ice storms are bewitching here, transforming the trees into crystal wind chimes. Spring is a battle between sharp light and fuzzy foliage, summer a narcotic and autumn a shameless display.

Nature occasionally hurls herself at you. When a moose steps onto the woodland path ahead, for instance, and fixes you with that implacable moose look; when a bow-legged bobcat suddenly appears in the mountain laurel or a bear trundles across the road at midday. But nature usually insinuates herself with a delicate midsummer firefly display or a distant coyote choral arrangement. And towns like New Salem, Warwick, Royalston, Templeton, Petersham, Barre, and Hardwick are equally sly, luring you into their shady commons, then bewitching you with their stillness and unforced beauty. The general stores and small country inns look real because they are, and you can drive for half an hour without meeting another car.

Routes 202, 122, and 32A don't sound romantic, but they form a beguiling circuit around the Quabbin where almost every back road is worth investigating for its stories as well as its beauty. On the North New Salem Road, for instance, the rocky gorge and cascading waters of Bear's Den on the Swift River were reportedly the site of King Philip's 1675 council of war that preceded the attack on Hatfield.

■ OLD STURBRIDGE VILLAGE *map page 162, F-4*

Situated far to the southeast of the Quabbin area on 200 acres of farmland, this re-creation of an early 19th-century rural New England community is meticulously researched and uniquely informative. Forty buildings were moved here from sites

The wool carding mill in Old Sturbridge Village.

across New England, and they include the 1704 Fenno House from Canton, Massachusetts, the 1735 Stephen Fitch House from Willimantic, Connecticut, and an 1832 Greek Revival church. The setting, village layout, and costumed inhabitants are convincing and there is real work going on. Villagers herd livestock and work in the tinshops, potteries, shoe shops, mills, and other enterprises that contribute to this miniature rural economy. A day flies by here without a trace of theme park fatigue. *At intersection of Route 20 and I-84; 508-347-3362.*

■ WORCESTER *map page 162, H-3*

Worcester—the region's second largest city—is frayed at the edges, but the lovely **Worcester Art Museum** houses one of the country's finest American collections and over 30,000 artworks ranging from Roman to impressionist; *55 Salisbury Street; 508-799-4406.*

Worcester's **Higgins Armory** is the only museum in the country dedicated to medieval and Renaissance arms and armory; *100 Barber Avenue; 508-853-6015.*

CONNECTICUT
CENTRAL & EASTERN

■ HIGHLIGHTS *page*

■ TRAVEL BASICS

Hartford is a business rather than a tourist city, but its Wadsworth Atheneum is one of the country's finest museums. Historic towns like Wethersfield, Farmington, and Suffield, though now suburban, are nonetheless charming. Central Connecticut is heavily developed but the quieter Woodstock valley to the east recalls a more rural past. The Connecticut River Valley, winding between Hartford and Long Island Sound, offers river views and cruises as well as eccentricities like East Haddam's Goodspeed Opera House and the playfully gothic Gillette Castle.

Getting Around: Bradley International Airport is just 15 minutes outside Hartford. Amtrak's rail service from Boston and New York serves Hartford, New Britain, Windsor, and Windsor Locks. Metro-North serves New Haven from Grand Central Station while Connecticut Commuter Rail runs between New London and New Haven. By car it is difficult to avoid Interstates 91 and 84 around greater Hartford where rush-hour delays are lengthy. Routes 169 and 14 in the Woodstock valley are a restful contrast. Choose minor roads that shadow the Connecticut River in the valley and skirt Interstate 95 along the coast, following Route 1 and its offshoots. A river ferry serves Glastonbury and Rocky Hill. The Hadlyme-Chester river ferry operates from April to October. Ferries for Block Island depart from New London.

Climate: Hartford and Central Connecticut seem to boil in summer (temperatures average in the high 80s) while the Woodstock valley is slightly cooler. Winter temperatures are often slightly less extreme than those of interior Massachusetts, although sudden blizzards and ice storms occasionally close stretches of the interstates. Spring and autumn are typically moderate, with pleasantly warm days and chilly nights.

Food & Lodging: Chain hotels are found everywhere, fine old inns in small historic towns. Dining runs from old-country ethnic to haute-nouvelle. Connecticut listings begin on page 354; towns are listed in alphabetical order. Listings map page 327; listings chart page 376.

John Trumbull's painting Norwich Falls, *1806. (Yale University Art Gallery)*

■ OVERVIEW

Connecticut may be one of the smallest states in the country (only Rhode Island and Delaware are smaller) but it is also one of the richest and most densely populated. As you sit in clover eating a summer picnic outside Woodstock village, you may sense that you are lounging not on land but on future real estate. Western Connecticut is, after all, New York's long-established bolt-hole and the eastern corner has been recently "discovered." But little Connecticut still has space and plenty of surprises left. Its graceful coast and elegant, leafy interior are old hands at anaesthetizing visitors with charm. There is real grit in cities like Hartford and New Haven, but the overall impression is one of softness. Emerging from a morning hike along the Metacomet Trail or an evening stroll by the Farmington River, you realize how smitten you are when you forget not only where you parked your car, but that you even had one.

■ HISTORY

Viewing the most rural part of the Connecticut River Valley today—with its lush meadows and gentle curves—you see what attracted Native Americans and the first European colonists. To the Nipmucks of northeastern Connecticut, to the Saukiogs of present-day Hartford, and to the neighboring Tunxis, Poquonocks, and Podunks, the valley was an ideal farming, fishing, and hunting site. But fertile land is also enviable land. The Pequots had invaded the territory of the Connecticut Algonquians before 1600 and there were also repeated attacks by the Mohawks. Such tribal rivalries would subsequently be exploited to great effect by the English settlers, particularly during King Philip's War of 1675–1676.

◆ DUTCH AND ENGLISH SETTLERS

Early encounters between Native Americans and Europeans foreshadowed no such conflict. Sailing up the Connecticut River around 1614, the Dutch explorer Adrien Block traded along the way with Native Americans. He christened the waterway Fresh River, but it was already called Quonitockuut, the Long Tidal River, a name that English settlers would later adopt as Connecticut. Two years later, a smallpox or measles epidemic killed one-third of the region's Native American population and the stage was set for white settlement.

That settlement was, ironically, facilitated by the people it would quickly subdue. In 1631, Chief Wanginnacut of the Podunks approached the English colonists at Boston and Plymouth, urging them to settle in Connecticut as his allies against the Pequots. The following year, Plymouth's Governor Edward Winslow visited the region and secured a grant from the Earl of Warwick to all land from Narragansett Bay to the Pacific Ocean. Little Connecticut already had delusions of grandeur.

Hearing of the English initiative, the Dutch of New Netherland established outposts at present-day Saybrook and Hartford. Defying Dutch guns, Plymouth's William Holmes and his followers established a palisaded trading post at Windsor. A year later, in 1634, John Oldham and other Watertown, Massachusetts, colonists settled Wethersfield. But the fertile valley could prove treacherous, as 60 Massachusetts families discovered when they almost starved and froze to death attempting to reach Windsor in 1635. They survived and retreated only with the help of the Native Americans.

The Rev. Thomas Hooker of Newtown (Cambridge) was more cautious, sending John Steel and his followers to establish a new colony and following with his congregation in 1636. Dissatisfied with aspects of the Massachusetts Bay Colony's theocracy and eager for "land and elbow-room," as Increase Mather termed it, Hooker was that peculiar Puritan hybrid—a fervent religious dissenter and hardheaded entrepreneur. His Fundamental Orders, drafted in 1638, foreshadowed constitutional democracy. Before they could be framed, however, the new colony had to address the Pequot problem.

◆ PEQUOTS FIGHT BACK

The only tribe to resist English encroachment, the Pequots, under Chief Sassacus, repeatedly raided the Connecticut Valley settlements, most ferociously in April 1637, when a war party killed at least six men and three women in Wethersfield and kidnapped two girls. On May 1, the settlers gathered at Hartford, declared war on the Pequots, and raised a band of 90 men under Capt. John Mason.

By June the war was won, most Pequots had been killed or sold into slavery, and Connecticut had witnessed the most decisive—and bloodiest—battles ever fought on its soil, at Fort Hill in West Mystic.

Historians Richard Slotkin and James K. Folsom note that the Pequot War "had showed the Indians that 'the English way of war had no limit or scruple or mercy' and that English weapons were greatly superior to those of the natives." When John Eliot came to preach to the Podunks in 1657, having translated the Bible into their language, it is hardly surprising that he was told, "No, you have taken away our lands, and now you wish to make us a race of slaves."

After the Pequot War, Connecticut had time to consolidate and expand before the next round of retribution. Hooker's Fundamental Orders were drawn up and adopted by Hartford, Windsor, and Wethersfield in 1639. Under its provisions, the towns formed "one publicke State or Commonwealth," with a legislative branch of government dominating the executive and judicial branches, presided over by the governor. But only a characteristic mixture of bluff and ingenuity would gain Connecticut legal status. In 1687 Sir Edmund Andros, appointed royal governor of New England by King James in 1686, arrived in Hartford demanding the return of the colony's charter.

The document was placed before Andros one October afternoon, and a lengthy wrangle about his jurisdiction ensued. At sunset, candles were lit, then mysteriously extinguished. In the confusion, the charter was snatched from the table and hidden in the hollow of a venerable tree which became known as the Charter Oak, "of which," Mark Twain once quipped, "most of the town is built." The charter remained hidden until 1715, by which time the colony's rights had been restored with the 1689 accession of William and Mary to the throne.

◆ COLONIAL CONNECTICUT AND THE REVOLUTIONARY WAR

Life in colonial Connecticut's isolated towns and homesteads fostered a provincialism that endured as conservatism. But it also taught self-reliance, thrift, ingenuity, and adaptability—qualities that would eventually make the state one of the manufacturing wonders of the world.

The colony's contribution to the Revolutionary War was critical. Almost 32,000 Connecticut men joined the Continental Army, and the expedition against Fort Ticonderoga was planned in Hartford. Israel Putnam of Pomfret was the ranking officer in the field at the Battle of Bunker Hill; Ethan Allen of Litchfield captured Fort Ticonderoga; and Benedict Arnold of Norwich became first a war hero, then the nation's most infamous traitor.

Emerging intact from the conflict, Hartford prospered as a shipping and trading center until the War of 1812 precipitated a maritime depression and shifted

At Riverside Cemetery lies the grave of Foone, one of the Amistad *Africans who died while the group was living in Farmington following their acquittal by the Supreme Court.*

the emphasis to manufacturing. Liberalizing certain religious tolerance laws, the new state of Connecticut nevertheless retained its insular conservatism and resisted change. There were, for example, no banks in the state until 1792, and slavery remained legal until 1784. Like the rest of the nation, the state would be propelled into the modern era by the Civil War.

◆ SLAVERY, AMISTAD, AND THE CIVIL WAR

The first Africans arrived as slaves in the 17th century. By 1850, however, when the fugitive slave law was passed, Hartford and Farmington in particular had become important stations on the Underground Railroad, aiding escapees from the South. In 1839, Farmington also provided refuge for enslaved Africans who had seized control of the Spanish slave ship, *Amistad,* and were subsequently tried and freed in the Connecticut courts. Following the outbreak of the Civil War in 1861, Hartford's banks loaned Connecticut's governor half a million dollars to equip a regiment, and the state ultimately contributed over 57,000 men in 30 regiments to the conflict, sustaining 20,000 casualties.

◆ THE PROSPEROUS 1800S

Inventive, adaptable Connecticut was well positioned to cater to the post-war nation. Home industries had, after all, been supplying local markets since the mid-17th century, and the 18th century saw the emergence of the Yankee peddler—a traveling vendor who originally sold tin goods, then "notions" such as buttons, combs, kettles, and clocks. He invariably returned home with crude sketches of new items requested by his customers. Translated into patterns and manufactured with handcrafted tools, the peddlers' orders kept numerous riverside workshops humming with invention.

By 1860, Hartford's population of 14,000 had more than doubled, and between 1850 and 1900, the manufacturing work force grew by almost 250 percent. As late as 1937 almost 70 percent of the city's population worked in its 300 manufacturing companies. Every imaginable item—from axes to aircraft engines—has been manufactured here, and since the Patent Office opened in 1790, Connecticut has received more patents than any other state.

Writing in 1813, Alexis de Tocqueville observed that one-third of U.S. senators and one-quarter of U.S. congressmen had been born in Connecticut and that the state had produced the clock peddler, the teacher, and the politician—"the first to give you the time, the second to tell you what to do with it, and the third to make your laws and civilization."

The Hartford Fire Insurance Company had been founded just three years earlier, so Tocqueville may be excused for neglecting Connecticut's other key player: the insurance man. "I do unhesitatingly affirm that Hartford companies will pay in full every claim made against them," Senator Morgan G. Bulkeley, president of Aetna Life Insurance Company, declared after the San Francisco earthquake. And Hartford companies did pay up, just as they had in the devastating New York and Chicago fires.

The fortunes made from insurance and manufacturing, along with the influx of immigrant labor, transformed an agricultural state into a sophisticated, multiracial society that rivaled Boston and New York as a literary and artistic center.

Connecticut's manufacturing decline began in the 1950s and accelerated through the 1960s as factories relocated, were swallowed by conglomerates, or simply closed. The richest state in the country is now a post-industrial economy with three out of four workers engaged in financial, government, retail, and other service jobs.

■ HARTFORD

As you leave Bradley International Airport—New England's second largest—on a midsummer day, everything seems suspiciously easy. There are no traffic snarls, no tunnels, no toll booths. Best of all, you seem to be in the country. On either side of the airport road, tobacco grows under acres of white gauze, giving the fields the prudish look of a maiden aunt wearing a hair net. Hartford is just 15 minutes away.

As you approach the city, however, ominous portents appear. Traffic grows thick and sluggish. A gigantic landfill, locally known as Mount Refuse, fills one horizon. The highway circling the city becomes a challenging work-in-progress apparently inspired by a demented Escher puzzle. The blue onion dome of the old Colt armory, once the worldwide symbol of Hartford's genius and energy, still stands out. But the building it crowns seems neglected and the famous Colt weathervane now sits in the Museum of Connecticut History on Capitol Avenue. A legendary symbol of endurance, the gilded colt holding a broken spear in his mouth represented the war horse fighting the losing battle after his rider has fallen.

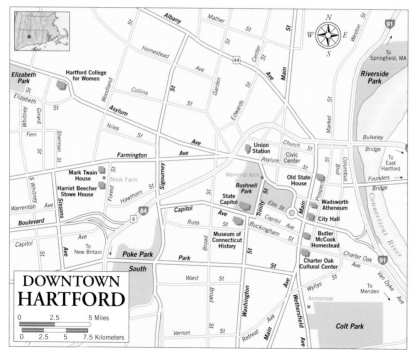

CONNECTICUT
CENTRAL & EASTERN

At a glance it is clear that Colt-era Hartford long ago lost its battle against the forces of redevelopment, although the Colt building is currently slated for restoration. Dominating the skyline, the city's expressionless office blocks look like extra-terrestrial slabs, lowered into place the night before by a celestial crane. Yet there is a symmetry to Hartford that remains pleasing. "They have the broadest, straightest streets in Hartford that ever led a sinner to destruction," Mark Twain wrote when he moved here in 1871. And even on a stifling July day, when most of those streets are clogged with traffic, the sense of space and airiness persists. Hartford may sit on a low bluff, but its wide thoroughfares and its Connecticut River breeze make the metropolis seem positively lofty.

◆ OLD STATE HOUSE

The pretty little Old State House on Central Row, cornered by glassy banking giants, appears besieged. Completed in 1796, this charming Bulfinch building replaced the 1720 State House that accidentally caught fire during the Revolutionary victory celebrations in 1783.

The Great Senate Chamber of the Old State House, where the first Amistad trial was held.

CONNECTICUT
CENTRAL & EASTERN

Today, the Old State House is surrounded by glass highrises.

Some of the costumed staff here are mediocre actors, but who can resist bumping into George Washington as he plans Revolutionary strategy with Rochambeau, Roger Sherman Baldwin as he defends the Amistad prisoners, or Joseph Steward as he launches his distinctly strange museum? "The patronage of the curious is still solicited to increase the collection," urged Steward, a deacon and painter, in 1797 when he needed, among other things, a two-headed calf. Today, that double-topped calf and other stuffed aberrations glower at you from the walls of Steward's tiny one-room museum in the State House, defying you to keep a straight face. *800 Main Street; 860-522-6766.*

Senate Chamber, Site of the Amistad Trial: The first Amistad trial was held in the magnificent Senate Chamber in 1839, and the twice-weekly, half-hour reenactment, based on the original transcripts, is both enlightening and stirring. In 1839, 53 Mende-speaking Africans who had been kidnapped in western Africa and illegally enslaved in Havana seized control of the slave-ship *Amistad* but were tricked into sailing into Long Island Sound, where they were arrested and charged with murder and piracy. A dramatic legal battle, first in the Old State House and later in the U.S. Supreme Court, freed the Africans, who were then housed in nearby Farmington before returning home. Hartford's Amistad awareness predates Steven Spielberg's 1997 film, by the way, and the city's African-American Freedom Trail has long included several Amistad-related sites.

Guided Tours of Hartford: A practical as well an inspirational starting point for a tour of the city, the Old State House stages thoughtful exhibits, and its extensive tourist information includes details of Hartford's guided tours. There are over 20, ranging from "Ivied Walls and Gothic Halls" to a "Post-Work Relaxation Excursion" and many of the city's notable sites are within easy walking distance. *Old State House: 860-522-6766.*

◆ WADSWORTH ATHENEUM

Once you enter the Wadsworth Atheneum, America's oldest continuously operated public art museum, time evaporates. After a few intoxicating hours, your growling stomach will recall you to the mundane world. But the superb museum cafe will instantly seduce you again. It is wise to leave a list of your financial,

Frederic Church's Thomas Hooker and Company Journeying through the Wilderness from Plymouth to Hartford in 1636, *painted in 1846. (Wadsworth Atheneum, Hartford)*

domestic, and social obligations with the Atheneum staff. That way they can manage your life while you are gone.

Being a Hartford institution, the Wadsworth Atheneum has a lot of "firsts" to its credit. Founded in 1842 by businessman and philanthropist Daniel Wadsworth and opened in 1844, this was the first American museum to acquire works by Frederic Church, Salvador Dalí, Joan Miró, Piet Mondrian, Joseph Cornell, Max Ernst, and Caravaggio. It mounted the first American museum exhibitions of Italian baroque paintings, neo-romanticism, and surrealism and the first comprehensive Picasso retrospective. It began screening films in 1929 and staged the first public performances by Balanchine's American Ballet Theatre in 1934. This is also the home of the earliest dated American portrait painting: *Elizabeth Eggington,* artist unknown, 1664.

Such achievements conjure up a vision of a streamlined showcase dedicated to artistic one-upmanship. But nothing could be further from the truth. Efficiently run and superbly organized, the Atheneum is also a friendly, refreshingly quirky place that bears the stamp of its individual patrons and its unique history. The central neo-Gothic Wadsworth building dates to 1844, the Tudor-style Colt Memorial and the Renaissance-revival Morgan Memorial both opened in 1910, the Avery Memorial in 1934, and the Goodwin building in 1969.

"You surprise me, at your age, to paint like this," Col. John Trumbull told landscape painter Thomas Cole in 1825, "You have already done what I, with all my years and experience, am yet unable to do." This was praise indeed, coming from the leader of the Hartford Wits, who passed Yale's entrance examination at the age of seven and entered the college at twelve. Cole's work is well represented in the museum's Hudson River Galleries, the largest collection of its kind in the country.

When Samuel Colt died in 1861 at the age of 47, his widow Elizabeth inherited over 3.5 million dollars, control of Colt's Patent Arms Manufacturing Company, and a leading role in the nation's cultural life. Overseeing the Hartford Table at the New York Metropolitan Sanitary Fair in 1864, where "loaf cake and Colt's revolvers were the articles most readily bought," Elizabeth visited the art gallery and was inspired to build a private collection at Armsmear, the Colt's Hartford mansion. In 1905, she bequeathed over a thousand objects to the Wadsworth Atheneum, including paintings and her husband's firearms collection. The painting collection is an invaluable reflection of America's post–Civil War taste.

The Atheneum's permanent collection comprises over 50,000 works of art spanning 5,000 years—from ancient Greek bronzes to contemporary mixed-media installations—and over 10 special exhibitions. The Amistad Collection documents African-American history from slavery to the present and offers continuous educational and children's programs. *Open Tuesday through Saturday, 11:00 A.M. to 5:00 P.M.; 600 Main Street (downtown); 860 -278-2670.*

◆ BUTLER MCCOOK HOMESTEAD

Farther down Main Street, the modest Butler McCook Homestead is the last of the private dwellings that once lined Main Street. The 1782 house stayed in the family until 1971, and its small, memento-crowded rooms make you feel as if Mrs. Butler McCook will bustle in any moment, offering tea. The kitchen was originally a butcher's and blacksmithing shop. *396 Main Street; 860-522-1806.*

◆ THE COLT FAMILY, COLT PARK, AND ARMSMEAR

Colt Park, on Wethersfield Avenue, was originally the camping ground of the Saukiog Native Americans and later a Dutch trading post. But the ostentatious Italianate mansion **Armsmear** (80 Wethersfield Avenue) has dominated this site since 1856, when it was built for Samuel Colt and his bride, Elizabeth Hart Jarvis. Armsmear is a private rest home today, but its estate once comprised elaborate gardens and commanded Hartford's finest view of the Connecticut River and of Colt's factory town. The brief but apparently happy Colt marriage was marred by the early death of three of their four children here. Photographs of the house in its heyday and a small collection of Colt items may be viewed in the drawing room.

"It is better to be the head of a louse than the tail of a lion," Samuel Colt always replied when asked his family's motto. Born in Hartford in 1814, the inventor and industrialist who revolutionized American manufacturing was a willful 16-year-old recently expelled from the Amherst Academy in Massachusetts when his father sent him to sea to learn discipline. En route to Calcutta, he whittled a wooden model of the revolver that would become the world's first repeating firearm.

"The gun that won the West" started out as an engraved prototype in 1835 and was refined into the famous 1860 Navy Revolver, a sleek weapon with just seven moving parts. Demand from the U.S Army and from the westward-bound pioneers made Colt a fortune practically overnight. His best-selling gun was one of his cheapest: a .31-caliber pocket pistol costing $10. "God made all men," a popular slogan had it, "And Samuel Colt made them equal."

In 1855, Colt built the world's largest armory on the reclaimed flood plain still dominated by the blue onion dome. Producing 1,000 arms daily, the factory transformed manufacturing by mass-producing gun parts on steam-powered, belt-driven machines, using interchangeable parts, and instituting a rigid division of labor. Before Colt, one gunsmith, working by hand, performed as many as 200 tasks. After Colt, each worker concentrated on a single part. The industrialist also revolutionized the workplace itself, building high-quality housing for his workers, as well as Charter Oak Hall for their instruction and entertainment. Slavery, he concluded from his travels in the South, could only retard industrial development.

Mrs. Colt's wedding cake had been decorated with pistols, and as a widow she remained faithful to the motif. Consequently, Hartford's Church of the Good Shepherd, dedicated to her husband's memory in 1869, is surely the only one decorated with revolvers, gunsights, bullet molds, and other firearm motifs.

To study the Colt phenomenon in detail, visit the **Museum of Connecticut History** which has approximately 1,000 firearms and Colt-related documents. Here you can also see Hartford's original charter (framed in wood from the Charter Oak), the first record (1636) of the General Court, and the table at which President Lincoln signed the Emancipation Proclamation. *231 Capitol Avenue; 860-566-3056.*

◆ BUSHNELL PARK

At this stage, Hartford may seem all granite and brownstone. The mating call of throbbing muscle cars at every intersection may also have begun to grate. If so, the nearest antidote is Bushnell Park on Trinity Street. Dominated by the magnificent 1878 State Capitol, the park on a summer evening is a grassy retreat. A few joggers pad laboriously by, and a leafy rustle replaces the traffic's hum. It seems a shame to go inside. But you must.

◆ STATE CAPITOL

The State Capitol, an exuberant, colorful Italianate feast, is one of the country's most surprising public buildings—as its early critics noted. "Nobody would ever imagine such a building to be intended for a State House," the *Hartford Times* railed against the 1872 plans, "All would require a signboard…[stating] 'this is a state house.' These plans are architectural delirium tremens…."

Hartford became Connecticut's capital in 1871, having shared the distinction with New Haven, and these marbled halls contain fascinating historical exhibits including Lafayette's camp bed, a canonball-encrusted tree trunk from a Civil War battlefield, and the winged *Genius of Connecticut* statue. The original 3.5-ton *Genius,* which topped the Capitol dome and wobbled erratically in high wind, was removed in 1938 and melted down for armaments during World War II. The Capitol's exterior is decorated with outstanding sculptures and features a relief of the ubiquitous Charter Oak. *210 Capitol Ave. (at Trinity); 860-240-0222.*

◆ NOOK FARM

"Every bush has it hair cut and face washed daily," Harriet Beecher Stowe wrote, "The evergreens are clipped into most precise decorum, the grass duly manured, rolled and shaved…Hartford is a very beautiful city." Driving the short distance from the city center to Stowe's house on Forest Street today, you see little of the gentility the writer described when she came to Nook Farm in 1871. But the Stowe House and its neighbor, the Mark Twain House, still transmit the charm and taste of a prosperous, highly cultivated 19th-century city.

In 1853, lawyer and abolitionist John Hooker and playwright Francis Gillette established Nook Farm, a community of like-minded intellectuals on 140 acres beside the Park River, attracting not only Harriet Beecher Stowe but Charles Dudley Warner, William Gillette, and Samuel Clemens (a.k.a. Mark Twain). *To reach the Stowe House and the Twain House, take Exit 46 (Sisson Avenue) off I-84; turn right on Farmington Avenue.*

Harriet Beecher Stowe House

Stowe, best known for Uncle Tom's Cabin, spent her final, troubled years here. Her son was missing in California, having been wounded in the Civil War, her husband was losing his mind, and years of senility lay ahead for the prolific writer. Her neighbor Mark Twain recalled that "she would slip up behind a person who was deep in dreams and musings and fetch a war whoop that would jump that person out of his clothes." Stowe's charming Victorian cottage and delightful gardens transmit not gloom, but the palpable sense of an agile life; *71 Forest Street (near Farmington Avenue); 860-525-9317.*

Mark Twain House

"To us our house was not insentient matter," Samuel Clemens wrote in 1896, "it had a heart and a soul and eyes to see us with…we were in its confidence and lived in its grace and in the peace of its benediction." So indelible is Clemens's mark, that the house on Farmington Avenue still seems sentient. Touring the Victorian extravaganza, you feel as if each lavishly decorated room is amused by your enthusiastic reaction.

Hartford police patrol Bushnell Park. The State Capitol stands in the background.

DAMN HARD-WORKING YANKEE

*I*am an American. I was born and reared in Hartford, in the state of Connecticut—anyway, just over the river, in the country. So I am a Yankee of the Yankees—and practical; yes, and nearly barren of sentiment, I suppose—or poetry, in other words. My father was a blacksmith, my uncle was a horse-doctor, and I was both, along at first. Then I went over to the great arms factory and learned my real trade; learned all there was to it; learned to make everything: guns, revolvers, cannon, boilers, engines, all sorts of labor-saving machinery. Why, I could make anything a body wanted—anything in the world, it didn't make any difference what; and if there wasn't any quick new-fangled way to make a thing, I could invent one—and do it as easy as rolling off a log. I became head superintendent; had a couple of thousand men under me.

—Mark Twain, *A Connecticut Yankee in King Arthur's Court,* 1889

Built in 1874 at a cost of $100,000, the vermilion and black Gothic/German-inspired folly has five balconies, three turrets, and the only remaining domestic interiors by Louis Comfort Tiffany. Its oddities include a window over a fireplace that enabled Clemens to watch snowflakes and flames at the same time. The author wrote some of his best-known works here, including *Tom Sawyer, Life on the Mississippi,* and *A Connecticut Yankee in King Arthur's Court,* and also found time to invest in the doomed Paige typesetting machine now displayed in the basement. *351 Farmington Avenue; 860-493-6411.*

◆ CONNECTICUT RIVER

The Connecticut is no Mississippi, but after a one- or two-hour cruise aboard the *Lady Fenwick,* you might develop a slight drawl. From Memorial Day to early October, this reproduction of an 1850s steam yacht departs daily from Hartford's Charter Oak Landing; *exit 27 off I-91; 860-526-4954.*

Far stranger is the subterranean canoe tour of the Park River, which has flowed under Hartford since it was buried in 1936 to prevent flooding and to accommodate a highway. Small guided tours offered by Huck Finn Adventures take you through concrete tunnels on two miles of shallow water (partly in darkness if you wish) before emerging on the Connecticut River for a further half-mile paddle; *860-693- 0385.*

◆ ELIZABETH PARK

"Money is another kind of poetry," Wallace Stevens once wrote, perhaps after he had walked the three or so miles from his office at the Hartford Accident and Indemnity Company to his house at 118 Westerly Terrace (now private) through glorious Elizabeth Park. From the time he moved here in 1916, the poet's daily route took him through the nation's first municipal rose garden, on Prospect Avenue, which peaks now (as it did then) in late June, when over 14,000 rosebushes compete to intoxicate visitors. The peony exhibit of over 100 varieties is the nation's only public collection. If Elizabeth Park causes symptoms of chronic euphoria you can always visit the **Menczer Museum of Medicine and Dentistry**, on nearby Scarborough Street, where displays of instruments and medications from the 18th century to the 20th prove an excellent corrective. In 1844, Hartford witnessed the first use of nitrous oxide gas as an anaesthetic, thanks to Dr. Horace Wells. *230 Scarborough Street; 860-236 -5613.*

■ TOWNS NEAR HARTFORD

◆ WETHERSFIELD

In this artfully preserved 18th-century town, people appear immune to the modern activity virus. Strolling along Main Street on a balmy spring evening, they greet you as you sit on a bench outside the Wethersfield Museum listening to the clock in the 1762 meetinghouse strike the half-hour. The only other interruption is a toddler across the street repeatedly shouting "Doggy!" at one of the indignant bears in the Olde Towne Doll Shoppe's window. Like so many old Connecticut towns, Wethersfield is blessed with huge maples that provide its broad streets with shade, birdsong, and soundproofing. But life was not always this peaceful. In April 1637, the "Wethersfield Massacre" by the Pequots sparked the Pequot War, and the Ancient Burying Ground behind the lovely Congregational Church on Main Street has some early settler graves.

Ideally situated on the Connecticut River, Wethersfield prospered from the West Indies trade until the mid-19th century, gaining particular fame for its red onions, which tolerated long Caribbean voyages.

CONNECTICUT
CENTRAL & EASTERN

Cove Park

Today, the 1690 Cove Warehouse, at riverside Cove Park, is the nation's only remaining 17th-century warehouse, and you emerge from its nautical exhibits expecting to see a forest of masts. Sadly, most vessels in the pretty river cove today are of the plastic, soap-dish variety.

Historic District Houses

The same skills that produced ships here starting in 1649 created some of the region's finest 18th-century houses, and the town's historic district—Connecticut's largest—contains over 140 of them.

The **Webb-Deane-Stevens Museum** at 211 Main Street comprises three houses on their original sites: a Georgian mansion built for Patriot and merchant Joseph Webb in 1752, the 1766 home of lawyer and diplomat Silas Deane, and the humbler 1788 house built for saddler Isaac Stevens. The red-flocked wallpaper in the Webb House was hung for George Washington's visit in 1781, when he discussed the Yorktown strategy here with General Rochambeau. There are many 18th-century flower varieties in the exquisite gardens, and next door, the Stevens House garden overflows with early medicinal and culinary herbs.

Capt. James Francis, who built over 20 Wethersfield houses, got around to one for himself at 120 Hartford Avenue in 1793. It remained a Francis home for seven generations and today offers a rare glimpse of one family's changing tastes over 170 years. The altogether different **Buttolph-Williams House**, with its hewn overhang and casement windows, looks like a 17th-century construction but probably dates to 1725. Whatever its birthday, its plain grace is clearly indisputable. *249 Broad Street; 860-529-0460.*

Like much of the historic district, Broad Street—actually a lengthy Common—is an ideal place for you to practice the Wethersfield stroll. It is not as easy as it looks, so allow plenty of time. Should guilt set in, you can always rush back to the 1820 **Comstock Ferre & Company**, the nation's oldest independent seed company, and become a horticulturally better person by rummaging in their antique seed bins. *263 Main Street; 860-571-6590.*

♦ GLASTONBURY

Glastonbury was part of Wethersfield until 1693 and became famous for its fruit, hygiene, and suffragettes. Hale peaches and commercial soap were first produced here, but the elderly Smith sisters had more than housekeeping in mind when they refused to pay their taxes in 1873: They demanded the vote. You can study their story and others at the **Museum on the Green** at Main Street, most easily reached by taking the Main Street exit off Highway 2 East. A four-mile walk along the **Shenipsit Trail,** which may be entered at the intersection of Hebron Avenue and Hill Street, reveals earlier upheaval. Glacial boulders, many of them studded with

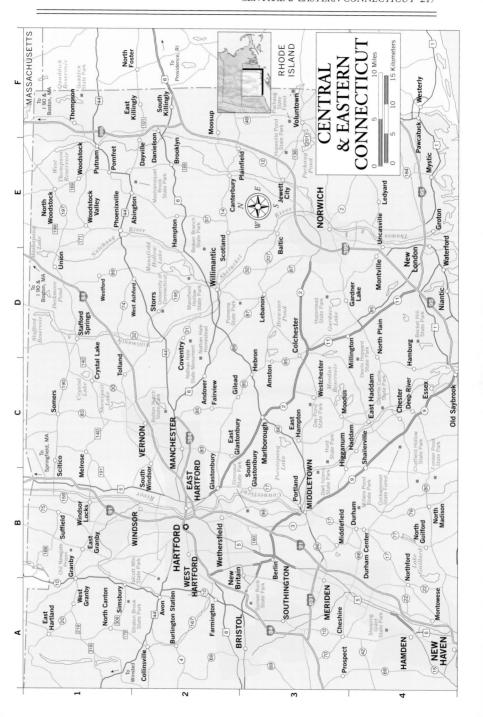

tiny garnets, litter the ridges here, giving the impression that you interrupted a giant in the middle of his tidying.

◆ FERRY TO DINOSAUR STATE PARK

More prehistoric celebrities lurk across the Connecticut River in Dinosaur State Park at Rocky Hill, and you can surprise them by taking the nation's oldest continuously operated ferry from Glastonbury. Running since 1655, today the ferry accommodates 20 passengers, three automobiles, and numerous bicycles from May 1st to October 31st, weather permitting. *On Highway 17 off Highway 2; 860-443-3856.*

If the ferry seems small, just see how you feel when you enter the largest dinosaur track site in North America, where the eternal question—"Feel like lunch?"—acquires fresh urgency. Hundreds of dinosaur tracks were uncovered here in 1966 and today an enormous geodesic dome protects the 185-million-year-old footprints and related exhibits. The full-size model of the carnivorous Dilophosaurus may dissuade you from exploring the park's 70 bird-filled acres of gardens and trails. If you do go, bring 10 pounds of plaster of Paris and a quarter cup of vegetable oil to make your own cast of a dinosaur footprint in the perfectly safe track-casting area. *Dinosaur State Park entrance on West Street, Rocky Hill; one mile east of Exit 23 off I-91; 860-529-8423.*

◆ NEW BRITAIN

New Britain graduated from making sleigh bells to earn the nickname "Hardware City," but the somewhat lifeless town is better known today for the **New Britain Museum of American Art.** A stucco mansion is home to an exceptional American collection including works by John Singer Sargent, Winslow Homer, Childe Hassam, Thomas Hart Benton, and members of the Hudson River School. There are true surprises here: Georgia O'Keeffe's 1928 *East River from the 30th Story of the Shelton Hotel,* Thomas Hart Benton's mural *The Arts of Life in America,* and the nation's first museum collection of American illustration from the 19th century to the present. There is also delicious humor in Barbara Falk's 1981 acrylic *Next to Grandma Moses my Favorite Artist is Rubens* and in Howard Freer's *Shrimp Cocktail.*

Small rooms ward off gallery fatigue, and most are furnished with a large, book-strewn table where you may sit in a comfortable Windsor chair reading about art or staring out the tree-filled windows. *56 Lexington Street. Directions: Columbus Boulevard Exit off Highway 72, left onto Lake Street, right at stop sign and left onto Lexington Street; 860-229-0257.*

◆ BRISTOL

Bristol presents different mechanical delights: 3,000 timepieces, at the beautiful **American Clock and Watch Museum**, and the nation's oldest amusement park, **Lake Compounce**, where the 1911 **carousel** still turns and the wooden **Wildcat roller-coaster** still prompts gratifying screams. Bristol is also where Everett Horton invented the collapsible fishing rod, which allowed him to flout the law and fish on Sundays. *Clock Museum: 100 Maple Street, off US 6; 860-583-6070. Lake Compounce: 860-583-3300.*

◆ FARMINGTON

Reaching Farmington, you enter a landscape that is green with trees, fields, and money. The town was founded in 1640 as "an ideal Christian commonwealth," but the 18th- and 19th-century mansions lining the shady Main Street prove that principle and profit were not mutually exclusive. Fortunes were made here from manufacturing, commerce, and trade, and the town was further enriched by the completion of the Farmington Canal in 1828.

The Stanley-Whitman House in Farmington, built in 1720, is a National Historic Landmark as well as a museum.

Farmington Historic Area

A leisurely walk down Main Street reveals not only Farmington's historic splendor but also its role as the Grand Central Station of the Underground Railroad. You will pass **Miss Porter's School** *(at 60 Main Street)*, founded in 1843, the **Day-Lewis Museum**, which features Native American artifacts, and the sublime **1771 meetinghouse** where the 38 exonerated Amistad Africans worshiped during their eight-month stay here. The artfully restored 1720 **Stanley Whitman House** is at 37 High Street.

Other Amistad-related sites in the town include **Union Hall**, where abolitionists rallied support for the captives; **Samuel Deming's Store** (still a store), where the Africans were educated; the **Austin F. Williams House**, their primary home; and **Foone's Grave** in Riverside Cemetery, where the Mende leader who drowned in the canal is buried. **The Farmington Historical Society** *(860-678-1645)* gives bus and walking tours, providing details of "The Lost Eight Months." One of the most charming houses on Main Street, by the way, is the 1690 **Cowles House**, with its crooked gable overhang and skewed doorway—an eccentric contrast to the architectural rectitude on every side.

Farmington River

Take practically any side street here and you quickly reach the Farmington River. In 1994, Congress added 14 miles of the waterway's west branch to the National Wild and Scenic Rivers System, but the Farmington was remarkable long before legislators made it official. Otters and bald eagles raise their young along its banks and the river also accommodates sedate canoeists and white-water fanatics.

Hill-Stead Museum

Leaving Farmington center on Mountain Road's gentle incline, you meet one of Connecticut's treasures. Hill-Stead Museum is an elegant 1901 mansion set on 150 acres of fields, gardens, and woodland, and it contains one of the country's most extraordinary French impressionist collections. Before reaching the paintings, however, you will be distracted by the estate's elegant sunken garden and sloping, tree-fringed pastures. (Picnicking is forbidden, however.) Theodate Pope Riddle, one of America's first female architects, clearly had as fine an eye for proportion as her father, Ohio iron tycoon Alfred Atmore Pope, did for art. Working with Stanford White, Theodate designed the family home of Hill-Stead in 1898, and today it offers a rare opportunity to view outstanding works by Degas, Monet, Manet, Cassatt, and Whistler in a domestic setting. Monet's haystacks never looked so daring.

Theodate survived the sinking of the HMS *Lusitania* off the Irish coast in 1915 to design, among other buildings, the landmark Old Farms School in neighboring Avon in 1927. Were she alive today, the restless innovator might fidget during the Sunken Garden Poetry Festival staged here each summer, but she surely would enjoy the Classic Car Dinner Dance in September. *Follow signs posted on Route 10; 35 Mountain Road; 860-677-9064 .*

◆ SIMSBURY *map, page 217, A-1*

Simsbury's first settlers were attracted in 1640 by the area's impressive stands of pine trees, which were critical to the shipbuilding industry, and the town later prospered with the discovery of copper in neighboring East Granby. Today the giant pines are gone, the old railway station has become the **One Way Fare restaurant**, and Simsbury wears the pastel gloss of an affluent suburb. It is relaxing, however, to sit at a shady table on the old station platform, eating an exceptionally good hamburger while you summon the energy to walk the few hundred yards to **Massacoh Plantation,** the town's small historic district. Here the furled bark of enormous sycamores crunches explosively underfoot as you proceed from the 1771 Phelps Tavern to the 1795 cottage, warning the meetinghouse, icehouse, barns, schoolhouse, and peddler's cart of your arrival.

◆ TALCOTT MOUNTAIN TRAIL AND HEUBLEIN TOWER *map, page 217, B-2*

A more eccentric sight awaits you when you hike the Talcott Mountain Trail to the Heublein Tower, a seven-story concrete and steel castle built for food and liquor merchant Gilbert Heublein in 1914 and now open to the public. The hillsides here are pockmarked with modern condominium-castles, but Talcott Mountain State Park, a reservoir watershed, offers pleasant views as you walk, bicycle, or ski its forested trails. *South of Simsbury off Route 10/US 202; 860-242-1158.*

◆ OLD NEWGATE PRISON *map, page 217, B-1*

When the copper mine at East Granby ceased production in 1773, another use was immediately found for the bleak underground warren. It became Newgate Prison. "Finding it not possible to evade this hard cruel fate," one inmate wrote, "they bade adieu to the world and descended the ladder....Here they found the inhabitants of this woeful mansion who were exceedingly anxious to know what was going on above."

Visiting the small Newgate complex on Newgate Road on a breezy, clear July morning, you feel the chill long before you explore the dripping labyrinth. Standing on the site of the whipping post and the treadmill, you try to look on the bright side. Ten lashes was the maximum allowance, and prisoners spent 30 minutes on the treadmill, working 10 and resting 5. Cider was provided daily, and rum for good behavior. Then you see a ladder disappearing into the ground and imagine surfacing each morning at 4 A.M. from the hellish depths. The small museum tells several prisoner's stories, and the admittance ledger is a catalogue of rape, incest, bestiality, and petty crime. When Tories and British soldiers incarcerated here during the Revolutionary War staged a mass escape in 1781, 16 of the 28 escapees were recaptured within one week. A resident vulture hovers over the delightful picnic area, which overlooks a rolling, wooded valley. *Located on Newgate Road in East Granby; one mile off Route 20, follow signs; 860-653-3563.*

❖

To gain ever more altitude, hike an adjacent section of the Metacomet Trail, paralleling Newgate Road, to Peak Mountain.

◆ TOBACCO COUNTRY AND SUFFIELD *map, page 217, B-1*

The Newgate Prison museum has a crude sketch on stone by one of Newgate's inmates depicting a man smoking a cigar. And driving along the quieter roads of the Connecticut River Valley above Hartford you see why. Tobacco has a long history here, beginning with the Native Americans who taught the settlers how to grow the crop that made this valley's worldwide reputation for premium cigar-wrapper leaf.

The recent cigar fashion has revitalized the industry, and even if there will never

A tobacco harvest: New England tobacco is used primarily for premium cigar-wrapper leaf.

again be 1,600 square miles of tobacco in this valley—as there was after World War II—it is astonishing to see tract housing and mini-malls interrupted by broad green swaths that launch perfumed waves at you as you drive by. The fertile red soil on either side of the road north from Granby to Suffield may now grow mostly lawn, but many fields around Suffield itself are still productive. On a spring afternoon, the charming town center even smells of manure. Stare long enough at the 1742 **Gay Manse** and you begin to wonder if the rolling fields behind it did not partly inspire the exquisite curves of its restrained Connecticut Valley doorway.

There is a fine tobacco and cigar collection in the 1764 **King House Museum** *(at 232 S. Main Street)*, but South Main Street is Suffield's chief delight—a broad, shady thoroughfare where even the outbuildings are splendid.

Behind its enormous sycamore and its ornate fence, the regal 1760 **Hatheway House** has presided over the street since it was a dusty Common. Its original furnishings include rare 1790s hand-blocked French wallpaper, and its restful garden is a spring treat; *55 South Main Street; 860-668-0655.*

◆ WINDSOR LOCKS *map page 217, B-1*

When a canal was built in 1829 to bypass the rapids of the Connecticut River at Windsor Locks, that town quickly became known as the bawdiest in New England, thanks to the scandalous behavior of its rivermen. Today Windsor Locks is a respectable Hartford suburb and its waterway offers innocent pleasures. Walking or bicycling its paved towpath, you pass the exhilarating **Enfield Rapids,** one of the best shad fishing spots in New England, and encounter wildflower and butterfly delights at every turn. Intermittent rumblings remind you that the towpath is on Bradley International Airport's flight path. "Even in my childhood…I dreamed about the possibility of going straight up," Igor Sikorsky, inventor of the helicopter, once remarked. Those harboring similar fantasies will want to visit the **New England Air Museum** and see how Sikorsky and other innovators turned theirs into reality; *Bradley International Airport; 860-623- 3305.*

◆ WINDSOR *map page 217, B-2*

Windsor has a long tradition of being first. Its settlers were the first (in 1647) New Englanders to hang a suspected witch, Alice Young, and the first Americans (in 1633) to transport a prefabricated frame house (from Plymouth to Windsor). The town's historic **Palisado Avenue** and **Palisado Green** are named after the settlement's

CONNECTICUT
CENTRAL & EASTERN

original stockade, and its most famous son is Capt. John Mason, hero of the Pequot War. The **Fyler House** at 96 Palisado Avenue is one of Connecticut's oldest, dating to 1640.

Tobacco has been grown around Windsor since 1640—over 3,000 acres of it in the 1930s—and from late summer through autumn you still see long barns filled with what appear to be thousands of sleeping bats hanging upside down to dry. Find out more in the tobacco-curing barn at the **Luddy/Taylor Connecticut Valley Tobacco Museum** on Northwest Park. The visionary minister Jonathan Edwards, born in neighboring South Windsor in 1703, would have heartily disapproved. *145 Lang Road; 860-285-1888.*

■ CONNECTICUT'S NORTHEAST CORNER

Connecticut's historically quiet northeastern corner is not as quiet as it once was. There are fewer "tractor crossing" signs these days and more "horse crossing" ones, fewer silos and more antique barns. But in much of the Woodstock Valley, cozy, pleated farmland still falls away from the road as you drive along winding, old Route 169 from Woodstock to Canterbury.

Connecticut's quiet northeast corner. (photo by Robert Holmes)

◆ WOODSTOCK AND
   ROSELAND COTTAGE
map, page 217, E-1

You may, of course, never
leave the starting gate if you
succumb to the beguiling
garden at Woodstock's
Roseland Cottage, which
has survived intact since
1850. Wispy cosmos, lively
petunias, exuberant snap-
dragons, and other exhibitionists wave at each other
across immaculate box-
wood hedges, luring you
through the green maze to a
summerhouse that begs to
host a romantic assignation.

Also known as the Bowen
House, the 1846 Gothic
cottage, with its blushing
walls, stained-glass, pointed
arches, and peerless Victorian interior, remained in the

Roseland Cottage in Woodstock.

Bowen family until 1970. Open from Wednesday through Sunday in season, it
also offers twilight concerts and Victorian teas on the lawn. The barn contains one
of the country's first bowling alleys, and the **October Festival** is one of the region's
liveliest arts and crafts events. *Roseland Cottage: 556 Route 169; 860-928-4074.*

◆ PUTNAM WOLF DEN *map page 217, E-1*

South of Pomfret is the Putnam Wolf Den, where Revolutionary War hero Major
Gen. Israel Putnam ("Old Put" to his men) shot what was later immortalized as
the last wolf in Connecticut. Follow the trail in the Mashamoquet Brook State
Park as it slopes toward the Wolf Den midway down an impressive cliff, and then
relax in the Indian Chair, a natural stone couch perched on a 20-foot ridge. A suitably heroic statue of Israel Putnam on horseback dominates the pretty town of
Brooklyn, to the south.

Route 14, heading west from Canterbury to Willimantic, is a lovely, swooping road that darts under trees and between lush meadows, throwing up scents of hay and honeysuckle along the way.

◆ SCOTLAND AND WILLIMANTIC *map page 217, D&E/2*

Arriving in Scotland and breaking abruptly for the **Olde English Tea Room,** you will be disappointed if you have not made a reservation. Pearl Dexter uses several rooms in her home for tea: one houses her teapot collection; another, tea-related tchochkes; and a third, a tearoom. *3 Devotion Road; 860-456-8651.*

Willimantic Brewing Company, in the altogether grittier town of Willimantic, requires no advance warning, however, and you are welcomed into the lofty old Post Office building by an impressive menu of outstanding beers. *967 Main Street; 860-423-6777.* Nearby to the southeast is **Natchaug State Forest,** known for its rhododendrons. *(See page 258.)*

◆ COVENTRY *map page 217, D-2*

When gardening became a competitive sport, nurseries became merciless testing grounds with frowning customers inspecting serried ranks of eager-to-please plants. But **Caprilands Herb Farm** is the opposite—a mercifully idiosyncratic 50-acre garden of herbs and woodland that soothes and inspires as it leads you from scented corner to scented corner, following its own eccentric logic. *534 Silver Street off US 44 in North Coventry; 860-742-7244.*

The Nathan Hale Homestead in Coventry.

CONNECTICUT
CENTRAL & EASTERN

A statue of American patriot Nathan Hale stands next to a stone garden wall at his homestead, built by his family in 1776, the year of Hale's death.

The Nathan Hale Homestead is another green sanctuary, surrounded by stone-walled meadows and mature forest. The patriot spy was executed before the 1776 house was completed, but the restored interior recalls his life as well as 18th-century decorative fashion. *On Coventry's South Street, off US 44 East and 6 West; 860 -742-6917.*

◆ **STORRS** *map page 217, D-2*

The biggest surprise on the **University of Connecticut**'s graceful campus at Storrs is not the 15-foot white shark in the fine Museum of Natural History, but the cattle grazing nearby as part of the Agricultural Program. Hikers with a taste for wilder life should hike three miles or so along the **Nipmuck Trail,** which can be entered at Gurleyville Road and may present, if you're lucky, acrobatically gifted troupes of flying squirrels.

■ HARTFORD TO OLD SAYBROOK

Traveling southeast from Hartford, following the Connecticut River to its destination on Long Island Sound, you enter an amphibious world where even the Goodspeed Opera House, a national treasure, has one foot in the water. Soon you are in the same condition. Lured by watery temptations that shimmer around each bend, you find yourself coaxing your car or bicycle onto a ferry regardless of the destination. Finally you abdicate responsibility, abandon your burdensome wheels, and submit to a steamboat ride or an island cruise.

Meander from Middletown downstream to Old Saybrook (described on page 267), then upstream from Old Lyme to Portland in one day and spend another couple of days exploring the Thames River Valley to the east.

♦ MIDDLETOWN'S WESLEYAN UNIVERSITY

Middletown, a former shipbuilding and trading port, was Connecticut's wealthiest town in the mid-18th century. Today it presents a blank face to the visitor, particularly in its arid, tree-starved downtown, where the few remaining 19th-century commercial buildings seem to have washed up on an alien, concrete shore. If they could manage the short journey uphill to Wesleyan University, they would feel completely at home. *General information: 860-685-2000.*

Founded in 1831 by Methodists but nonsectarian from the outset, Wesleyan is small enough to be explored in a leisurely walk and grand enough to necessitate frequent admiring stops. Its grassy, tree-shaded thoroughfares also present fine lolling opportunities. You may earn these by investigating the **Davison Art Center**, at 301 High Street, beside the visitor's parking area, which displays prints and photographs in the 1838 Alsop House; the adjoining **Zikha Gallery,** which exhibits contemporary art; and the **General Mansfield House** (at 151 Main Street), an 1810 mansion displaying period furnishings and Civil War memorabilia. "Nothing could exceed the luxury of my quarters," orator Edward Everett wrote when he stayed at Samuel Russell's house, now Honors College, in 1859—and Wesleyan's varied architectural richness is equally impressive today.

♦ MEANDERING SOUTH ALONG THE RIVER *map page 217, C-3, C-4*

Rather than vaulting back onto Highway 9 to travel south from Middletown to Higganum, meander along the old highway—an extension of Main Street—that turns into Route 154 and shadows the river to Long Island Sound. Modest **Higganum** has a suitably limp dog napping on the porch of its feed store, and you sense the sleepy town barely opening one eye as you pass through.

The small town of **Haddam** is equally subdued on a midsummer afternoon, and the **Thankful Arnold House** seems grateful for company. Built in 1794 and restored to its 1810 appearance, the house's period furniture, charming garden, and restrained decoration present a striking contrast to the modern "trophy houses" now lining many of Haddam's—and the region's—back roads. The museum also houses the Arnold family's Civil War correspondence. *14 Hayden Hill Road, off Route 154; 860-345-2400.*

The Connecticut River is at its most sedate on the outskirts of Haddam, sliding between the broad expanse of Haddam Meadows on one side and a defunct nuclear power plant on the other. If the bulbous giant guarding the opposite bank unsettles you, picnic by the lily pond or head downstream taking one of the narrated cruises of the Connecticut River offered by Camelot Cruises in Haddam. *Dock opposite the Goodspeed Opera House; 860-345-8591.*

A riverboat cruises up the Connecticut River near East Haddam. (photo by Robert Holmes)

◆ GOODSPEED OPERA HOUSE

Crossing the bridge at Terryville to **East Haddam,** you are greeted by one of Connecticut's most exuberant treasures. The Goodspeed Opera House is a six-story Victorian music hall that looks more like an overdressed bathing beauty about to take the plunge. This remains the tallest wooden building on the river, and when shipping and banking entrepreneur William H. Goodspeed built it in 1876 it served a variety of purposes. The Goodspeed housed a theater, a steamboat terminal, a general store, and various professional offices before becoming a State Highway Department depot and facing demolition in 1958.

Artfully restored between 1960 and 1963, it is now one of the nation's most whimsically charming musical theater venues with a particularly cozy **Victorian Bar and Ladies' Drinking Parlor.** The **Goodspeed Library of Musical Theatre,** accessible by appointment only, is one of the finest in the country, with a comprehensive collection of scripts, scores, sheet music, cast recordings, and theatrical ephemera. Goodspeed produces three musicals from April through December in

East Haddam and develops new musicals at Goodspeed-at-Chester, an old factory building reopened in 1984. Tours of the Goodspeed Opera House are offered from June to October. *Exit 7 off Highway 9, follow signs; 860-873-8668.*

❖

To get out of your car and enjoy the countryside, visit **Devil's Hopyard State Park—** on Hopyard Road off Highway 82, east of East Haddam— where water and rock have collaborated to produce the exquisite Chapman's Falls.

The Goodspeed Opera House in East Haddam.

◆ GILLETTE CASTLE
map page 217, C-4

The wonders at Gillette Castle, south of East Haddam, are manmade, the product of a Connecticut actor and playwright's imagination. William Gillette grew up next door to the Mark Twain House at Nook Farm in Hartford, a fact that may have contributed to the youngster's eccentricity. The teenage Gillette built his first steam engine at home and fully indulged his mechanical passion when theatrical success—in particular his portrayal of Sherlock Holmes—allowed him to build Seventh Sister, now known as Gillette Castle, in 1915.

The Gillette Castle in East Haddam was built in 1915.

Whether viewed from the river below or approached by road, the fantastic Rhenish castle seems to lurk in its wooded grounds, daring visitors to probe its secrets, an effect that playful Gillette doubtless intended. Specifying in his will that the property not fall into "the possession of some blithering saphead who has no conception of where he is or with what surrounded," the playwright would be delighted today by the astonishment greeting his innovations. An elaborate mirror system allows someone in the bedroom to monitor the entrance below, furniture runs on railway-like metal tracks, intricate locks and ingenious lighting challenge even the most sleuthlike visitor. *67 River Road, East Haddam.*

Hike along the well-marked trail, which is dotted with Gillette's trademark stonework features and bridges and affords tantalizing river views; *Gillette Castle State Park; 860-526-2336.*

A few miles from the castle, you can set yourself and your car adrift on the tiny **Hadlyme-Chester ferry**, which materializes like an eager dog whenever it is summoned and is content to fetch and retrieve passengers all day long between April and November; *860-443-3856.*

◆ CHESTER *map page 217, C-4*

Once a manufacturing and shipbuilding town, pretty little Chester is today dominated by theater and art. The **Connecticut River Artisans Cooperative** (at 69 Main Street) is an eclectic gallery, the **Goodspeed-at-Chester** occupies a former knitting-needle factory, and the award-winning **National Theater of the Deaf** performs in both sign language and spoken language throughout the year.

◆ COCKAPONSET STATE FOREST

But the ferry trip may have whetted your appetite for less confined spaces. If so, the 15,000-acre Cockaponset State Forest, stretching from Chester north to Haddam, is the perfect destination. Following the Cockaponset Trail, you can wander for hours, through snowdrifts of mountain laurel in the spring or ankle-deep in golden leaves during the autumn. And if you are lucky, the electric blue flash catching your eye by a riverbank is a kingfisher.

◆ DEEP RIVER

Nourishment of an equally transcendent variety is available in the small town of Deep River, to the south on Route 154, where **Pasta Unlimited** at 159 Main Street provides not only superb pasta dishes and sandwiches (the chicken salad would convert any meatball extremist) but picnics that may be ordered, spring through autumn, on the morning of your excursion. Seating is limited to a few chairs on the busy street, but you will be spending most of your time on your knees anyway, adoring the almond bars and raspberry tarts.

Casting about for a reason to stay in Deep River for another snack, you will be relieved to discover the **Stone House** at 245 Main Street, a museum of local history that reveals, among other things, that the town once made ivory combs and piano keys.

◆ ESSEX AND ITS STEAM TRAIN *map page 217, C-4*

If you find regression distasteful then you should bypass Essex, where the steam locomotives of the Valley Railroad turn responsible adults into enthralled children.

Standing beside Engine No. 40 as the 1920 giant does some preparatory breathing exercises, you wonder if it is too late to become an engine driver. Probably. But
the consolation prize is substantial: The **Essex Steam Train and Riverboat Ride**
takes you on a two-and-a-half-hour journey, first on rail, then on water as the train
hands you over to a steamboat at Deep River (you see Gillette Castle and the
Goodspeed Opera House from the water). When that whistle blows, even the
fainthearted will find themselves secretly willing the iron horse to bolt. *Take exit 3
off Highway 9, then head west a quarter mile to Railroad Ave; 860-767-0103.*

The Dinner Train serves brunch, lunch, or dinner during a two-hour ride on
the luxurious North Cove Express; *800-398-7427.*

The Essex Steam Train. (photo by Robert Holmes)

CONNECTICUT
CENTRAL & EASTERN

❖

Essex was a major shipbuilding town from the mid-18th to the mid-19th century and has the oldest continuously operating waterfront in the country. In 1987, Wesleyan archaeologists uncovered evidence of Robert Lay's wharf, built in 1650 on the site of the present-day Steamboat Dock. The dockside **Connecticut River Museum** focuses on maritime and river history and includes a replica of the 1775 *American Turtle,* America's first submarine, which David Bushnell built in Old Saybrook; *67 Main Street; 860-767-8269.*

For more varied local information, visit the Essex Historical Society at **Hill's Academy Museum** (22 Prospect Street) or the **Pratt House** (20 West Avenue), part of which may date to 1648. Or you could just sit on the spacious porch of the 1776 **Griswold Inn** at 36 Main Street and watch Essex going about its leisurely business.

If you continue south to the coast, you'll arrive in Old Saybrook, described on page 267.

■ HARTFORD TO NORWICH *map page 217, B-2 to E-3*

An alternate journey from Hartford to the coast begins on soothing Highway 2, which takes you to Norwich, at the head of the Thames River (pronounced "Thaymes" not "Tems" here). Much of Highway 2 is flanked by working farms, as it was 30 years ago. But **Norwich,** gloriously situated on a rocky bluff overlooking the river, has declined since its glory days in the 1850s, when the town had the world's largest paper mill and the country's largest cotton mills.

Downtown Norwich is a patchwork of elegant facades and boarded-up storefronts. There are, however, remarkable survivors. Leffingwell Inn, built around 1645 and a meeting place for patriots including George Washington, peeps shyly out from under the highway at the junction of Highway 2 and Route 169. Now a museum, the imposing **Leffingwell House Museum** still has clay pipes by the fireplace and a fine collection of period furniture; *348 Washington, 860-889-9440.* Neighboring **Norwichtown Green** is ringed by pleasing 18th-century houses. Site of the first English settlement, the Green was part of the "nine miles square" given by Uncas, chief of the Mohegans to Thomas Leffingwell, a Saybrook soldier, as payment for English assistance in routing the attacking Narragansetts in 1645.

Uncas is buried in the Indian Burial Ground at Sachem Street and commemorated with an 1833 obelisk. Reminders of Norwich's past affluence, on the other hand, are everywhere. Broadway is the most evocative: an airy thoroughfare lined with superb 19th-century houses in a variety of styles from Greek Revival to English Gothic, terminating in a charming Green.

The gardens that once surrounded these houses earned Norwich the title "Rose of New England" and the **Memorial Rose Garden** in Mohegan Park on Judd Road maintains the fragrant tradition from June through September. A more tangible legacy is displayed at the 19th-century **Slater Memorial Museum,** whose extensive collection ranges from Greek, Roman, and Renaissance casts through American, European, and African art, Native American artifacts, furniture, and firearms. *108 Crescent Street, 860-887-2505 or 2506.*

Following Route 12 south along the river, turn east onto leafy Route 214, to **Ledyard,** which has a water-powered, up-and-down sawmill in a pleasant park to the east of the town. The site is open weekends in April, May, October, and November, water levels permitting. Once famous for a late-18th-century female preacher named Jemima who sprang out of her own coffin to impress her zealous "Jemimakins," Ledyard now attracts different believers, praying for different miracles, at **Foxwoods Casino** on Route 12, where the gaming area alone covers 314,000 square feet.

Suddenly filling the horizon like a candy-colored spaceship, Foxwoods is an enterprise of the Mashantucket Pequot Tribal Nation and Connecticut's biggest individual source of revenue. Visitors who tire of its mammoth attractions may catch a shuttle bus to the nearby **Mashantucket Pequot Museum and Research Center,** opened in 1998, where high-tech exhibits transport you from the glacial period to the present, illustrating Native American life not only in traditional villages but in the trailers that were pre-casino home to many of the 550 Pequots. *Pequot Museum: 800-411-9671.*

Across the river at Uncasville, the Mohegan Sun on Mohegan Sun Boulevard and the Tantaquidgeon Indian Museum on Route 32 are more modest Native American gaming and historical institutions.

To continue along the coast, see the "CONNECTICUT COAST" chapter, page 254; Mystic Seaport, page 260; New London, page 262.

CONNECTICUT
THE NORTHWEST CORNER

■ HIGHLIGHTS

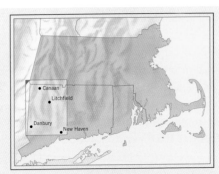

■ TRAVEL BASICS

Northwestern Connecticut is a noticeably tilted place. From the state's highest point—Bear Mountain in the northwest corner—the land tumbles down to form the rugged slopes and alpine meadows of the Litchfield Hills before finally reclining along the shore of Long Island Sound. The contrasts too are often dizzying. You can spend the morning exploring hill country that is scarified by ice and civilized by chamber music festivals and take your mid-afternoon coffee in what seems to be a New York suburb.

New York—just an hour away—creates its own gravitational field. And northwestern Connecticut, more than any other part of the state, is heavily tilted toward its neighbor. Its hills have long been summer retreats and its coast a commuter's paradise. Appearances here are consequently deceptive. That grain silo is actually an art gallery, the Victorian farmhouse beside it is a conference center, and the general store is exclusively gourmet. But any region with a thousand lakes is sure to keep a few charms in reserve. To discover some of them, wander through the Litchfield Hills during spring or autumn, taking back roads whenever possible, and explore the coast when the elements, not the crowds, are in charge.

Climate: Temperatures in the Litchfield Hills are not unlike those in the Berkshires, to the north. Summer temperatures often rise to the 90s during July and August with high humidity, while winter temperatures can drop well below zero at night and into single digits in the daytime. Autumn is particularly lovely with moderate temperatures.

Food & Lodging: Historic inns in the Litchfield Hills range from tasteful to cloying, as do the menus in the region's sophisticated restaurants. Connecticut listings begin on page 354; listings map on page 327; chart on 375.

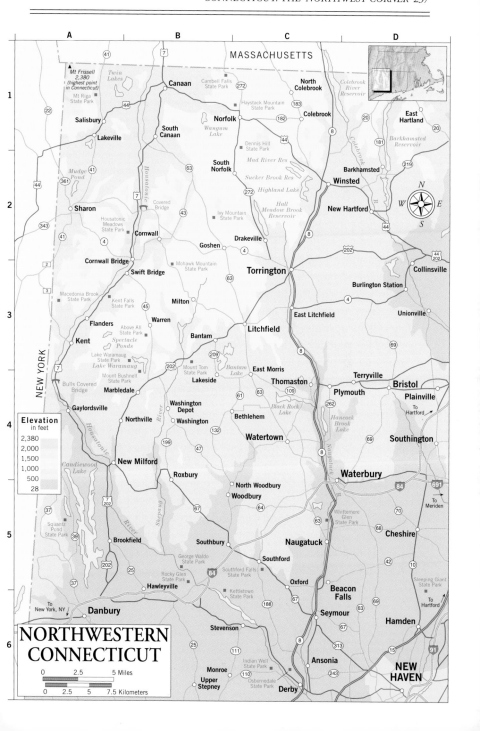

NORTHWESTERN
CONNECTICUT

0   2.5   5 Miles
0   2.5   5   7.5 Kilometers

Elevation
in feet
2,380
2,000
1,500
1,000
500
28

MASSACHUSETTS

NEW YORK

NEW
HAVEN

■ HISTORY

Traversing the northwest corner's quiet back roads today, it is hard to imagine this as one of New England's most industrialized regions. But the 18th-century discovery of rich iron ore deposits near towns like Kent and Lakeville quickly stripped the now reforested hills bare and turned the valleys into roaring, puffing blast furnaces as early as 1730. An astonishing variety of metal objects—everything from firearms to cooking pots—was manufactured in even the smallest towns while larger cities like Bridgeport and Stamford became as famous for their locks, machine guns, and sewing machines as Danbury was for its hats.

The region's first white settlements had been established with similar energy and pragmatism. Fanning out from new communities then thriving along the rich Connecticut Valley, English settlers first established themselves along the coast, at Fairfield and Bridgeport in the late 1630s and at Stamford, Greenwich, and Norwalk over the next decade. The desired territory was typically purchased from the resident Native Americans for an agreed number of coats and trinkets and a community of farming, fishing, and shipbuilding families established. The Pequot War was settled less amicably in the Great Swamp Fight outside Fairfield, where most of the tribe was annihilated or scattered.

Evidence of that colonial past is somewhat thin and scattered, thanks in part to devastating British raids during the Revolution, a conflict to which this small western corner made a significant contribution.

Most eligible men enlisted in the Connecticut Army, and the area's list of its Revolutionary War heroes is particularly impressive. Ethan Allen was born in Litchfield and manned his forge in Lakeville, while Washington chose two western Connecticut men—David Humphreys of Ansonia and Benjamin Tallmadge of Litchfield—to be his closest advisers. The region paid a high price for its zealotry. In July 1779, British forces under New York governor William Tryon launched a series of coastal raids, landing at New Haven and going on to burn Fairfield, Norwalk, and Greens Farms, having destroyed over 40 houses and barns in Danbury two years earlier.

■ TOURING THE LITCHFIELD HILLS

Driving at an ambling pace, you can see much of the Litchfield Hills in a couple of days. Whether your starting point is New York, Boston, or somewhere in between, the main routes are easily plotted. In any case, directions and timetables soon seem irrelevant. This corrugated landscape encourages even the most disciplined visitor to lose weeks in its upland meadows and comfortable inns. Anxiety and urgency drain away as the road lulls you with its gentle, rhythmical curves. In this chapter we make a circuit from Winsted (reached from Hartford on US 44) down to Litchfield and New Milford, returning north on US 7 and Route 41 to US 44, Canaan, and Norfolk.

Not surprisingly, this hill region bred strange beliefs. **Winsted,** for example, was not only a 19th-century clock-making center but a hotbed of witchcraft, superstition, and outlandish sightings. "Wild men" reportedly roamed the hillsides, along with five-legged cows and talking owls. It all started when the Beach family found cloven hoof tracks in the snow and "a slight mark as if a forked tail had been drawn across the powdery surface"—enough to have a parishioner whipped for witchcraft. Today's visitors must content themselves with admiring the 19th-century houses on Main Street and the impressive Solomon Rockwell colonial mansion on Prospect Street.

A Girl Scout camp overlooking the Litchfield Hills,
circa 1930. (Underwood Photo Archives, San Francisco)

The wilderness also harbored outlaws and outcasts. In **Barkhamsted,** east of Winsted, Molly Barber, a white woman from Wethersfield, and her Narragansett husband, James Chaugham, established an outcast village in 1740 where Native Americans, African-Americans, and wayward whites found refuge. An archaeological site in People's State Forest recalls the community that survived for 120 years, until 1860.

Route 272 passes through tiny **Drakeville,** skims over the glassy expanse of Stillwater Pond, and is swallowed up in the once heavily industrialized town of **Torrington.** Once known as Mast Swamp for its exceptional pine trees used in shipbuilding, Torrington was one of the region's early brass towns, producing among other things the country's first brass kettles and cartridge brass for export to Spain and Russia. The fine historical society at the **Hotchkiss-Fyler House** displays period furnishings and decorative art and, in an adjacent building, an exhibit on the history of the Hendley Machine Company; *192 Main Street, approached on Route 4, 860-482-8260.*

John Brown, the famous abolitionist, was born in Torrington in 1800, and the pikes used by Brown and his men in the 1856 raid on the U.S. arsenal at Harper's Ferry, Virginia, were made by the Collins Company in Canton. A marker on John Brown Road, accessible from University Road off Route 4, commemorates his birthplace.

More hilltop legends lurk to the south, at **Leatherman Cave** in **Thomaston.** Rivaling George Washington in the number of his reported stopovers, the Old Leatherman was a Connecticut wanderer first noticed in 1862. A Frenchman named Jules Bourglay who had failed in the leather business and been jilted, he traversed the state in all seasons wearing only leather clothing, sleeping only in caves. You may hike to one of his retreats along the Mattatuck Trail, a mile southwest of Thomaston, where Crane Lookout affords spectacular views. The trail passes through Leatherman Cave at the foot of Crane Lookout, intersecting with the Jericho Trail. *Trailhead is in Mattatuck State Forest, a mile southwest of Thomaston off Reynold's Bridge Road.*

■ LITCHFIELD AREA *map page 237, C-3*

Litchfield, to the north on US 202, is perfectly situated and perfectly charming, its broad, tree-lined streets and a large, shady Green dominating a generous hilltop.

West Street in downtown Litchfield.

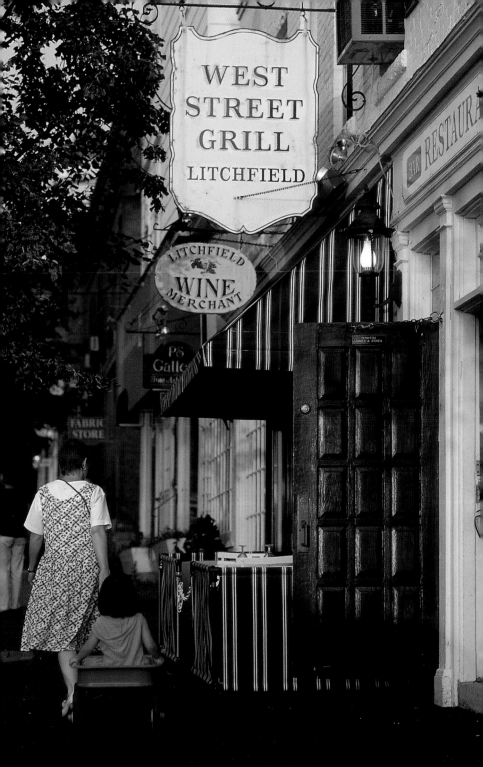

Long popular as a summer retreat for affluent New Yorkers, Litchfield had a shaky start. Bought from Native Americans for 15 pounds and settled in 1720, the town was repeatedly subject to attack, and in 1722, Joseph Harris was captured and scalped on what is now known as Harris Plain. The quiet agricultural and trading town was most active during the Revolution, when many of its residents, including Oliver Wolcott, held key military and governmental positions. A Continental Army store on the main route to Boston, Litchfield prospered after the Revolution and became an intellectual center of Federalist New England.

When railroads bypassed the town in the 19th century, Litchfield became a sedate backwater. In 1938, the *WPA Guide to Connecticut* noted: "When the mail comes in, townsfolk gather at the post office....Just across the Green...is the county jail, seldom occupied except by some backwoodsman who has been intemperate....The dog warden usually basks in the sunlight near the harness store,...his golden badge polished bright."

(above) The Tollgate Hill Inn in Litchfield was once a tavern, but is today a bed-and-breakfast.

(opposite) Litchfield Congregational Church.

Litchfield Green

The scene today is a little different. Fashionable all-terrain vehicles circle the Green at lunchtime and chalkboards outside the many restaurants announce a daunting variety of pastas, salads, and vegetarian alternatives. To savor the atmosphere on a summer afternoon, take the easy way out. Buy a sandwich (as gourmet as you wish) at the 1886 Granniss and Elmore General Store on the Green and eat it under a tree, watching three elderly gentlemen in shirtsleeves playing bocce nearby, and the Easy Rider, probably a vacationing CEO, "blatting" back and forth on his Harley.

Litchfield Historical Society

Farther along the Green, at the corner of South Street and East Street, the Litchfield Historical Society is a good starting point for a more strenuous exploration. Founded in 1856, the museum presents permanent and changing exhibits of paintings, textiles, photographs, clothing, and decorative arts. Admission here also covers the Tapping Reeve House nearby on South Street, America's first law school, which was founded in 1773 and played a pivotal role in shaping the new nation. The school's list of graduates includes two U.S. vice presidents, 101 congressmen, 28 senators, and three supreme court justices. Tapping Reeve also championed more enlightened legal status for married women, working toward legislation that would eventually allow wives to transfer property without their husband's permission. *7 South Street; 860-567-4501.*

Litchfield's other prominent residents included Pastor Lyman Beecher, father of Harriet Beecher Stowe and of Reverend Henry Ward Beecher, and Benjamin Tallmadge, chief of the Intelligence Service during the Revolution and a friend of Nathan Hale. Ethan Allen was born here in 1737 but his family later moved to Vermont.

Open House Day

The Tallmadge House on North Street, like most of the town's houses, is a private residence. You may visit it and Litchfield's other mansions on Open House Day in July, which is organized by the Historical Society. Should you miss that opportunity, a walk around the Green and down elegant South Street will still give you a sense of the town's uninterrupted prosperity.

White Flower Farm

South Street will lead you to White Flower Farm, the leading nursery in a region where competition is particularly tough. Passing equestrian centers that look more like luxury condominiums, you turn into a modest parking lot and immediately change from a rational person into a creature ruled by its senses. Colors and smells erupt from every corner of the 10-acre display garden and from the 30 acres of growing fields, especially in the peak blooming season from June to September.

Babbling to yourself or the nearest stranger, you are drawn past glorious perennial beds, through arbors, and under copper beeches until you stumble upon the nationally famous display of English tuberous begonias—outrageous plants that look like roses on steroids. But there are subtle varieties here as well as show-offs, and real work goes on under rows of black plastic in the horticultural sweat shops. No matter where you live, you will leave with something in a pot, resolving to have your soil tested. *On South Street (Route 63) 3 miles south of town center; 860-567-8789.*

Topsmead State Forest

Topsmead, east of Litchfield off Route 118, is harder to find but even more intoxicating. Apple trees line the rustic path leading to a small English Tudor cottage perched in a highland meadow, the former summer home of Edith M. Chase and one of the loveliest places in New England. It is not just the elevation or the summer breezes, it is the scale of the half-timbered stone house. After the grandiosity of Litchfield, the cottage's dainty walled gardens and exquisite architectural details restore the human perspective. The most perfect picnic spot imaginable, the park also tempts you with woodland walks. *Off Route 118; call for directions; 860-567-5694.*

White Memorial Foundation

The 4,000-acre White Memorial Foundation provides a more challenging variety of trails as well as a campground, marina, and nature museum. Every preference— whether for meadow, river, forest, or marsh views—is catered to here with an accompanying seasonal soundtrack of cricket, grasshopper, and cicada harmonies in summer, leaf-rustle during autumn, and ice-crunch in winter. *Two and a half miles west of Litchfield on US 202; 860-567-0857.*

■ SMALL TOWN DETOURS *map page 237, B-4, C-4*

US 202 dips and climbs its way southwest from Litchfield to New Milford, but you may want to make a detour south on Route 47, to the small town of **Washington,** where the **Gunn Memorial Museum** mounts local history exhibitions in a 1781 house. *Corner of Wykeham Road and Route 47; 860-868-7756.*

Just to the north in the town of **Washington Depot,** the **Institute for American Indian Studies** animates the Native American past. The indoor longhouse exhibit is the main attraction here. There is also a simulated archaeological site and a re-creation of a 17th-century Algonquian village, both of which suffer from their proximity to the parking lot and the museum's concrete abutments. *38 Curtis Road; 860-868-0518.*

Bethlehem, a short distance to the east on pleasant back roads, is the site of the fine 18th-century **Bellamy-Ferriday House** and formal garden on Main Street, whose history spans 1740–1990. Farther south, the 18th-century **Glebe House** on Hollow Road in Woodbury was the home of America's first Episcopal bishop and today displays the only extant garden in the country designed by landscape artist Gertrude Jekyll.

Roxbury, south of Washington on Route 199, is the high, isolated place to which writer James Baldwin retreated in 1961 while working on his novel, *Another Country*, a task that probably prevented him from appreciating the pretty sweep of Route 67 between Roxbury and New Milford. Settled in 1707 by John Noble of Westfield, Massachusetts, and his eight-year old daughter, New Milford attracted Roger Sherman, signer of the Declaration of Independence, who arrived here from Newton, Massachusetts, in 1743 and opened a cobbler's shop. A neat yet substantial town today, New Milford's attractions include the Litchfield County First Bank, the 1796 Elijah Boardman Store, and the fine **Historical Society Museum** at *6 Aspetuck Avenue; 860-354-3069.*

■ HOUSATONIC RIVER AREA *map page 237, A-4, B-5*

US 7, one of the region's loveliest roads, runs north from New Milford to the Massachusetts border, following the course of the Housatonic River for much of its run and competing for beauty with the equally lovely Route 41 and US 44 to the west. "There is no tonic like the Housatonic," U.S. Supreme Court Justice Oliver Wendell Holmes once observed. And he was right. Dawdling is the point here. The road's curves and the sleepy villages along the way demand it. You may, of course, drive singlemindedly through unassuming **Gaylordsville**. But then you would miss Brown's Forge, an authentic 1871 blacksmith shop on Brown's Forge Road not far from the 1843 Merwinsville Hotel and the one-room Little Red Schoolhouse on Schoolhouse Road, both managed by the local historical society; *860-354-3069.*

This rugged terrain is ideal ambush country and weaving your way north to Kent on a spring afternoon you become a willing victim. The glinting Housatonic River makes repeated forays at the road, banks of purple loosestrife suddenly catch your eye, then **Bulls Covered Bridge** forces you to stop and admire both river and foliage framed in its dark windows.

Kent, settled in 1738, was one of the area's leading iron-producing towns, and the **Sloane-Stanley Museum** on US 7 displays an 1826 furnace along with an extensive collection of tools. From Flanders Cemetery just north of the town, you see what attracted 19th-century landscape painters like George Inness. You may also contemplate the gravestone of Capt. Jirah Swift, killed during the Revolution, which reads "I in the Prime of Life must quit the Stage or Nor see the End of all the Britains Rage." Over 100 Schaghticoke warriors, descendants of the Pequots,

Kent Falls State Park in the Housatonic Valley.

also joined the Continental Army. Acting chiefly as a signal corps, they relayed messages from Stockbridge, Massachusetts, to Long Island Sound, using drumbeats and fires on Candlewood Mountain, Straits Mountain, and Pickett Rock.

Today, part of the **Appalachian Trail** crosses the Schaghticoke Indian Reservation west of Kent off Route 341, providing an often steep hike which affords fine views of the Housatonic Valley, particularly from Indian Rocks. Far less rugged is Kent Falls State Park, on the edge of town, where stair pathways allow visitors to view the cascades, and picnic tables encourage sloth.

■ CORNWALL AREA *map page 237, A-2, B-2*

"Only the very poor or the very brave settled here," the *WPA Connecticut Guide* observed of rocky, icy Cornwall in 1938. An updated assessment would, however, include the very gifted and the very rich. A favorite summer retreat of New York intellectuals and even the odd movie director, this isolated town deep in the Taconic highlands attracted writers Mark and Dorothy Van Doren in summer and James Thurber all year round. Thurber and his wife, Helen, settled in Cornwall in

CONNECTICUT
NORTHWEST

For decades, Cornwall has attracted artists and intellectuals. (photo by Robert Holmes)

Cornwall Bridge over the Housatonic River.

1945, and the writer lived here until his death in 1961, completing *The Thurber Carnival* and other late books in the house that still stands near the Cathedral Pines section of the **Mohawk State Forest.** The summit tower of 1,683-foot Mohawk Mountain commands a 360-degree view, but various hiking trails, some originating from the dramatic Cathedral Pines stand, provide equally fine perspectives as they cross swamps, woodland, escarpments, and abandoned villages.

The sleepy villages of **Cornwall Bridge** and **West Cornwall** (both on US 7) and Cornwall to the east on Route 4 form a triangle of treats that includes the lovely covered bridge in West Cornwall. The charming town of **Sharon,** farther west on scenic Route 41, is another pleasing diversion; the vibrant 18th-century manufacturing center produced shoes, tools, mousetraps, and practically everything in between. Here Benjamin Hotchkiss invented exploding shells, a fact that is hard to imagine when you walk down Sharon's peaceful Main Street and explore the magnificent 1775 **Gay-Hoyt House Museum** or when you visit the 758-acre **Sharon Audubon Center** on Route 4, where the loudest sound is usually that of bees on assignment in the wildflower and herb gardens. *Gay-Hoyt Museum: 860-364-5688.*

A blanket of snow, a picket fence, and twilight conspire to turn a Connecticut field into an austere geometric pattern. Over 100 inches of snow fall each year in the Litchfield Hills.

■ LAKEVILLE AREA *map page 237, A-1*

It is equally hard to imagine Belgian-born writer Georges Simenon spending five years in nearby Lakeville. But the creator of Inspector Maigret did indeed live at Shadow Rock Farm from 1950 to 1955, producing *Maigret and the Headless Body* among many other novels. "In the United States I learned shame," Simenon wrote, referring to the "alcoholic consciousness" that overcame him when he traded wine for martinis. Shadow Rock remains a private residence. The novelist would doubtless have been shocked by the outrageous, pugnacious Ethan Allen who became co-owner of the Lakeville iron forge in 1762 and scandalized the town with his behavior. Not that Lakeville was genteel. Its ironworkers were fortified with unlimited supplies of meat and rum, so critical was their output of cannons and shot to the Revolution.

Iron and rock are constant presences as you reach Salisbury and, depending on your fitness, you may choose either a hike following the **Appalachian Trail**—accessible from the Undermountain Trail parking area off Route 41—to the peak of Bear Mountain or a more leisurely exploration of the early-19th-century Mount

Riga Blast Furnace off US 44. High and mighty in its own right, the furnace occupies a thousand-foot ledge, and in its day manufactured anchors for the USS *Constitution* among other warships. It may be viewed from the road only. Bear Mountain, on the other hand, welcomes explorers, particularly in the kinder seasons when wild blueberries and mountain laurel decorate the slopes.

In **Salisbury** itself you'll find the **Salisbury Cannon Museum**, a Revolutionary museum for children, standing near the site of the first iron blast furnace on US 44. The **Holley-Williams House** on Upper Main Street, built in 1768 for an iron tycoon, conjures up the atmosphere and wealth of the time. **Pocketknife Square** recalls the product that revitalized Lakeville in the late 19th century. *Cannon Museum: 860-435-2878.*

■ CANAAN AREA *map page 237, B-1*

Advertised as "a land flowing with milk and honey" when it was auctioned off at New London in 1738, the town of Canaan, northeast of Salisbury, was—and still is—a mountainous outcrop redeemed only by some fertile valleys along the

Collin's Diner has been a fixture in North Canaan for more than half a century.

Housatonic River. Any trace of early hardship has been erased by prosperity, however, as has the public Sunday drinking and brawling that earned neighboring Sodom its name in the 18th century.

More respectable pleasures are provided these days by **Music Mountain,** the nation's oldest continuous summer chamber music event, that takes place on 120 acres at Falls Village to the south, another former iron-producing town that shows a softer face to today's visitor. *Music Mountain; follow signs from US 7 or Route 63; 860-824-7126.*

■ NORFOLK *map page 237, C-1*

Norfolk is a pleasant pause. Once a wild, rugged outpost, this pretty, compact town sheltered by surrounding hills is perhaps best known today for the summer and autumn **Chamber Music Festival** held in the Music Shed at the Ellen Battell Stoeckel Estate. Beginning in 1899, annual concerts attracted composers like Coleridge Taylor, Sibelius, and Henry Hadley, and internationally renowned ensembles and artists continue to play for audiences who are usually sated with the estate's beauty and with the traditional picnics on the lawn; *860-542-3000.*

The charmingly fishy **Joseph Battell Memorial Fountain** on the Green was designed by Augustus Saint-Gaudens and commemorates the town's most influential 18th-century entrepreneur.

■ WATERBURY *map page 237, C-4*

The town of Waterbury presents a sharp contrast to the Litchfield Hills. Comfortably lodged in the valleys of the Naugatuck and Mad Rivers, it tempts you off manic I-84 with its soaring display of redbrick mill buildings and church spires. Known originally to the Native Americans as Mattatuck, meaning "badly wooded region" the area was surveyed—somewhat pessimistically—in 1674 by English settlers who expressed doubts that it could support more than 30 families. Today it appears to support twice that number of shopping malls and brick must now share the skyline with concrete. The country's leading brass-producing city from the 19th century through the early 20th century, Waterbury provided America with about five million of Robert Ingersoll's famous one-dollar pocket watches annually until 1922; supplied copper and brass for the Boulder Dam in Colorado and coinage for South America; and revolutionized metallurgical technology in its own factories.

Remnants of that industrial legacy are still visible. Grand Street, with its venerable municipal buildings, is still rather grand and the Green is still green despite the traffic. The **Mattatuck Museum** on the Green at West Main Street offers a comprehensive and imaginative view of the city's history, particularly in its permanent Brass Roots exhibition, which takes you from the earliest days of white settlement through Waterbury's subsequent industrial and social development. Charles Goodyear's rubber desk is among the local products on display here, but the museum also devotes airy galleries to 18th-, 19th-, and 20th-century American artists including Frederic Edwin Church, John Frederick Kensett, Maurice Prendergast, Josef Albers, and Arshile Gorky. *Mattatuck Museum: 144 West Main Street; 203-753-0381.*

The city's **visitor center** is on Church Street, across the Green from the Mattatuck Museum, and its historic districts are also nearby. Turning from the Green onto Central Avenue, you reach Hillside, home to the wealthiest 19th-century industrialists, and just above it, Overlook, a 148-acre suburban community laid out in the 1890s and completed by 1930. Fulton Park, designed by Frederick Law Olmsted, is still the chief recreation area here, and streets like Buckingham, Pine, Willow, and Upper Fiske have a lived-in rather than a preserved appearance. No two houses are alike and practically every American architectural style is represented.

Descending into Waterbury's challenging one-way traffic puzzle, you understand why James Thurber's hero Walter Mitty lapsed into one heroic fantasy after another as he negotiated the city while running his nagging wife's errands in *The Secret Life of Walter Mitty.*

◆ RAILROAD RIDE

To let someone else do the driving, visit the **Railroad Museum of New England**. The Naugatuck Railroad Company will take you on an 18-mile ride along the river, through state forest and across the face of the dramatic Thomaston Dam, an excursion that is particularly memorable in October when outrageous autumn leaves do their best to distract the stolid locomotives. *176 Chase River Road; 203-575-1931.*

CONNECTICUT
THE COAST

■ HIGHLIGHTS   *page*

■ TRAVEL BASICS

Stonington is one of the state's loveliest villages, but the coastal cities seems somewhat faded—though New London has a rich maritime history and New Haven is home to Yale University. Mystic Seaport shows how life was carried on here in more rugged, seafaring times, while Yale University and sedate Old Lyme have particularly fine art museums.

Getting Around: Avoid Interstate 95 whenever possible, instead following Route 1 and its offshoots and the pretty Merritt Parkway. The Chester–Hadlyme river ferry operates from April to October. Ferries for Fishers Island depart from New London.

Climate: Coastal Connecticut typically has hot summers (60s to 80s) and stormy winters (20s to 40s). Offshore winds make moderate spring and autumn days feel chilly. Bring layers of clothing.

Food & Lodging: Older shore towns are filled with historic inns, and you'll find the best dining in these towns, too. Large hotels dot the coast more and more frequently close to New York. Food varies from the authentically fishy to minimalist suburban. Connecticut coverage begins on page 354; towns are listed in alphabetical order. Listings map page 327; listings chart page 376.

CONNECTICUT
COAST

■ OVERVIEW

Connecticut's eastern shore retains its seafaring state of mind, particularly in small fishing villages like Stonington, which were largely spared the industrialization that transformed New Haven, New London, and numerous inland towns. Gauging that seafaring mentality is simple. Count the number of fishing boats in the harbor. Then count the number of people staring at those boats and at the surrounding sea for hours on end, for no discernible reason.

Locals have had years to refine this skill. You may only have the weekend. You can, however, become reasonably proficient by meandering from Middletown downstream to Old Saybrook, then upstream from Old Lyme to Portland in one day and by spending another couple of days exploring the Thames River Valley to the east, taking in Mystic Seaport, Stonington, and New London. If your reflexes grow sluggish as your staring ability improves, don't worry. There is always the coastal run to New Haven with its flood tide of New York traffic to snap you back into competitive shape.

■ HISTORY

In 1635, a group of English settlers under John Winthrop Jr., erected a fort at Saybrook, but New Haven was the region's first substantial English settlement. Founded in 1638, the year following the Pequot War, New Haven had a generous harbor that attracted minister John Davenport, merchant Theophilus Eaton, and about 500 followers. The brutal conflict of the preceding year had removed any Native American threat, and smaller settlements quickly flourished along the coast, spreading throughout the Connecticut River and Thames River Valleys. Their development followed a familiar New England pattern.

Subsistence farming, fishing, and craftwork grew into profitable agriculture, shipbuilding, whaling, trade, and manufacturing in the 18th century. In the early 19th century, the West Indies and China trade bestowed architectural splendor on even the smallest ports, while the subsequent industrial revolution turned Norwich, New Haven, New London, Essex, and other towns into centers not only of manufacturing but of invention. Soon rivaling Hartford, the region's products included Winchester rifles, pianos, bicycles, cigars, combs, cotton, and paper.

Trade and enterprise have never been the sole concerns here. Besides supplying the Continental Army with men and provisions during the Revolution, the region also witnessed Connecticut's only significant Revolutionary War battle, in 1781

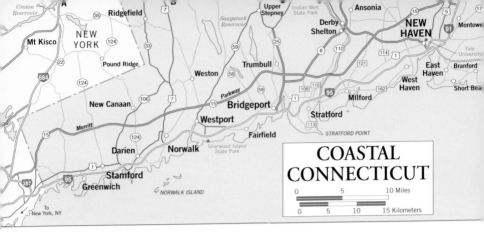

when native son Benedict Arnold led an ignominious attack on New London and Groton. Fueled by revolutionary zeal, Saybrook inventor David Bushnell in 1775 designed the first submarine and, inspired by this century's wars, Groton became a modern naval manufacturing center, launching the world's first nuclear-powered submarine in 1954.

Not all creative energy was shackled to defense. Yale was founded in Branford and located in Saybrook in 1701, before being moved to New Haven in 1717, while Wesleyan University was founded in Middletown in 1831. New York artists discovered their neighbor's picturesque charms at the turn of the 19th century, and art colonies like Old Lyme have been admiring themselves on canvas ever since.

Final light of day over Stonington Harbor.

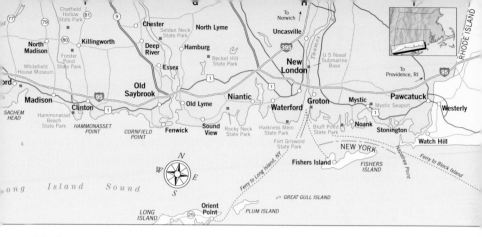

■ STONINGTON

Stonington, one of the loveliest villages on the Connecticut coast, is an old whaling and fishing port that still has work boats in its harbor and magnificent Greek Revival mansions lining the narrow, pretty streets leading to the water. At the **Captain Nathaniel B. Palmer House,** guided tours of the Antarctic explorer's Victorian home are offered; *40 Palmer Street; 860-535-8445.*

Old Lighthouse Museum displays whaling, nautical, and military equipment; portraits; and oriental artifacts. *7 Water Street; 860-535-1440.*

Leaving the museum on an autumn evening, you should linger on the quay

In downtown Stonington stands a memorial to the defenders of the port during the War of 1812.

until sunset, perhaps contemplating the words of Chief Canonchet, who was executed here in April 1676 declaring: "I like it well that I should die before my heart is softened and I say things unworthy of myself." If that seems too maudlin, try chanting the defiant cry that became Stonington's anthem when its two cannons defeated 140 British naval guns in 1814: "It cost the King ten thousand pounds to have a dash at Stonington."

◆ Natural Areas Near Stonington

Should Stonington frown on your enthusiasm, retreat inland to hike the **Narragansett Trail,** which opens at the Ledyard–North Stonington line and winds northeast to Rhode Island. Or lose yourself in **Pachaug State Forest** to the north, the state's largest, which covers almost 24,000 acres and includes a rhododendron sanctuary that during late June and early July forms outlandish 20-foot walls of blossom. *See map page 217, F-3.*

Stop in tiny North Stonington for sustenance and you will find it mixed with history at **Randall's Ordinary Landmark Inn,** once a stop on the Underground Railroad. Staff can still show visitors where fugitive slaves were hidden, and there is still cooking on the open hearth. *US 2; 860-599-4540.*

Instead of joining the traffic on I-95, take US 1 and head west toward New Haven. Sections of it follow the old **Shore Path,** one of the most heavily traveled of the Native American trails that once connected Manhattan and Boston. The coastline it traverses is today the most developed in New England, so don't expect dreamy expanses and windswept solitude. There are, however, pretty coves, soft marshes, and islands punctuating the glinting ocean.

Much of the shoreline here is privately owned, but you can walk without anxiety for a couple of sandy miles at **Hammonasset Beach State Park** between Clinton and Madison. Appallingly crowded in summer, the beach, dunes, and tidal marshes are best explored in early spring or late autumn. In May, a multicolored assortment of ducks sample the marsh's weed of the day, while perfectly poised snowy egrets, apparently disgusted by duck manners, stand aloof in the reeds. If you are lucky, you'll hear the hysterical giggle of a loon or see osprey chicks. Camping, boating, scuba diving, and saltwater fishing facilities are provided.

◆ MYSTIC AQUARIUM *map page 257, H*

Mystic Aquarium is an unlikely apparition, particularly when approached on the small woodland roads that putter along in the slipstream of Interstate 95. A spiky, futuristic disc served by a vast (and in summer, packed) parking lot, this still-expanding research, educational, and exhibition center is not solely—or even mainly—concerned with teaching dolphin acrobatics. The discovery of ancient Roman shipwrecks in the Mediterranean, seal rehabilitation, and an outreach program to inner-city schools are just some of the institute's activities. But there are also the crowd pleasers: shameless somersaulting dolphins, applause-hungry beluga whales, strait-laced penguins, and an astonishing variety of finny creatures swimming around you in a wide range of imaginatively designed exhibits. *In the town of Mystic; take Exit 90 off I-95 and follow signs; 860-572-5955.*

The adjacent **Denison Pequotsepos Nature Center**, a 125-acre sanctuary encompassing seven miles of hiking trails, houses feathered exhibitionists in its outdoor flight enclosures, where swooping birds of prey attempt to upstage their watery relatives.

African black-footed penguins at the Mystic Aquarium.

Mystic Seaport is home to the world's largest collection of historic vessels. (photo by Robert Holmes)

■ MYSTIC SEAPORT   *map page 257, H*

Mystic Seaport is the nation's leading maritime museum, with the world's largest collection of historic vessels and maritime photography. A visit here is bewitching, particularly in early spring, late autumn, or winter, when crowds have thinned and the only sounds along the waterfront and in the 19th-century streets are the screeching of gulls and the creaking of the port's leviathans, rocking gently at anchor.

Mystic Seaport is best known for its three largest ships—the 1841 ***Charles W. Morgan,*** America's last surviving wooden whaleship; the 1882 training vessel ***Joseph Conrad;*** and the 123-foot fishing schooner ***L.A. Dunton,*** built in 1921— and for its 19th-century village and waterfront. The museum also includes a preservation shipyard, a research library, exhibition galleries, a planetarium, and a children's museum. The range of daily activities, many of them seasonal, is equally impressive, including steamboat cruises on the 1908 *Sabino,* whaling reenactments, carriage rides, garden tours, nautical demonstrations, concerts on the Green, and conversations with meticulously researched 19th-century characters. You can even sample the definitive New England chowder at the museum's Columbus Day weekend Chowderfest. *Mystic Seaport: north of the town of Mystic; take Exit 90 off I-95 and follow signs; 860-572-5315.*

All of this may sound daunting, even phony. But it's not. Standing outside the Spouter Tavern, looking back at the harbor as a chilling November mist shrouds the masts of the *Charles W. Morgan,* you feel as if a hand is about to land on your shoulder, condemning you to a five-year whaling voyage. The museum is a working as well as a uniquely atmospheric place, and in March 1998, its shipyard began constructing a replica of the 80-foot *Amistad,* due to be completed in the year 2000 and currently on view as a work-in-progress. Aside from the maritime museum, Mystic's other chief delight is the **Carousel Museum of New England** (on Green-manville Avenue), which displays the world's finest collection of antique carousel art along with miniature carousels and an antique carving shop.

◆ SIDETRIPS ALONG US 1 *map page 257, H*

Make a couple of diversions to visit the charming little **harbor at Noank** and the more grandiose summer "cottages" at **Groton Long Point,** south of Mystic on US 1.

Groton itself witnessed one of the Revolution's most horrific engagements when over 80 of the 150 young Patriots defending Fort Griswold against Benedict

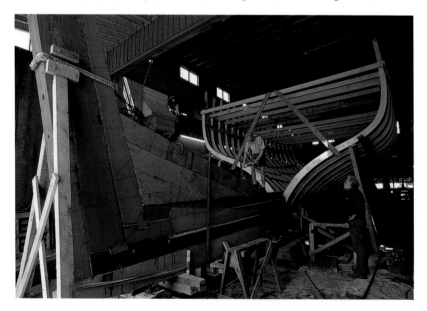

New England's ship-building tradition is carried on with the construction of the schooner Amistad II, *a replica of the original slave ship.*

Arnold's assault, having inflicted heavy casualties on the British, were killed when they surrendered. The ramparts at **Fort Griswold State Park** are intact. Students of modern military history will be equally impressed by the **Submarine Force Library and Museum** at the Naval Submarine Base, where the world's first nuclear-powered submarine, the USS *Nautilus,* is among the exhibits. *Off Highway 12 in Groton; 860-694-3174 or 800-343-0079.*

■ NEW LONDON *map page 257, H*

Humming the sea-chanties recently learned at Mystic Seaport, you may be disappointed as you cross the bridge to New London, to see not whalers and schooners below but fragile yachts, blowing about like paper scraps on the Thames below, and brick-shaped ferries plying their route to the green, watery retreat of Fisher's Island. The pendulum of decline and redevelopment has eviscerated New London, as it did Norwich, and much of the waterfront is now dominated by parking garages and office buildings. Not everything of value, however, has been scuttled.

Settled in 1646 by John Winthrop, Jr., New London commanded the largest and deepest harbor on this coast, profited from the West Indies trade, and became one of New England's largest whaling centers in the early 19th century, when its

A women's eight from Connecticut College rows by the school's sailing team on the Thames River.

fleet of some 80 vessels was outnumbered only by those of Nantucket and New Bedford. "Now," the *New London Gazette* exhorted as early as 1775, "my horse jockeys beat your horses and cattle into spears, lances, harpoons, and whaling gear, and let us all strike out; many spouts ahead! Whale plenty, you have them for the catching."

Fine Mansions

On Huntington Street you'll find Whale Oil Row, a breathtaking stand of four Greek Revival mansions that testify to the golden days when a year-long voyage could bring $150,000 in profit. Capt. Lyman Allyn, however, preferred Williams Street, buying a mansion here in 1851. Today the **Deshon-Allyn House Museum** has as its neighbor the beautiful **Lyman Allyn Art Museum**, which exhibits contemporary American art, American impressionist paintings, drawings, and special collections. *Lyman Allyn Museum: 625 Williams Street; 860-443-2545.*

The 1833 **Custom House** on Bank Street is still glorious as is the 1887 **Union Station** on the waterfront, the latter designed by Henry Hobson Richardson. Washington and Lafayette visited the 1756 **Shaw Mansion** on Blinman Street, the state's naval headquarters during the Revolution and a superb museum today. Business here was brisk—and lethal—at its peak. New London, after all, harbored more privateers during the Revolutionary War than any other New England port and was burned and blockaded for its temerity.

Monte Cristo

Playwright Eugene O'Neill once wrote a daily column for the *New London Telegraph* and spent summers at Monte Cristo, his parents' house. Now open to visitors, the modest cottage overlooks the harbor, and the room in which O'Neill set *Long Day's Journey Into Night* has been reconstructed from his stage directions. Even today, the somewhat lifeless house seems to exude O'Neill melancholy. *325 Pequot Avenue; 860-443-0051.*

Joshua Hempsted House

Joshua Hempsted wrote far jollier prose in his diary, and visiting the exquisite Joshua Hempsted House today, you imagine a robust, energetic man striding through these plain rooms. This is New London's oldest dwelling—its earliest portions date to 1678—and one of New England's loveliest, with heavy framing, casement windows, and simple furnishings that give an immediate sense of life in the early settlement. The 18th-century stone Hempsted House beside Joshua's is another rarity, built in 1751 of granite quarried on the site by Hugenot refugees. *11 Hempstead Street; 860-443-7949 or 247-8996.*

Connecticut College Arboretum

If the Hempsted Houses don't dispel the O'Neill gloom, you can always try the Connecticut College Arboretum, where the trees, plants, ducks, and even more dignified birds do everything they can on 750 verdant acres to entertain their visitors. *On Williams Street across from the college; 860-439-5020.*

New London is the point of embarkation for a number of ferries, including the following *(see map page 257, H-1):*

>**Block Island, Rhode Island:** car ferry, auto reservations required, one trip daily, June to September, 401-783-4613.
>
>**Fishers Island, New York:** car ferry, year round, 516-788-7744.
>
>**Montauk, Long Island, New York:** passenger ferry, 516-668-5709.

The town of **Waterford**, adjacent to New London on US 1, is home to the Eugene O'Neill Theatre Centre and to the splendid **Harkness Memorial State Park,** a former summer estate with Italianate mansion, formal gardens, and a beach that welcomes walkers but not swimmers.

Beach Scene, New London, *by William J. Glackens, 1918.*
(Columbus Museum of Art, Ohio, gift of Ferdinand Housald)

Buoys, used by lobstermen to locate their pots, decorate a lobster pound in Noank.

■ OLD LYME *map page 257, G*

The merchants and shipbuilders who made Old Lyme a vibrant trading center in the 18th century would never have tolerated recreational seafaring. The wealth created by their enterprise, chiefly in the West Indies trade, still pervades the town, which has long been an affluent summer retreat. And in the fading light of an October evening, the 18th- and 19th-century mansions along Lyme Street seem like ships themselves, anchored by their taut shadows in a harbor of meticulously groomed parkland.

Florence Griswold Museum

Artist Willard Metcalf came to board at Florence Griswold's house at Old Lyme in 1901 "because he was poor and had heard of the four vegetables she was famed for serving with each meal." Scores of artists were similarly drawn to "Miss Florence's" art colony in the 1817 mansion on Lyme Street to explore a surrounding landscape described by the colony's founder, Henry Ward Ranger, as "only waiting to be painted." Today, the Florence Griswold Museum provides a rare opportunity to see not only what painters like Childe Hassam, Will Howe Foote, Matilda Browne, Charles Ebert, and others created, but how they lived and worked. The Griswold dining room is lined with over 30 panels painted by the boarding artists who ate the famed four vegetables here. Viewing the panels of landscape scenes and humorous self-portraits is like catching Henry James writing his holiday postcards; *96 Lyme Street; 860-434-5542.*

The restored **Chadwick Studio**, overlooking the Lieutenant River a short distance from the house, was the workplace of impressionist William Chadwick from 1920 until his death in 1962, and so strong is his presence that you expect him to burst in any minute and upbraid you for snooping. Indignant catbirds will meow similar accusations when you linger in the museum's lovely gardens.

Lyme and the Fine Arts

Lyme Academy of Fine Arts is a fine arts college with galleries housed in the 1817 John Sill House; *84 Lyme Street.* **Lyme Art Association** is the nation's oldest summer art colony; *90 Lyme Street; 860-434-7802.*

◆ NATURAL LANDSCAPES NEAR OLD LYME *map page 257, G*

To test your own aesthetic reflexes, make a short detour west of Old Lyme on Route 156, first to the **Great Island Wildlife Area** and then to **Rocky Neck State Park**. Both are at their best in spring and autumn, when they are denuded of crowds and reveal such marshy, shoreline treasures as herons, teal, osprey, and scurrying sandpipers.

Route 156 north from Old Lyme to Hamburg winds between inviting coves on one side and salt marshes on the other. Swans glide, herons stalk, reeds catch the afternoon sun, and you see what captivated the American impressionists. **Hamburg Cove** is a light-filled composition of glassy water, sloping meadows, and cool forest, and **Selden Neck State Park,** north of Hamburg off tiny Joshuatown Road, is a shady preserve that inspires even the most reluctant walker with views of the surrounding marshes and creeks.

Fenwick Point Community in Old Saybrook.

■ OLD SAYBROOK *map page 257, H*

The wind from Long Island Sound that flays this coastline in winter cools demure Old Saybrook on a summer afternoon, and there is nothing in the peaceful scene that you can imagine having inspired David Bushnell in the late 18th century to start blowing things up underwater. Bushnell experimented in Saybrook's Otter Cove, submerging and igniting gunpowder-filled barrels before testing his submarine, *American Turtle,* in front of an enthusiastic Benjamin Franklin. Today's aquatic outings from Saybrook Point are less incendiary. Deep River Navigation Company offers several cruises daily to Essex, Duck Island, and the lighthouses. Mystic Whaler Cruises entice voyagers with lobster-dinner cruises and one- to five-day voyages—or you can sail for a half-day to a week on the elegant *Odyssey. Deep River Navigation: 860-526-4954; Mystic Whaler: 860-572-5315.*

■ GUILFORD *map page 257, E*

Guilford is a solid place. Granite from its quarries formed part of the Brooklyn Bridge and the Statue of Liberty, but the **Henry Whitfield House** is the town's most impressive rock formation. Built in 1639, the oldest stone house in New England was part dwelling, part fortress, and the 1930s restoration artfully conveys the preoccupations and atmosphere of the early settlement. Beautifully situated on a sloping orchard field just outside town, the house is furnished with exceptional 17th- and 18th-century pieces and is a cool retreat on a humid summer's day. *2488 Old Whitfield Road at Stonehouse Lane, half-mile south of the town green; 203-453-2457.*

The green heart of Guilford is one of the area's loveliest commons, bordered by historic houses and commercial buildings. The stores cater mainly to affluent shoppers craving organic cotton and handmade chocolates, but most of the town's several hundred 18th- and 19th-century houses are privately owned. Spared destruction by the British during the Revolution largely because its militia successfully defended nearby Leete's Island, Guilford retains an intact architectural face. Boston Street off the Green contains two particular treasures, the 1660 **Hyland House,** a beautiful saltbox with exceptional furnishings, and the 1774 **Thomas Griswold House,** which was a Griswold family home until 1958. Harriet Beecher Stowe spent a year here as a child on her grandmother's Guilford farm, where she met her first African-Americans, the household's indentured servants. *Hyland House: 203-453-9477; Griswold House: 203-453-3176 or 4666.*

Abandon US 1 in Guilford and take Route 146, which snakes along the coast between soothing marshes, passing the sandy outcrop of Leete's Island and teasing you with Sachem Head and the Thimble Islands, which seem within wading distance. Sachem Head earned its name when the Mohegan chief, Uncas, exhibited his enemy's head in a tree during the Pequot War, while Captain Kidd is reported to have buried treasure on the Thimble Islands in 1699. Stony Creek and tiny Branford Harbor afford some of the finest sea views, despite the fact that development straggles to the water's edge. It also extends inland to where the fine 1720 Nathaniel Harrison House seems marooned on Branford's Main Street; it would doubtless feel more welcome on the quiet town Green.

■ NEW HAVEN

New Haven and the surrounding territory were bought from the Quinnipiac tribe for the sum of 23 coats, 12 spoons, 24 knives, 12 hatchets, and assorted hoes when John Davenport and Theophilus Eaton settled here in 1638. To appreciate the bargain, take the Lighthouse Point Park exit off I-95 on the city's outskirts to the 82-acre preserve, which commands spectacular views of the bay, harbor, and city.

Two forts here—**Black Rock Fort,** dating to the Revolutionary War, and **Fort Nathan Hale,** dating to the Civil War—are reminders of New Haven's turbulent history. Three thousand British troops invaded the city in 1779, hoping to lure George Washington out of New York. They quickly retreated, having burned Black Rock Fort and the nearby **Pardee Morris House** *(at 325 Lighthouse Road),* which was rebuilt between 1780 and 1820 and is now the city's best-preserved 18th-century dwelling. *Black Rock Fort and Fort Nathan Hale: 203-946-8790; Pardee Morris House: 203-562-4183.*

◆ YALE UNIVERSITY

Swooping off I-95 to Yale University, you feel as if you have gone underwater. The traffic's roar is suddenly muffled and the light is greenish, leaf filtered. The true "haven" in New Haven, Yale's campus borders the 18-acre Green and seems hermetically sealed off from the surrounding, somewhat grim metropolis. Its buildings face each other, their backs to the 20th and 21st centuries. You should walk rather than drive around the small campus, starting at the **Yale Visitor Center,** on Elm Street, which is housed in the oldest of the three 18th-century wood-frame houses on the Green and provides parking and touring information; *203-432-2300.*

Founded in 1701 and permanently established here in 1717, Yale University is a pleasing arrangement of gothic tracery, grassy parks, and shady courtyards. **Phelps Gate,** facing the Green, leads to the Old Campus, built between 1842 and 1928. **Connecticut Hall** is the oldest university building, dating to 1717, but Yale's most ancient-looking buildings were in fact erected between 1919 and 1941.

Beinecke Library

The most alien and perhaps most architecturally honest presence here is also one of the most glorious—the Beinecke Rare Book and Manuscript Library, one of the largest in the world, housed in a massive block of Vermont marble and granite, bronze, and glass that is more starship than building. Huge "windows" of translucent marble protect the 180,000 volumes in the central tower, while more than 500,000 books and several million manuscripts reside underground. Padding around the bridge of the starship *Beinecke,* you circle this book aquarium, admiring particularly ancient bindings and titles while students in the reading room below peruse their daily catch, which is served up by library staff.

In addition to its astonishing general collection, the library also houses collections of Western Americana, German literature, and English literary and historical manuscripts. The Gutenberg Bible and Audubon's *Birds of America* are permanently displayed alongside special exhibitions. Research at the Beinecke may reveal why James Fenimore Cooper was expelled from Yale, why Sinclair Lewis briefly dropped out, and the secrets of other graduates such as Jonathan Edwards, Nathan Hale, and Thornton Wilder. Cole Porter, a cheerleader who graduated in 1913, once confessed "I delight in being chatty with New Haven's literati." *Beinecke: 121 Wall Street; 203-432-2977.*

Yale University Art Gallery and Theaters

A short stroll from Beinecke Library, the Yale University Art Gallery—the country's oldest university art museum—is quiet even on a busy August afternoon, and there is plenty of room to survey Picasso's *First Steps,* Van Gogh's *Night Cafe,* Seurat's tiny *Cow,* and other marvels, not all of them on canvas. The gallery's collection of American furniture and silver, for example, is outstanding. *On Chapel Street; 203-432-0600.*

Across the street, the **Yale Centre for British Art** will effortlessly steal your time and thoughts with its equally impressive collection of works by J. M. W. Turner, William Blake, Joshua Reynolds, Anthony van Dyck, Thomas Gainsborough, and others. The museum shop will also drive Anglophiles to distraction. The neighboring **Yale Repertory Theatre,** along with the 1914 **Shubert Performing Arts Center** (on nearby College Street), and the **Long Wharf Theatre** (on Sargent Drive) makes New Haven one of the region's richest theatrical venues.

◆ New Haven Sights

Once so elm-shaded that it earned New Haven the nickname "Elm City," the **Green** supports less majestic trees today and is bisected by heavy traffic. Its three 19th-century churches, however, are still glorious.

The Harkness Tower on the Yale University Campus. (photo by Robert Holmes)

To get a sense of New Haven's sedate past, follow Hillhouse Avenue north of the Green to the delightful **Peabody Museum of Natural History** at 170 Whitney Avenue, where a gigantic Brontosaurus skeleton dwarfs the other fine exhibits. A leisurely walk along one of the city's most splendid avenues also takes in the **Yale Collection of Musical Instruments** at 15 Hillhouse Avenue, on view from September through June; while farther down at 114 Whitney Avenue the **New Haven Colony Historical Society** displays Eli Whitney's cotton gin and other exhibits covering 350 years of the city's history. On the opposite side of the Green on Chapel Street, **Wooster Square Green** between Academy and Wooster Place is another architectural showplace enhanced in spring by flowering cherry trees.

A surprisingly short distance from downtown New Haven lies the **Sleeping Giant**, a 1,500-acre state park that follows the line of the city's surrounding volcanic hills and allows you to refill your lungs along a 32-mile trail of woodland and rock.

❖

An exploration of the back roads to the north reveals the intensifying, unequal struggle between land and concrete. Pockets of farmland, however, have survived the suburban pincer movement from New Haven and Hartford, particularly on Route 68 between Wallingford and pretty Durham, where the smell of manure still overpowers that of asphalt.

An early and rather fanciful rendition of New Haven's railroad station.

Frederic Church's West Rock at New Haven, *1849. (New Britain Museum of American Art, New Britain, Conn.)*

■ ABOUT THE WESTERN SHORE

Connecticut's western shore, from Milford to Greenwich, and the neighboring uplands between Danbury and Waterbury have, to a large extent, been mercilessly developed. Here only state parks, wildlife reservations, and increasingly rare stretches of farmland offer the breathing space that the Litchfield Hills so generously dispense. Even the back roads in this busy place too often reward the meandering visitor with views of spanking new 30-room mansions squatting on bare one-acre building lots. You will, however, be consoled when you drive along lovely Highway 8 south from Waterbury to Bridgeport and slip onto the even lovelier **Merritt Parkway**, which takes you westward to Norwalk. You may then veer northward to Danbury, digressing as you go.

◆ MERRITT PARKWAY *map page 256, A to C*

Route 95, running along the shore of Long Island Sound, looks tempting on the map but is more of an endurance test than a scenic treat. Take the beautiful Merritt Parkway (Highway 15) instead and deviate whenever necessary to explore the coastal towns. Opened in 1938 and restricted to automobiles, the exquisitely land-scaped parkway is such a leafy, shaded relief that you might easily stray into New York without noticing. On a late autumn day, showers of russet leaves bombard your windscreen, a plump woodchuck nibbles contentedly on the grass verge, and you have a sense of how the region's first highways looked when asphalt had just conquered clay.

To learn more about the parkway and to be assaulted by further vernal delights, visit **Boothe Memorial Park and Museum** in **Stratford**, where a Merritt Parkway tollbooth exhibit is among the many historical displays on the 32-acre former home-stead of the Boothe Family, who flourished here from 1663 to 1949. *Boothe Museum: 134 Main Street Putney, 203-381-2046. Open Tuesday and Friday, for tours only.*

A battle site in the Pequot War, Stratford preserves its Native American history in the local historical society, which adjoins the 18th-century Capt. David Judson House. *Stratford Historical Society: 967 Academy Hill; 203-378-0630.*

◆ FAIRFIELD *map page 256, C*

The Pequots fleeing west in 1639 were defeated in the Great Swamp outside pre-sent-day Fairfield and are commemorated with a granite monument marking the battle site in Southport on US 1. Later destroyed by Tryon's July 1779 raid (more than 100 Revolutionary soldiers are interred in the **Old Burying Ground** on Beach Road), Fairfield recovered to become a prosperous farming, whaling, and shipping center.

The town's **Southport Harbor** district contains nearly 200 houses built in the 18th and 19th centuries, and the historical society conducts walking tours as well as presenting 350 years of the port's life. The 18th-century **Ogden House** and 19th-century **Bronson Windmill**, both on Bronson Road, also reanimate a vibrant past. The region's natural history is explained in the **Connecticut Audubon Bird-craft Museum** on Unquowa Road, the country's first nature center, opened in 1914. *Fairfield Historical Society: 636 Old Post Road; 203-259-1598.*

◆ WESTPORT *map page 256, B*

Briefly forsaking the Merritt Parkway, you may follow US 1 to the affluent town of Westport, where upscale designer stores line the main thoroughfare and fragile-looking women drive four-wheel drive vehicles more suited to a safari than a shop-ping expedition. A long-established artist's and writer's retreat, Westport is not

The Easton Congregational Church in Fairfield County.

solely a spending opportunity. Various arts centers including the Westport Country Playhouse offer cultural distractions, while **Sherwood Island State Park** and the **Nature Center for Environmental Activities** provide the simpler pleasures of a solitary beach walk or a woodland ramble with live animal exhibits and an aquarium as a reward.

Bigger fish and mammals lurk at the **Maritime Aquarium** on North Water Street in Norwalk, which also allows you to watch fellow humans building boats.

◆ NORWALK *map page 256, B*

Settled in 1649, burned by Governor Tryon in 1779, and subsequently an important manufacturing center, Norwalk is not as elegant today as it was in 1864 when New York financier Le Grand Lockwood had his four-story, 50-room mansion built here on West Avenue at a cost of 1.2 million dollars. Approached in heavy traffic, on somewhat derelict streets, America's first chateau, with its elaborately stenciled walls, inlaid woodwork, and skylit rotunda seems glaringly—yet magnificently—out of place. Similarly, the WPA murals in City Hall on East Street, one of the country's largest collections, appear to be relics of a distant era.

Lockwood Mansion in Norwalk.

Commuters line the platform at the Greenwich train station.

Ocean Views and Ferry Rides

The restorative ocean is nearby, and practically any peninsula here affords lovely views of the islands scattered along the sound. To escape even more fully, board the ferry from Hope Dock in South Norwalk, which will take you on a soothing voyage to Sheffield Island Lighthouse, a three-acre park and wildlife sanctuary with a fine picnic area and 1868 lighthouse. *Norwalk Seaport Association: 203-838-9444.*

◆ DARIEN AND STAMFORD *map page 256, A*

Darien has the **Bates-Scofield Homestead** on the Old Kings Highway, a restored 1736 homestead that artfully evokes early Connecticut life, while Stamford has the **Museum and Nature Center,** a 118-acre park that demonstrates every imaginable form of 19th-century agriculture and devotes seven galleries to Native American cultures, fine art, Americana, and natural history. *Bates-Scofield: 45 Old Kings Highway North; 203-655-9233. Nature Center: 39 Scofieldtown Road; 203-322-1646.*

The first friction clutches, steam-powered wagons, and cylinder locks were Stamford inventions, and the Stamford Historical Society explains this history as well as offering tours of the 1699 Hoyt-Barnum House, a restored blacksmith's dwelling; *203-329-1183.*

◆ CHAMPION AND NORTH STAMFORD

The **Whitney Museum of American Art** at Champion is militantly modern, presenting 20th-century art drawn largely from the Whitney Museum of American Art in Manhattan. On a bright spring day, however, you may conclude that the blazing rhododendrons and wildflowers in the 63-acre **Bartlett Arboretum** outside North Stamford provide all the enlightenment you need. Even Eugene O'Neill may have found the spectacle cheering when he boarded at Stamford's Betts Academy for four years, but there is no evidence that the Arboretum did anything to ease tensions between Edmund Wilson and Mary McCarthy, who married here and remained until 1941. *Whitney Museum: One Champion Plaza; 203-358-7630. Bartlett Arboretum: 151 Brookdale Road; 203-322-6971.*

◆ GREENWICH *map page 256, A*

Stamford's wealthier neighbor, Greenwich has long attracted its share of writers. Ring Lardner and Willa Cather lived here, Truman Capote and Thomas Flanagan attended Greenwich High School, and Clare Boothe married Henry Luce in the First Congregational Church. The surrounding suburbs also provided the setting for novels and stories by Sloan Wilson, John Cheever, and Richard Yates. Greenwich's more distant history is recalled at the Putnam Cottage at 243 East Putnam Avenue; previously known as Knapp's Tavern, this was the site of Gen. Israel Putnam's daring escape from British dragoons in 1779 when he rode his horse over a cliff. The 18th-century Bush-Holley House was a boarding house for Connecticut's first art colony, and the exhibits here include a fine collection of American impressionist paintings. *Bush-Holley House: 39 Strickland Road; 203-869 6899.*

◆ NEW CANAAN *map page 256, B*

North of the Merritt Parkway, the rocky slopes and forested valleys of the uplands attracted land-hungry settlers in the 17th century, witnessed bloody skirmishes during the Revolutionary War, and later attracted writers and artists seeking rural rejuvenation. Leaving the Merritt Parkway to reach New Canaan, you see little evidence of any of these historical phases. But the **New Canaan Historical Society Museum** on Oenoke Ridge does a fine job of re-creating the town's 18th- and 19th-century past, in a complex of five buildings that contains seven museums and a library; *203-966-5598.*

BRIDGEPORT'S BARNUM MUSEUM

Bridgeport is a busy, somewhat chaotic city that requires all your navigational skills to reach your destination; finding the Barnum Museum, however, is easy. You simply follow the signs to the gloriously silly Romanesque building on Main Street where the line between bad taste and art is blithely erased. Built by Bridgeport resident Phineas Taylor Barnum in 1890, the museum is dedicated to inventors. "The Greatest Show on Earth" displays, among other things, an Egyptian mummy; a hand-carved, miniature five-ring circus with half a million figures; clown paraphernalia; and mementoes of Barnum, General Tom Thumb, and Jenny Lind. An oddly touching evocation of an era when most freaks appeared not on television but in traveling shows, the exhibits make even the most wary visitor's jaw drop, just as Barnum intended.

Known for his declaration that "everybody likes to be humbugged," the sensationalist was born in nearby Bethel in 1810. When he was 15, Barnum's father died, leaving Phineas to support his mother and five sisters and brothers. A few years later, he became publisher of a Danbury weekly newspaper, the *Herald of Freedom;* during his tenure there he was arrested three times for libel. In 1834 he purchased John Scudder's American Museum in New York City, and turned the five-story marble building into a theater for beauty contests, freak shows, and other outrageous events. First exhibiting Joyce Heth as George Washington's 160-year-old nurse (she died in 1836 at age 70), the showman achieved worldwide fame with General Tom Thumb, the 25-inch-high Charles Stratton, who was presented to Abraham Lincoln, Queen Victoria, and various European monarchs. In an effort to upgrade his public image, Barnum imported Swedish soprano Jenny Lind, and, without first seeing her or hearing her sing, dubbed her the "Swedish Nightingale" as part of a huge publicity campaign. After her nine-month concert tour in the United States, Jenny Lind was a household name and Barnum was an even richer man.

Meanwhile, Barnum served two terms in the Connecticut legislator and was elected mayor of Bridgeport, during which time he fought union discrimination against blacks, improved railroad service, expanded the harbor, and developed municipal parks. At his Bridgeport home, an ornate mansion he named Iranistan, he hosted visitors such as Mark Twain, Horace Greeley, and Matthew Arnold.

"The Greatest Show on Earth"—a combination of circus, freak show, and menagerie—was launched in 1871 and made Barnum's name known worldwide long before his death in 1891. Barnum and Charles Stratton are both buried in Bridgeport's Mountain Grove Cemetery on North Avenue. Alongside Stratton, who died at age 45 in 1883, is the body of the spouse who survived him by more than 30 years and who was interred in an infant casket beneath a tiny headstone that reads simply "Wife." *Barnum Museum: 820 Main Street; 203-331-9881.*

R H O D E   I S L A N D

■ TRAVEL BASICS

Coastal towns such as East Greenwich still feel more seafaring than
suburban, and the variety of restaurants, inns, and shops reveals a lively summer
tourist trade. Providence has one of the finest historic districts in the country, outstanding art museums, superb Italian food, and a lively arts scene centered on Brown
University and the Rhode Island School of Design. Southern Rhode Island, encircling
Narragansett Bay, has flawless white beaches, picturesque villages, outlandish mansions, and a worldwide sailing reputation. Historic Newport is the best-known attraction, but the quiet corners are equally charming: lovely towns like Wickford, the
sleepy Tiverton area, Jamestown Island beside Newport, and enchanting Block Island,
12 miles offshore.

Getting Around: There are regular bus, train, and air services to Rhode Island from
Boston and New York. Smaller coastal roads skirt Narragansett Bay as does the bicycle
route from East Providence to Bristol (this is ideal bicycling terrain). Take the ferry to
Block Island from Point Judith (401-783-4613), with seasonal sailings from Newport
and Providence. There is daily ferry service from Bristol to Prudence and Hog Islands;
401-253-9808.

Climate: Summer temperatures are in the 80s; spring and autumn are typically moderate, with temperatures in the 60s and 70s. In winter, temperatures can descend
below freezing, and Block Island is occasionally isolated by severe storms.

Food & Lodging: Restaurants and accommodations are as sophisticated or as plain as
you desire. In Newport B&B's are upscale, some being former gilded age mansions.
There are numerous culinary festivals throughout the year, and Providence has some
of the region's best food. Rhode Island listings begin on page 367; towns are in alphabetical order. Listings map on page 327; listings chart page 376.

RHODE ISLAND

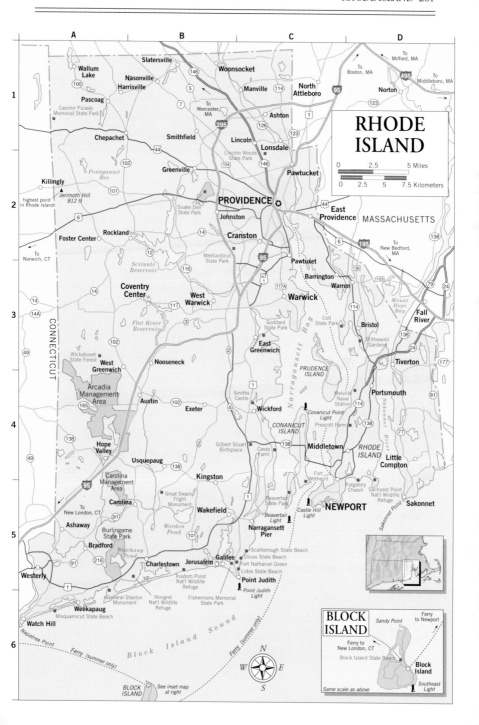

RHODE ISLAND

0	2.5		5 Miles
0	2.5	5	7.5 Kilometers

Slatersville
Woonsocket
Wallum Lake
Nasonville
Harrisville
Manville
North Attleboro
To Milford, MA
To Boston, MA
Norton
To Middleboro, MA
Pascoag
Ashton
Chepachet
Smithfield
Lincoln
Lonsdale
Casimir Pulaski Memorial State Park
Lincoln Woods State Park
Greenville
Pawtucket
Killingly
highest point in Rhode Island
Jerimoth Hill 812 ft
Ponaganset Res
Snake Den State Park
PROVIDENCE
Johnston
East Providence
MASSACHUSETTS
Foster Center
Rockland
Cranston
To Norwich, CT
CONNECTICUT
Meshanticut State Park
Pawtuxet
To New Bedford, MA
Barrington
Warren
Scituate Reservoir
Coventry Center
West Warwick
Warwick
Flat River Reservoir
Goddard State Park
Colt State Park
Bristol
Blithewold Gardens
Fall River
West Greenwich
Nooseneck
East Greenwich
PRUDENCE ISLAND
Tiverton
Wickaboxet State Forest
Arcadia Management Area
Austin
Exeter
Smiths Castle
Wickford
Melville Naval Station
Portsmouth
CONANICUT ISLAND
Conanicut Point Light
Prescott Farm
RHODE ISLAND
Little Compton
Hope Valley
Usquepaug
Gilbert Stuart Birthplace
Casey Farm
Middletown
Purgatory Chasm
Sachuest Point Nat'l Wildlife Refuge
Sakonnet
Carolina Management Area
Kingston
Fort Wetherill
Carolina
Great Swamp Flight Monument
Wakefield
Beavertail State Park
Castle Hill Light
NEWPORT
Ashaway
Burlingame State Park
Worden Pond
Beavertail Light
Narragansett Pier
Bradford
Watchaug Pond
Scarborough State Beach
Olivos State Beach
Fort Nathaniel Green
Lidos State Beach
Point Judith
Westerly
Charlestown
Jerusalem
Galilee
Trustom Pond Nat'l Wildlife Refuge
Point Judith Light
General Stanton Monument
Ninigret Nat'l Wildlife Refuge
Fishermans Memorial State Park
Weekapaug
Misquamicut State Beach
Watch Hill
Napatree Point
Block Island Sound
Ferry (summer only)
Ferry (summer only)

N
W E
S

BLOCK ISLAND
See inset map at right

BLOCK ISLAND

Sandy Point
Ferry to Newport
Ferry to New London, CT
Block Island State Beach
Block Island
Southeast Light
Same scale as above

■ OVERVIEW

"The sewer of New England," Cotton Mather called it—speaking as a 17th-century Puritan, not as a casual visitor. He was referring to Rhode Island—the Haight-Ashbury of the colonial era—later known as "Rogue's Island" and viewed as a low-lying sinkhole into which all New England wickedness and corruption drained. But even Mather might have softened had he spent time in this tiny, beautiful place.

Tucked unobtrusively into New England's southeast corner, the smallest state in the union is approximately 48 miles long and 37 miles wide. Texans point out that it would fit into Texas 200 times. They are, however, missing the point. Fitting in is not a Rhode Island characteristic, and the state pities giants like Texas who are practically landlocked by comparison.

The smallest state in the union contains, after all, 420 miles of coastline and New England's largest estuary. One-quarter of the nation's national historic landmarks and some of its most outrageous mansions are here. And those are just the physical paradoxes. There is also the fact that Rhode Island, founded on the principles of democracy and religious freedom, prospered from the slave trade.

Rhode Island would, of course, be easy to ignore. Just stay on Interstate 95 and you can pass through it in about an hour. Stray off the major highways, however, and this modest state has its sweet revenge, hypnotizing you with shimmering water and undulating meadows until it seems imperative that you wait for the sunset. And then for dawn.

■ HISTORY

Rhode Island's earliest English settlement was founded on principle by Roger Williams, who was banished from the Massachusetts Bay Colony in 1635 for opposing (among other things) the Crown's seizure of Native American lands. Williams established a settlement he named Providence, on land purchased from the Narragansetts. Later persuading the Narragansetts to support the colonists in the brutal Pequot War of 1636–37, Williams also provided a remarkable account of Native American life, in his *Key Into the Language of America*, published in 1643.

Committed from the outset to religious tolerance, Providence Plantation soon attracted dissenters like John Clarke and William Coddington, the pair who purchased Aquidneck Island in 1638 and called their settlement Portsmouth. When

Landing of Roger Williams *by Alonzo Chappel.*
(Museum of Art, Rhode Island School of Design)

visionary Massachusetts exile Anne Hutchinson arrived with her followers in Portsmouth the following year, Coddington, Clarke, and others moved on to settle Newport. In 1644, Aquidneck was renamed Rhode Island, perhaps harking back to an early navigator's observation that an island in the vicinity resembled the Greek island of Rhodes.

The first Quakers arrived in 1657 and the first Sephardic Jews came from Holland in 1658. The security of these settlers was later enhanced by the 1663 royal charter stating "that all and every person...may from tyme to tyme and at all tymes hereafter freelye and fullye enjoye his and their own judgements and consciences in matters of religious concernments."

With its superb harbors and flourishing settlements, Rhode Island developed a vibrant seafaring economy by the mid-17th century. By the mid-18th century, the infamous Triangle Trade in rum, molasses, and slaves had developed that economy

RHODE ISLAND

into a goldmine. Between the 1740s and '60s, Rhode Island's captains also made fortunes sailing as privateers during England's wars with France.

During the Revolutionary War, piracy became patriotism when Rhode Island's mariners attacked English ships, beginning in Newport when impressed sailors burned a Crown vessel in 1775. The first colony to react violently, Rhode Island was also the first to declare independence—in May, 1776—and it seems fitting that Paul Revere's horse was a Narragansett Pacer. Reports of the Battle of Lexington reached Rhode Island the night of Revere's ride, and the following morning saw 1,000 men ready to fight (a response that would be echoed almost a century later when Rhode Island citizens formed the first volunteer battery of the Civil War).

In 1793, Samuel Slater constructed the nation's first water-powered textile mill in Pawtucket. During the next century, Rhode Island would become one of the country's largest textile-producing states and one of its leading jewelry manufac-

The living room in the 1730 home of Captain Potter, slave trader and counterfeiter, along the Old Post Road south of Wakefield.

Young women sunbathe on Narragansett Beach in the 1930s. Despite appearances, the gal on the left is not known to be related to actor Bruce Willis. (Underwood Photo Archives, San Francisco)

turers. By 1910, when the population had grown to over 500,000, Rhode Island was an established summer destination not only for the new rich but for the growing middle class. By the mid-1930s, Rhode Island was the most highly industrialized state in the country, with over half its inhabitants engaged in manufacturing. The subsequent industrial decline has been followed by a sizeable growth in tourism.

■ BLACKSTONE RIVER VALLEY *map page 281, C-1*

The Blackstone River, which provided drinking water to the Narragansetts, doesn't look revolutionary. For much of its 46-mile course from Worcester, Massachusetts, to Providence, Rhode Island, the river behaves like any other lazy, occasionally restless waterway. When its falls turned the first wheels of the Industrial Revolution at Pawtucket, however, the Blackstone changed American life. And in northern Rhode Island, that change is still detectable as you drive a few miles from a tough-looking mill town like Woonsocket to nearby farming villages that still feel like backwaters.

Blackstone River Valley Heritage Corridor

Traveling south into Rhode Island from the Massachusetts border, you drive through one of the nation's most unusual state parks. Covering 250,000 acres between Worcester, Massachusetts, and Providence, the Blackstone River Valley Heritage Corridor encompasses not only marshes, meadows, and forests but also cities, towns, villages, and a half-million people. Here you may track turbines in the morning and woodcock in the afternoon, or board the riverboat *Explorer* for a Blackstone River cruise. *Blackstone Valley Tourism Council: 800-454-2882 or 401-724-2200.*

Slatersville

You won't find the turbines working at Slatersville, west of Woonsocket, where the forbidding mill building, dating to 1826, is now derelict. But the mill houses are still occupied in this pleasant green village where Samuel Slater of Pawtucket started his enterprise in 1805. Some of the details—the fanciful winged urns carved on the doorway at No. 20, for example—recall the inventiveness of the early industrial era. The area immediately east and south of Slatersville is, for the most part, an undramatic landscape of relatively poor farmland dotted with small mill towns like Harrisville and Foster, where hand-lettered signs announce the availability of "Creative Pies" and "Exotic Poultry."

Lime Rock Preserve

To escape the mechanical world for an hour or so, explore the **Lime Rock Preserve** on Wilbur Road, south of Woonsocket off Highway 146. A botanical powerhouse in late spring and early summer, this often soggy haven sits on huge outcrops of dolomite marble and supports delightful populations of lilies, ladyslippers, trilliums, baneberry, and other shy beauties.

Breakneck Hill Road

Farther south on Highway 146, take the ominously named Breakneck Hill Road exit and descend intact to the Great Road in Lincoln. Originally a Native American trail and one of the earliest roads built in America, the thoroughfare dates to the 1660s and retains its antique character. An hour is sufficient for a leisurely exploration, and should you consult a map in public, passing residents will likely spring to your assistance.

Lincoln

The **Eleazor Arnold House,** restored to its 1687 appearance, is Lincoln's oldest dwelling, and its tiny windows are worlds away from the grandeur of **Hearthside,** one of the state's finest Federal-style mansions and still a private residence. Thanks to a $50,000 win in the Louisiana lottery, Stephen H. Smith was able to commission this house near Breakneck Hill Road in 1810, when he was besotted with a woman who craved the grandest house in Rhode Island. Hearthside failed to impress, however, and Smith died a bachelor. Sublimely plain by comparison, the **Friends Meeting House** at 374 Great Road was built by the Quakers in 1704 and is New England's oldest meetinghouse in continuous use. Lincoln's agricultural tradition is preserved at the Chase Farm, purchased by the town in 1979, while noisier skills are demonstrated in the adjacent Hannaway Blacksmith Shop. *All three houses are located on Great Road, Lincoln's main street.*

Blackstone River State Park

Between Ashton and Lonsdale, Blackstone River State Park shadows the Blackstone River, incorporating one of the longest remaining sections of the Blackstone Canal. Dug by Irish immigrants between 1824 and 1828, the canal was once vital to the region's industrial growth, as evidenced by the textile mill and brick row houses in the town of Ashton. Today, however, walkers, cyclists, and canoeists are attracted to the tranquil three-mile stretch that is shaded by some of the state's largest sycamores. *East of Lincoln off Route 122.*

William Blackstone Memorial Park

Blackstone Park, just north of Lonsdale off Route 114, honors Rhode Island's first white settler, an Anglican clergyman who came to present-day Valley Falls in 1635 and is credited with planting the first orchards in Rhode Island and Massachusetts. Although somewhat reclusive, Blackstone is also said to have traveled the countryside on a white bull, dispensing apples to astonished children.

Pawtucket

To the Narragansetts, Pawtucket had always meant "the place by the waterfall," a favorite fishing and camping ground. To Samuel Slater, arriving in 1790, it meant money. A former manager in England's innovative Arwright Mills, Slater constructed America's first successful water-powered cotton-spinning mill at the Pawtucket Falls in 1793 and initiated one of the biggest transformations in American society. Today the hilly city that grew up around the textile industry exhibits the signs of subsequent industrial decline.

Even if Pawtucket is fractured and faded, the Blackstone River still roars impressively at the **Slater Mill Historic Site** on Roosevelt Avenue. The birthplace of American industry, on the other hand, is surprisingly demure. Comprising the 1793 Slater Mill, the 1810 Wilkinson Mill, and the 1758 Sylvanus Brown House (moved to the site in the 1960s), the complex would fit in one corner of one of Lowell's mills; *800-454-2882.*

■ PROVIDENCE

Viewed from the scrambled heights of Interstate 95, Providence looks unappealing—especially at rush hour, when the city's sluggish digestive system stalls and you can be trapped in one section of its intestine for hours. Interminable construction projects also give you a misleading sense of sprawl. At street level, however, Providence is a relatively small, compact metropolis. Its chief attractions—Benefit Street, Federal Hill, the State Capitol, and the waterfront area—are within walking distance of one another; following the example of the Independent Man astride the State Capitol, you should liberate yourself from your car and proceed on foot as soon as you reach the center of town.

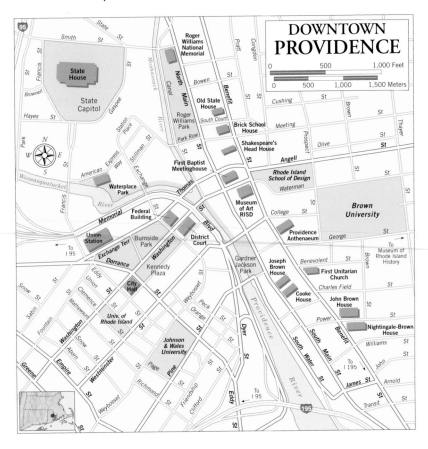

The College Hill and Benefit Street districts are reflected across Waterplace Park.

To escape I-95, take the Memorial Boulevard exit and cross the river to the historic Benefit Street district. Two streets uphill from Benefit Street on Congdon Street is Prospect Terrace, the burial place of Roger Williams, and a small 1930s WPA park that offers a superb view of the city below. You may even find an unrestricted parking place on the street.

◆ PROSPECT HILL

Providence is built on three steep inclines, and the earliest English settlement arose on the slopes of Prospect or College Hill, above Benefit Street. Today, this is one of America's loveliest historic neighborhoods, rivaling Boston's Beacon Hill and Salem's Chestnut Street. Beyond appreciating the astonishing variety and beauty of the architecture—from early-18th-century houses, mansions, and churches to Brown University's 19th-century campus—you can also take buoyant pleasure in strolling at such an airy height in a place that seems to truly enjoy its visitors. Walking south along Benefit Street from its intersection with Jenckes Street, for example, you notice that even the dignified State Capitol across the river cannot resist playing peekaboo, filling each gap between the houses with its enormous white dome.

RHODE ISLAND

88 Benefit Street

Tree-lined, brick-paved, and entirely golden on an autumn morning, Benefit Street forbids you to hurry. Edgar Allan Poe learned how to linger in the garden of No. 88, at the corner of Church Street, when it was the home of Sarah Helen Whitman. Poe's stories caused Whitman "a sensation of such intense horror that I dared neither look at anything he had written nor even utter his name." She did, however, send him a poem. Vowing "never again to taste wine" and having attempted suicide in despair of winning her, Poe won a betrothal to Whitman in 1848 after an intense courtship in Providence. His "To Helen" and "Annabel Lee" are Whitman-inspired. But the engagement

Benefit Street near Brown University.

was short-lived, and within one year of his disappointment, Poe was dead. It is easy to imagine the rejected suitor, hurrying blindly down Church Street to the river, the poetic scar tissue already forming over his romantic wound.

Roger Williams National Memorial

Roger Williams would probably have advised Poe to get on with things (see above). Williams was that sort of chap, you can conclude from the video presentations and publications at the Roger Williams Memorial; *office on North Main Street at the foot of Smith Street; 401-521-7266.*

Ejected from the Massachusetts Bay Colony in 1635 and paddling his canoe down the Seekonk River a year later, the robust dissenter settled near a spring on the site of the present memorial. "Having a sense of God's merciful providence unto me called this place Providence," Williams later wrote, "I desired it might be for a shelter for persons distressed for conscience." On a visit to England, Williams met John Milton and Oliver Cromwell, whose influence may be discerned in Williams's plea for religious and political freedom, *The Bloudy Tenent of Persecution* (1644). One early convert to Williams's views was the Rev. Chad Browne, who arrived in Provincetown in 1638 and whose descendants would become the city's most prominent citizens. Roger Williams's house is believed to have stood opposite the park on North Main Street, where a plaque commemorates the site.

Old State House

Back on Benefit Street, you soon reach the 1762 Old State House, which was the seat of state government until 1904 and now houses the Rhode Island Historical Preservation and Heritage Commission. On May 4, 1776, Rhode Island renounced its allegiance to the Crown here; George Washington, Thomas Jefferson, and Marquis de Lafayette were later entertained here. The Old Senate Chamber on the second floor is the only one retaining its 1762 appearance. *150 Benefit Street; 401-222-2678.*

"Shunned House"

A short distance away, 135 Benefit Street is known as the "Shunned House" thanks to horror writer H. P. Lovecraft. The writer was born at 454 Angell Street (in 1890) but set one of his most famous stories here. Following the 1926 failure of his marriage, Lovecraft lived with his aunt at 1012 Barnes Street, where he wrote "The Dunwich Horror" and other "tales of fantasy and supernatural horror." His final dwelling now stands at 65 Prospect Street, at the corner of Meeting Street, and he is buried at Swan Point Cemetery on Blackstone Boulevard, beneath a gravestone proclaiming "I Am Providence."

Historic School and House

The small Brick School House on Meeting Street played a Revolutionary War role, serving as a munitions dump and as a Brown University classroom when French troops occupied the campus.

The Old State House, partially obscured by a modern office building.

On the opposite side of the street, the equally modest Shakespeare's Head House was built in 1763 and used as the print shop for the *Providence Gazette,* the city's first newspaper.

First Baptist Meetinghouse

Roger Williams founded the country's first Baptist congregation in 1639, although he later became disillusioned with all organized faiths and died an unrepentant "seeker." The glorious First Baptist Meetinghouse was built in 1775 as the third building to be used by Providence's Baptist community. *75 North Main Street, extending to Benefit Street.*

RISD Area

The early center of Providence's costume-jewelry industry, Waterman and Thomas Streets later became the city's 19th-century arts district, a development that is most whimsically commemorated in the 1885 medieval-style Fleur-de-Lys building at 7 Thomas Street and perpetuated at the **Rhode Island School of Design**, or RISD (pronounced "Rizdee"). The school constructed its Venetian fantasy at 11 Waterman Street in 1893 and has subsequently expanded its presence without dwarfing its neighbors on Benefit Street and the surrounding hillsides; *401-454-6100.*

The RISD **Museum of Art** houses a collection that ranges from the ancient, medieval, and Renaissance eras to the present, and includes one of the world's largest Buddhas, galleries of impressionist paintings, and outstanding period furniture. The museum presents a deceptively modest face to the street. But don't be misled by the shallow entrance pavilion. This is in fact a five-story establishment making clever use of its hillside site. *224 Benefit Street; 401-454-6500.*

Providence Athenaeum

You can see what attracted Edgar Allan Poe and Sarah Helen Whitman to the Providence Athenaeum the moment you enter the cozy temple. On a raw November afternoon, the warmly lit corners and reading galleries invite a prolonged stay and whispered confidences. Founded in 1753, this is one of the nation's oldest libraries; its other famous but unromantically linked visitors include John James Audubon, Bronson Alcott, Ralph Waldo Emerson, Henry Wadsworth Longfellow, Jacqueline Onassis, and Archbishop Desmond Tutu. *251 Benefit Street; 401-421-6970.*

After the intimacy of the Athenaeum, the splendid **First Unitarian Church** on Benefit Street, built in 1816 and combining Renaissance and Federal elements, seems almost melodramatic. This prepares you somewhat for the sight of its neighbor—the **John Brown House**, which occupies the corner of Benefit and Power Streets.

John Brown House

One of the country's finest 18th-century residences, this is also one of the few still flanked by tall elms. John Quincy judged it to be "the most magnificent and elegant private mansion that I have ever seen on this continent," a conclusion that would doubtless have pleased its first owner.

A large, energetic, ruthless, and, one suspects, eminently dislikable person, Brown died in 1803 leaving an estate valued at $600,000—most of it from the West Indies and China trade and from privateering. Referring to himself as "the cleverest boy in town," Brown monitored his ships entering the harbor below as he surrounded himself with the finest available furniture from America and Europe, much of which is still displayed. A man of action as well as guile, he led the 1772 raid on the English revenue ship *Gaspee* seven miles south of Providence, burning it and emerging with

The spire of the First Baptist Meetinghouse towers over the College Hill area

souvenirs, among them six silver wine goblets now on display in the house. The city still celebrates **Gaspee Days** with parades, a colonial muster, and a gala ball, all during May and June.

Tours of the Brown House are informative, lively, and honest. Brown's lengthy involvement in the slave trade, for example, is candidly discussed, as is the lawsuit initiated by abolitionist Moses Brown against his brother when John continued to import slaves after such trade was outlawed by Congress in 1807. But it is hard to imagine the era's misery when you contemplate the beauty of a unique 18th-century nine-shell desk and bookcase by Robert Townsend or the perfect sweep of the elaborate staircase. Traces of the house's subsequent owners remain, most noticeably in the exotic bathroom additions by utility tycoon Marsden J. Perry, who reportedly entertained Sophie Tucker and other spirited ladies here. *52 Power Street (at Benefit); 401-331-8575.*

Other Houses of Note

The John Brown House has competition at the southern end of Benefit Street, where its substantial neighbors make the earlier houses you have passed seem fragile by comparison. The most striking include the **General Ambrose Burnside House** at 314, curving sinuously around its hilly corner; the lovely **Nightingale-Brown House** at 357, another Brown residence; and the **Thomas F. Hoppin House** at 383, an Italianate palazzo built for the painter and sculptor who died in 1873.

◆ BROWN UNIVERSITY

Much of this neighborhood's vitality is attributable to Brown University. Founded in nearby Warren in 1764 and moved here in 1770, Brown now dominates College Hill. Along with RISD, the university is chiefly responsible for the unlikely sight of body-pierced youth emerging from some of the nation's most decorous buildings. An airier place than low-lying Yale or Harvard, Brown has a pleasantly windblown atmosphere. And on a blustery autumn afternoon, when leaves rush the Van Wickle Gates, the harmonious buildings lining College Green seem to be the only things tethering the campus to the ground.

The 1904 **John Carter Brown Library** is considered the university's jewel, but University Hall is its oldest building, dating to 1770 and used to billet American and French troops during the Revolution. A collection of American art and printed ephemera is on display at the **Annmary Brown Memorial** on Brown Street.

Humorist S. J. Perelman grew up in Providence, graduated from Brown University in 1925, and later married Laura West, sister of his college friend Nathanael West. Perelman went on to write for the Marx Brothers in Hollywood and later for

Banners announce upcoming events at Brown University.

The New Yorker magazine. "From the moment I picked up your book until I put it down, I was convulsed with laughter," Groucho Marx wrote in a blurb for Perelman's *Dawn Ginsbergh's Revenge,* "Some day I intend reading it."

A short walk away, the **Museum of Rhode Island History** presents changing exhibits in four galleries where past subjects have ranged from World War II veterans to the evolution of diners in Providence. *110 Benevolent Street; 401-331-8575.*

◆ FEDERAL HILL AND ATWELL'S AVENUE

If the mention of food—even ancient food—has a predictable effect, cross the river to Federal Hill, Providence's Italian-American neighborhood. Running the gauntlet of impatient traffic and "urban renewal" is worthwhile when you reach Atwell's Avenue and pass underneath the neighborhood's enormous pinecone-topped arch. Italians began arriving here in the late 19th century, but the largest immigration occurred between 1900 and 1915, when natives chiefly of Naples, Palermo, Campobasso, and Frosinone formed the tight, influential communities that flourish in a city proud of its Italian influence. There are even gondolas on the river at the Waterplace downtown.

On Atwell's Avenue you may eat, shop for plaster saints and smoky chianti, speak Italian, and contemplate some of the finest hairstyles in town. The doorman at **The Blue Grotto** restaurant is sure to have a prize-winning look. But the coiffed grandmother presiding over a family lunch party at **Angelo's Civita Farnese** is also in the running. Angelo's is a noisy, no-frills place that has valet parking because it makes sense, not because it makes an impression. **L'Epicureo,** farther up the avenue, started out as a butcher shop and is now one of Providence's most sophisticated bistros. But wherever you stop on "the Avenue" you will be hard-pressed to find bad food. Eating is not your only duty here. There are bakeries, food markets, and wine stores to be inspected, among them **Venda Ravioli,** an irresistible food store at 265 Atwell's, and, at 361 Atwell's, **Gasbarro's,** which boasts one of the best Italian wine selections in the country. *Venda Ravioli: 401-421-9105; Gasbarro's: 401-421-4170.*

An Italian-owned Federal Hill grocery, circa 1920. (Courtesy of Joe Fuoco)

Saturday evening bonfires blaze along Providence's river walk. (photo by Carol Glover)

◆ STATE CAPITOL

"There was nothing you could do about anything, but then nothing was so bad that you felt a burning urge to do anything about it," A. J. Liebling wrote of Providence when he began working here as a journalist. He was referring to the city's often scandalous government, which typically behaved as if it were auditioning for the role of colorful thug in a bad Hollywood movie. The luminous State Capitol, however, shows no signs of ethical wear and tear. Completed in 1904, this giant supports the second largest dome in the world (after Saint Peter's in Rome) and floats its marble balloon alongside the highrises studding the skyline.

◆ WATERPLACE PARK

Not all Providence's energies have been directed skyward. In recent years the city uncovered, redirected, and landscaped the Woonasquatucket, Moshassuck, and Providence Rivers. Formerly paved over, these now constitute a delightful river walk that begins at **Waterplace Park**, a four-acre natural amphitheater below the State Capitol. This is also where the river blazes on Saturday evenings throughout the summer, lit by at least 40 bonfires that appear to float rather disturbingly on its surface; *401-621-1992.*

RHODE ISLAND

◆ ROGER WILLIAMS PARK AND ZOO

Children and nervous adults will prefer the reassuringly natural spectacles at the Roger Williams Park and Zoo, where polar bears, giraffes, and other creatures perform the usual exercise routines. A beautiful as well as an entertaining place, the park covers 430 acres and includes an 1896 casino, an antique carousel, the Museum of Natural History, a Queen Anne–style boathouse, and the Benedict Temple to Music, where outdoor concerts are held in summer. *1000 Elmwood Avenue; recorded directions at 401-785-3510.*

■ BIKE ROUTES AND BRISTOL *map page 281, D-3*

The Providence suburbs extend south to East Greenwich and across to the East Bay. There are, however, welcome interruptions along the way. Pawtuxet, Warwick, and East Greenwich provide a variety of townscapes, ranging from colonial to 19th-century, while the **14-mile bike route** along Narragansett Bay from Providence to Bristol presents you with undemanding gradient and superb watery views.

No matter how much you enjoy the bicycle route, it is a relief to reach Bristol, a genteel yet lively sailing town at the tip of the East Bay, and to discover that refreshments are taken seriously in its High Street coffee shops and waterfront pubs. Freewheeling past the 18th-century mansions on Hope, High, and Thames Streets, you also realize that Bristol has always taken profit seriously—much of it derived from the slave trade.

According to some estimates, over a fifth of all slaves crossed the Atlantic to colonial America in Rhode Island vessels—and Bristol slavers carried the largest percentage of that cargo. James DeWolf, owner of a Cuban sugar plantation, was one of the town's richest captains, and the house at 56 High Street (private) was built in 1793 to showcase his wealth.

If thoughts of the DeWolfs and their associates cast a gloomy shadow on your view of Narragansett Bay and Prudence Island, head down to the water and the **Herreshoff Marine Museum**, where the story is more uplifting. Struck blind at 18 years of age, John Brown Herreshoff nevertheless continued as a boatbuilder, establishing his Burnside yard in 1863 at the age of 22. Equipped with a phenomenal memory and a pictorial imagination, he dictated specifications to his brother, Nathaniel, who did the handwork, and established a name that later became synonymous with America's Cup defenders. The museum displays a unique collection of 50 classic sailing and power vessels built between 1859 and 1947. *One Burnside Street; 401-253-5000.*

To limber up for your 14-mile bike ride back to Providence, try the more merciful bike path in the **Colt State Park,** off Route 114, where a three-mile drive follows the shoreline of the former Colt family estate. Or stroll down the wooded path at **Blithewold Mansion,** which is graced with a Japanese water garden and the largest redwood tree east of the Rockies. From a small wooden landing at Blithewold, you may observe the sea dousing the setting sun and cormorants hurrying home from a day's gluttony. *101 Ferry Road; 401-253-2707.*

■ ABOUT SOUTHERN RHODE ISLAND

From Sakonnet Point in the east to Watch Hill in the west, it is as if salt water has selected this place as the laboratory for its myriad experiments. Forming tidal ponds, tidal rivers, salt marshes, coves, and inlets, the Atlantic tirelessly inserts itself into every scene and activity. Even grass-loving cattle stare longingly at the waves here, preparing themselves perhaps for the day when water vanquishes their pastures and they can set sail.

Travel in these areas is a pleasantly circular business as you meander from Bristol across to Little Compton and back to the mainland, or from Newport to Watch Hill, before losing your mind—in the best possible sense—on Block Island.

■ TIVERTON AREA *map page 281, D-3 to D-5*

There should be a flashing sign on the Sakonnet Bridge warning you of the outrageous beauty ahead in Tiverton and Little Compton. What looks like a bland cutlet of land terminating in the bony tip of Sakonnet Point is, in fact, Rhode Island's most bewitching mainland secret. You suspect as much when you are halfway across the Sakonnet River. Below you swans glide through the reeds, yachts balance on mirror-still water, and tree-fringed meadows roll their way into neighboring Massachusetts.

In spring and autumn particularly, this quiet corner has the pleasingly schizophrenic look of a farming community that would rather be fishing. As you follow Route 77 south along the coast from Tiverton, you notice upturned boats grazing alongside dairy cattle in the fields or sunbathing on grassy hillocks. Few traces of the once thriving textile industry remain. It is equally hard to imagine the charming fishing village of Tiverton in tumult. During the Revolutionary War, however, this was a mustering point for colonial soldiers and the site of Maj. Silas Talbot's daring capture of *Pigot,* a 200-ton British galley humiliated by Talbot's small sloop.

◆ CYCLING COUNTRY

This is perfect cycling country for those with scenic rather than aerobic tastes. To sample one of the most pleasing routes, turn left onto Neck Road at Tiverton Four Corners, circle Nonquit Pond, and branch out onto beautiful Fogland Point before returning to Route 77 on Pond Bridge Road. You may even bicycle the 25 miles from Tiverton to Little Compton in about four hours without suffering. None of which is painful enough to earn you a glass of **Sakonnet Vineyard** estate wine in Little Compton. But New England's largest winery doesn't care. Ignoring your mileage and your pulse rate, it offers generous tastings, informative tours, cooking classes, even bed-and-breakfast accommodations. *162 West Main Road; 401-635-8486.*

◆ LITTLE COMPTON *map page 281, D-4*

The road from Sakonnet Vineyard to Sakonnet Point passes 18th-century houses and modest farms before reaching Little Compton, a dormant town with a graveyard at its center. Note the gravestone to "Elizabeth, who should have been the wife of Simeon Palmer"—a caustic reference by her husband to the fact that Elizabeth confined herself to housekeeping. The grave of renowned Indian fighter Benjamin Church recalls the important role played by this region in King Philip's War, first when "squaw-sachem" Awashonks signed a peace compact with the British in 1675 and later when Church led the small group that captured Metacom.

Fishing boats and modest summer houses huddle around Sakonnet Harbor, and beyond it the wind-whipped outcrop of Sakonnet Point holds its own against the encroaching ocean. When you turn inland toward Adamsville the water seems to follow you, creating marshes and ponds that glint through the trees and punctuate the meadows. Pay your respects to the Rhode Island Red hen, imported from China then developed in Little Compton in the 1850s and commemorated with a bronze plaque in the center of Adamsville. Then follow Route 81 north, skirting Stafford Pond and returning via Newport to explore Conanicut Island, South County, and Block Island.

RHODE ISLAND

■ PORTSMOUTH *map page 281, D-4*

Banished from the Massachusetts Bay Colony in 1637 for "the troublesomeness of her spirit," Anne Hutchinson reached Portsmouth in 1638, accompanied by her husband, her 16 children, and numerous followers. Established the previous year by John Clarke and William Coddington, the settlement pledged that no inhabitant would be found "a delinquent for doctrine" and began a pleasantly sleepy existence, interrupted most notably by the Battle of Rhode Island in 1778. Historical markers indicate battle sites and the earliest encampment at Founder's Brook (near the intersection of Boyd's Lane and Highway 24). Portsmouth retains its soporific properties. The windsurfers off Sandy Point Beach seem to bob rather than scoot, and in the **Green Animals Topiary Garden** (380 Cory's Lane off Route 114), the elephants, giraffes, and other sculpted creatures require little stalking.

South of Portsmouth the road runs through acres of corn and nursery plantations. Plowed fields slope down to the sea and **Glen Farm** gives you a sense of an 18th-century Rhode Island plantation. Now a public sports ground complete with polo field, the estate retains the lovely tree-lined avenues and broad, level fields that characterized the colonial landscape; *on the right off Glen Road, outside Portsmouth; look for signs; 401-846-0200.*

■ MIDDLETOWN AREA *map page 281, C-4*

Middletown has long been a transcendent place. Bishop George Berkeley, one of the fathers of metaphysical philosophy, lived here from 1729 to 1731, and the **Whitehall Farm Museum** evokes not only his life but the turbulent Revolutionary days when Whitehall served as tavern and billet for British soldiers. *311 Berkeley Avenue; call for directions; 401-846-3116.*

Another rich view of colonial agrarian life is provided at **Prescott Farm**, on Middletown's West Main Road.

To awaken your own metaphysical insights, spend hours exploring the astonishing watery terrain of the **Norman Bird Sanctuary, Sachuest Point National Wildlife Refuge,** and **Purgatory Chasm,** all in the Middletown area. The 450-acre bird sanctuary encircles tiny ponds and jabs the ocean with its rocky fingers, while Sachuest's peninsula juts defiantly into Rhode Island Sound. Fleets of migrating waterfowl crowd these preserves in spring and autumn, while the 150-foot Purgatory Chasm to the west attracts daring humans who enjoy watching the ocean's perpetual assault on this narrow gorge. *Norman Bird Sanctuary: 401-846-2577.*

❖

Between Middletown and Newport, Route 138 is a wasteland of strip malls and fast-food outlets. **Tommy's Diner**, a lovely example of its exuberant species, is the only redeeming feature. *159 E. Main Road (Route 138).*

■ NEWPORT

Between May and September each year, Newport's population of 28,227 quadruples and the seaport is swamped by visitors drawn to its mansions and upscale shopping precincts. There is much more to Newport than either of those attractions, however, and to explore the small, fascinating town in comfort you should arrive in early spring or late autumn. Roses bloom here into late November, after all, and the housemaid's welcome at the Astor's Beechwood mansion is still warm in February.

A bird's-eye view of Newport, circa 1878. (Library of Congress)

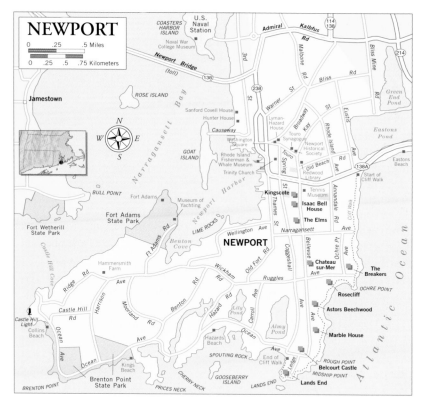

Museum of Newport History

The Museum of Newport History is a good starting point. It is not simply the superb nautical, military, artistic, and social exhibits but the voices resonating throughout the building that bring Newport's history to life. Pick up a headset to listen to Doctor Ezra Stiles and Mary Gould Almy reacting passionately in their diaries to the Revolutionary War siege that lasted from 1776 to 1780. Examining a land deed signed by William and Mary Dyer in 1644, you hear Roger Williams describing Narragansett customs, Anne Hutchinson questioning authority, and Mary Dyer defending her Quaker beliefs before being hanged on Boston Common in 1660. For light relief, you may then board a reproduction of an 1890s omnibus for a video tour of Bellevue Avenue and its palaces. *127 Thames Street at Washington Square; 401-841-8770.*

Armed with the museum's **walking tour maps**, you may choose a theme—colonial Newport, seafaring, religion—and follow its trail only to be distracted at every turn by overlapping history and humorous incongruity.

Friends Meeting House

The Friends Meeting House, for example, which dominates the corner of Farewell and Marlborough Streets, has Ruby's tattoo parlor as a neighbor. Newport's oldest religious building, the Meeting House dates to 1699 and is an elegant reminder not only of the town's religious tolerance but of the Quakers' status as the dominant religious group during the colony's first 100 years. Their numbers declined by 1840 to approximately 1,000 statewide, a fact that drew wry comment from the 1842 *Dublin University Review*. "Rhode Island has been urged by the other states to co-operate with them in expelling Quakerism," the review observed, "They declined on the following grounds: The Quakers were a people that delighted to encounter persecution, and quickly sickened of a patient audience; and had already begun to loathe Rhode Island as a place where their talent for patient suffering was completely buried."

Opposite the Meeting House, at 26 Marlborough Street, is the **White Horse Tavern**, which opened its doors to the thirsty public in 1673 and is the oldest surviving tavern in the United States; its dark, creaky interior still has an anaesthetic effect. Carpenters working on the nearby **Wanton-Lyman-Hazard House** in the 1690s, perhaps cheered by the tavern's proximity, built a house that seems genial today and uninflated by its status as Newport's oldest house. *17 Broadway.*

Touro Synagogue

The first Jews arrived in Newport from Spain and Portugal in 1658. Built in 1763, the Touro Synagogue is the oldest in North America and one where Sephardic ritual is still followed. When George Washington addressed the newly enfranchised congregation here in 1790, he pledged that independent America "gives to bigotry no sanction, to persecution no assistance." But the Revolution ruined the fortunes of shipping magnates like Aaron Lopez, and many Jewish families left Newport during the turmoil. Closed in the early 19th century, Touro Synagogue reopened in 1883 when industrial expansion attracted new Jewish immigrants. *85 Touro Street; 401-847-4794.*

Newport Historical Society

The historical society is a fine research and exhibition center incorporating the Seventh Day Baptist Meeting House, built in 1729 by Richard Munday, who went on to design the glorious 1739 Old Colony House at the center of town. *82 Touro Street; 401-846-0813.*

Perry Mansion

The Perry Mansion, at 29 Touro Street, was the Newport residence of naval hero Oliver Hazard Perry, who is now commemorated with a statue in Washington Square. The house became an African-American restaurant around 1900. Like most of its neighbors, it is now a private residence.

Trinity Church

Intersecting at odd angles and rambling down toward the water, the tangle of streets winding around the historical society seems to hoard the afternoon light, particularly in late autumn when the spire of Trinity Church appears spotlit. Built by Richard Munday in 1725 and regarded as one of the nation's finest colonial churches, Trinity was modeled on Boston's Old North Church, and its triple-decker pulpit is the only one remaining from that period. *Spring Street at Queen Anne Square.*

Spring Street Houses

Winding thoroughfares illustrate Newport's rapid growth from settlement to seaport. Spring Street's outstanding 18th-century residences, for example, include the **Bull-Mawdsley House** (No. 228), the original rear section of which dates to the late 17th century, and the far grander **Redwood House** (No. 69), home of merchant and sugar baron Abraham Redwood. In 1766 Redwood owned 238 slaves, most of whom worked on his Antiguan sugar plantation. By the mid-18th century, Newport slaves were permitted to hold elections for a black governor in Liberty Tree Park, at the intersection of Thames and Farewell Streets, which is still a park today.

Thames Street

Littered today with specialty stores and restaurants, Thames Street nevertheless retains its anarchic waterfront character. Home first to colonial artisans, the neighborhood soon attracted sea captains. The **Francis Malbone House** (No. 392) built around 1758, is a fine example of a merchant townhouse, while the early-19th-century **Samuel Whitehorne Museum** epitomizes the popular Federal style.

Chopped up for firewood during the Revolutionary War siege, Newport's crowded wharves may resemble malls on stilts today. But there are genuinely nautical things happening at the **International Yacht Restoration School**, which welcomes visitors to its premises at 449 Thames Street. There is also genuinely good seafood in oilcloth-and-ketchup-bottle-style upstairs at **Salas's** restaurant. *I.Y.R.S.: 401-848-5777.*

RI Fishermen and Whale Museum

Equipped with such ballast, you might want to try piloting a fishing boat at the Rhode Island Fishermen and Whale Museum, where visitors may handle the whale skeletons; *Bowen's Wharf; 401-849-1340.*

Washington Square

Washington Square, above Long Wharf, is Newport's center today as it was in the colonial era, although its modern activities and establishments might confound Oliver Hazard Perry, who died at the age of 34 from yellow fever and who oversees town business from his pedestal in the park. Some things, however, he would surely condone: the outstanding blueberry muffins and breakfast specials at **Ocean Coffee Roasters,** for example, and the superb pints of Guinness at **Aidans.** And much of Washington Square, previously known as the Parade, would be familiar to him. The exquisite Colony House—considered one of the nation's oldest capitol buildings—still dominates the scene from all angles. The **Rivera House,** 18th-century home of the whale-oil tycoon Abraham Rodriguez Rivera, still stands as the Newport National Bank, and the charming house beside the Jane Pickens Theater has settled so comfortably on its 18th-century foundations that its facade now balloons exuberantly out onto the street and its windows seem ready to pop.

Hunter House

It is just like Newport, somehow, to surprise you with an antiquated baseball field—Cardines Field on America's Cup Avenue—as you head toward the Hunter House, one of the nation's finest 18th-century mansions.

Built in 1784, the Georgian house was home to Lt. Governor Wanton and later the headquarters of French admiral le Ternay, who died here during the Revolution.

Many of the its neighbors on Washington Street have been sacrificed to crass waterfront development, but nothing can diminish the restrained elegance of the Hunter House and gardens and the playful eccentricity of the carved pineapple over the doorway. This popular symbol of hospitality originated when colonial sea captains signaled their return by placing a fresh pineapple outside the house to declare an open house. Today, visitors who left winter behind them that morning in Massachusetts are similarly amazed to see roses blooming here beside the water. *54 Washington Street; 401-847-1000.*

Thames Street in Newport. (above)
Trinity Church stands in the center of old Newport. (opposite)

Redwood Library

Fortunately for Newport, the new rich who arrived here during the 19th century's Gilded Age had little interest in the old town, which was consequently spared their improving zeal. They preferred to indulge their tastes on Bellevue, Ocean, and Harrison Avenues, where several existing buildings bolstered their aristocratic fantasies. The Redwood Library is a magnificent example.

Established in 1747, this is one of the nation's oldest libraries and one guaranteed to delight bibliophiles who resent the encroachment of computer banks, videos, and gourmet coffees onto bookshelves nationwide. There are no videos in the Redwood. There are, however, outstanding special collections that include the library's original volumes from 1749, a world-renowned collection on 18th-century furniture and decorative arts, and a Venetian Bible from 1487. Superb 18th- and 19th-century portraits line the walls. Nonetheless, the atmosphere is that of a friendly rather than a rarefied lending library.

Understanding staff smile reassuringly as you attempt to hug the card catalog. They beam when you are struck dumb by the intricate beauty of the Claggett clock that was manufactured in 1728 and marks not only the time but days of the week, phases of the moon, high tides, and other influences; they love you to ask about its repeater chord. Cool off in the library's charming gardens and contemplate what is surely one of the nation's finest colonial exteriors. *50 Bellevue Avenue; 401-847-0292.*

♦ NEWPORT TENNIS

The Spanish tennis champion Arantxa Sanchez Vicario once declared that "grass is for cows." But the green heart of the Newport Casino, on Bellevue Avenue, was planted for sporting rather than agricultural purposes. American tournament tennis was born on these grass courts in 1881, and impeccably clad Lawn Tennis Club members and visitors still pound the impeccable turf, deferring to international stars like Jimmy Connors and Zina Garrison during Newport's Tennis Week in July. Art critic Mariana Griswold Van Rensselaer judged Newport Casino to be "a mere summer-house for 'society's' amusement," but architect Stanford White's Shingle-style country club is unpretentious and pleasingly airy. The complex originally included a riding ring, an indoor tennis court, and a theater where Oscar Wilde and Basil Rathbone appeared. Today it houses the **International Tennis Hall of Fame and Museum,** where lively exhibits cover social as well as sporting history and where you may view your favorite matches on video. *194 Bellevue Avenue; 401-849-3990.*

RHODE ISLAND

◆ NEWPORT MANSIONS *map page 303*

The James family lived in Newport briefly when Henry, the 16-year-old budding novelist, was forming his literary opinions. He also served as a volunteer fireman and suffered what he referred to as an "obscure hurt" on duty, an injury that has preoccupied certain psychologists ever since. Though he was convinced that "Saratoga is a hotel. Newport is a realm," James later dismissed the proliferating mansions as "white elephants...queer and conscious and lumpish...really grotesque."

You don't have to be a Jamesian to notice, as you proceed down Bellevue Avenue, that there is something elephantine and out of scale about the creations in this palatial subdivision, where a French hunting lodge sits next door to an Italian villa on land that seems to have shrunk around its occupants.

Testaments not only to the wealth but to the competitive instincts of their owners, Newport's mansions—like the interminable movements of a Bruckner symphony—became increasingly elaborate as they build up to that great architectural crescendo, The Breakers.

The Breakers

Built for Cornelius Vanderbilt between 1892 and 1895, this vast marble Renaissance-style palace dominates the headland at Ochre Point Avenue and allows even today's humble visitors the illusion of commanding the ocean that ineffectually pummels the cliff below. *Ochre Point Avenue; 401-847-1000.*

Excess and Harmony

To put Newport's infectious excess in context, start with **Kingscote**, a relatively modest 1839 Gothic-style "cottage" designed by Richard Upjohn for Savannah planter George Noble Jones and the first summer residence to appear on Bellevue Avenue. Move on to the harmonious **Isaac Bell House**; built in 1883, it is one of the finest Shingle-style structures in America.

The Elms

The Elms, built in 1899 for coal magnate Julius Berwind, contains outstanding 18th-century French furniture.

Chateau-sur-Mer

Then consider Chateau-sur-Mer, a gigantic granite block that threw down the style gauntlet in 1852, when it proclaimed how kind the China trade had been to William Shepard Wetmore. Mining, railroad, and Wall Street fortunes spawned the later houses of the Gilded Age as the Vanderbilts, Astors, Belmonts, and their peers elevated this summer resort and turned it into the seedbed for similar architectural outbreaks in Narragansett, Bristol, Providence, Florida, and California.

Rosecliff

Newport's mansions are undeniably wonder-filled. Rosecliff, built in 1902 for Mrs. Herman Oerlichs and modeled on Grand Trianon at Versailles, contains Newport's largest ballroom.

Beechwood

An incurable anglophiliac, Mrs. William Astor mimicked Queen Victoria and even crowned herself the "Queen of American Society," reigning over its elite circle known as "The 400"—the number accommodated by the Astor ballroom. Visiting the Astors' Beechwood mansion today, you become one of the 400, as actors portraying the family's staff and guests guide you through the house and even smuggle you into the servants' quarters. The year is 1891, twittery Miss Drexler describes one of Mrs. Astor's dinners (only death—your own—excused you from attending), and you leave laughing—but resolving to dress more appropriately for your next visit. A sprig muslin, perhaps. Beechwood also stages murder mystery tours, Christmas feasts, and the Astor Ball; *580 Bellevue Avenue; 401-846-3772.*

Marble House

The Marble House, which cost William K. Vanderbilt $2 million to build and $9 million to furnish in 1892, is a harmonious concoction of Versailles-inspired salons, Siena marble hallways, and gilded everything. A few years after its completion, Alva Vanderbilt won Marble House in a divorce settlement, added a sublime China teahouse overlooking the water, and then married Oliver Hazard Perry Belmont, who lived down the road at Belcourt Castle.

Belcourt Castle

Built in 1892, Belcourt is now crammed with the antique collection of its current owners, but Alva's mark endures. When she learned that most old English libraries have warped floors, for example, she ordered that Belcourt's library floor be appropriately distorted. The deliberate hump remains. For his part, Mr. Belmont installed Newport's first shower and insisted that his horses dress for dinner, supplying them with embroidered bed linen; *401-846-0669.*

Land's End

Between 1890 and 1914, the summer season at Newport was an exercise in excess. A single ball might cost over $100,000, and flaunting was mandatory until the introduction of income tax and other economic changes signaled the end of the Gilded Age. Few writers portrayed that age as acutely as Edith Wharton, who bought Land's End as a summer house in 1893. Here she began the collaboration with Boston architect Osgood Codman on house and garden design that would lead to Wharton's *Decoration of Houses,* published in 1897. Wharton later decamped to The Mount at Lenox. Still a private residence, Land's End may be viewed from the shore when you travel past the mansions to the southern end of Bellevue Avenue and take Ledge Road to the left.

Corinthian columns front Marble House, on Bellevue Avenue.

Cliff Walk, with the Breakers in the background.

◆ AQUARIUM, CLIFF WALK, AND OTHER DIVERSIONS

To restore your confidence after visiting Beechwood, visit the **Newport Aquarium** at Easton's Beach, where, compared to Mrs. Astor, the sharks seem like kittens; *175 Memorial Boulevard at Easton's Beach; 401-849-8430.*

Then hike along the three-mile **Cliff Walk**, which runs between Easton's Beach and Bailey's Beach and is one of the most remarkable trails on any American coast. Ocean winds bully you from one side, mansions glower at you from the other, and in between, cloudbanks of wild roses reassure you with their sweetness. Originally a fisherman's trail, the walk was barricaded by mansion owners and then restored to the public when fishermen's shore rights were judged in court to overrule money.

Glowing with virtue and windburn, you should reward yourself by motoring along the 10-mile-long **Ocean Avenue**, which offers continuous sea drama and passes **Hammersmith Farm**. Known as the Kennedy's "Summer White House" between 1961 and 1963, this was the site of the reception that followed the marriage of John F. Kennedy and Jacqueline Bouvier in Saint Mary's Church on Spring Street.

On a fine autumn afternoon, a picnic at either **Brenton Point State Park** or

Fort Adams State Park seems just as stylish. Fort Adams hosts the Ben & Jerry's Folk Festival and the JVC Jazz Festival each August, so don't be surprised to hear the ghostly strains of Bob Dylan's shocking 1960s electric guitar debut here. Fend off afternoon snoozes by visiting the **Museum of Yachting**, at Fort Adams State Park, where sailing exploits and their social backgrounds are chronicled. If you don't feel up to circumnavigating the globe afterwards, you can board the *Aurora*, Newport's largest schooner, or one of the many other charter vessels, for a harbor tour. More serious naval activities are examined in the **Naval War College Museum**, founded in 1884 as a research and training center for naval officers. The museum is located in the 1820 Founder's Hall, originally Newport's poorhouse. *Coasters Harbor Island; call for directions; 401-841-4052 ext. 1317.*

■ CONANICUT ISLAND *map page 281, C-4*

Conanicut, also known as Jamestown Island, appears on the map as a mere stepping-stone to the mainland. But its rare delights should make you linger. A favorite summer ground of the Narragansett tribe, the island was named after their sachem, Conanicus, when it was settled by Quakers in the 1650s.

Beavertail Light, the oldest lighthouse in Rhode Island, stands on Conanicut Island.

Watson Farm

To get a powerful sense of how the island looked during the early years of its development, visit the 280-acre Watson Farm, owned by the Society for the Preservation of New England Antiquities.

When five mannerly, ecstatic border collies greet you in the Watson barnyard, you fear they may be costumed interpreters. But this is not that kind of farm. Don and Heather Minto, the enthusiastic managers for the last 20 years, are real, too, and will start you off on your farm hike as they attend to everything from neurotic guinea fowl to complacent eggplants. The Watson Farm booklet explains the agrarian history of the island and the farmland you are crossing. Reading becomes difficult, however, when you are distracted by the stunning views of Narragansett Bay, the beauty of the land, and the dolphin-like antics of the five collies, who take turns herding you and ambushing unsuspecting sticks. *Turn right onto North Road after crossing the Newport Bridge; 455 North Road, 401-423-0005.*

The **Jamestown Windmill**, across the road from Watson Farm, was built in 1787, continued grinding through the 19th century, and today has cattle for company as it contemplates the Newport Bridge, soaring across the bay.

Shoreside Pleasures

Fort Getty State Park, the adjacent **Fox Hill Salt Marsh**, and **Beavertail State Park** (at the island's southern tip), take you to the water's edge and unroll the Rhode Island coastline for your perusal. **Beavertail Lighthouse**, built in 1749, is one of the nation's oldest.

Sheep at Watson Farm. Border collies stand vigil in the background.

■ SOUTH COUNTY

The area extending from Jamestown west to the Connecticut border and north to West Greenwich from the coast is helpfully referred to by Rhode Islanders as South County. Confused? Don't worry. Just be grateful that practically any road within this mythical county leads to glorious open spaces and pleasingly eccentric towns. The coast from Watch Hill to Point Judith is certainly pocked with the blight of motels and malls, but it is also graced with antiquated summer resorts and magical beaches. The only thing that proceeds in a straight line here is Interstate 95, which should be avoided whenever possible. So abandon your linear ambitions and criss-cross from Kingstown up to West Greenwich, down through Arcadia to Carolina, to Westerly and Watch Hill in the western corner, and then along the coast to Point Judith and Block Island.

◆ SMITH'S CASTLE *map page 281, C-4*

Approaching this 1678 plantation house north of Wickford off busy US 1, you enter a hushed retreat on a shimmering estuary where kingfishers flash between the reeds, ducks sun themselves on the bank, and a gigantic white mulberry tree offers welcome shade. Originally a trading post, the house was a garrison during King Philip's War. It was burned during that conflict, and a tablet on the grounds marks the grave of 40 men who died in the Great Swamp Fight of 1675. *North of Wickford off US 1; 401-294-3521.*

◆ WICKFORD AREA *map page 281, C-4*

Beauty—as we all know—makes people hungry. And hungry people go to Wickford. Situated off US 1 on the mainland shore west of Conanicut, this small, picturesque town is home not only to some of the finest 18th- and 19th-century houses in the state, but also to **Wickford Gourmet Foods** (on West Main Street), an emporium that displays its heavenly lunch specials alongside pastries, cheeses, and other tempting comestibles. Eat on the small terrace or take your sustenance down to the pretty Municipal Wharf. The **Wickford Diner** on Brown Street is a treat for connoisseurs of the breed.

Suitably fortified, you should stroll down Wickford's main thoroughfare, a pleasing composition of old storefronts and 18th-century houses, and stray onto its leafy side streets. Notice that the lovely Old Narragansett Church, which was built in 1707 and looks so at home on Church Street, was in fact moved from the outskirts of town to its present location in 1800.

❖

South of Wickford off Route 1A, two adjacent sites conjure up a less fractious past. The **Gilbert Stuart birthplace** recalls the work of New England's famous 18th-century artist (best known for his portrait of George Washington long used on the one dollar bill), who was born in 1755 in this pleasing house beside a snuff mill. And the **Casey Farm**, run by the Society for the Preservation of New England Antiquities, is an early-18th-century plantation now operating as an organic farm.

An obelisk off Route 2 in West Kingston marks the battle site of the **Great Swamp Fight**, in which Massachusetts, Connecticut, and Rhode Island militias attacked the Narragansett's winter camp, killing hundreds of men, women, and children and prompting revenge attacks. Today, the Great Swamp is one of Rhode Island's many natural jewels. This 3,000-acre wetland borders the 1,000-acre Worden Pond. Accessible by dirt roads and dikes, the swamp is intoxicating when the dogwoods bloom in spring and when the maples and tupelos blaze in autumn. Don't be surprised to see nesting ospreys—the state's largest colony—glaring down at you from their untidy households.

◆ KINGSTON *map page 281, B-5*

Kingston itself displays elegant structures, particularly on Kingston Road, where 18th- and early-19th-century houses predominate and where even the Old Washington County Jail, built in 1792, is gracious enough to welcome innocent visitors into its cells. Kingston also preserves the 18th-century Oliver Watson House, in which the University of Rhode Island has established an agricultural college.

❖

Passing through **Usquepaugh** on the Queen's River west of Kingston, you may visit the 1750 **Kenyon Grist Mill**, where cornmeal for johnnycake—a Rhode Island culinary speciality along with quahogs and greening apples—is still ground on massive granite wheels.

Eighty percent of West Greenwich, to the north, is woodlands, since the township includes the **Arcadia Management Area**—14,000 acres of forest and varied wildlife habitat. The beech trees alone would make this a state treasure. But Arcadia also has Stepstone Falls careering over granite ledges, the trout-filled Wood River, and 40 miles of trails for riders, who may camp with their horses at Legrand G. Reynolds Horseman's Area. Those seeking steeper thrills may wish to climb the daunting Rattlesnake Ledge at **Wickaboxet State Forest** to the north.

◆ NARRAGANSETT TO WATCH HILL *map page 281, C-5, A-6*

Narragansett Beach is one of New England's finest. The coastline from Point Judith to Watch Hill is densely populated but nonetheless graced with timeless resorts like Weekapaug; with the major conservation areas of **Burlingame State Park;** and with the National Wildlife Refuges of **Trustom Pond** (near Green Hill) and **Ninigret** (near Charlestown). Here fishing villages like Galilee and Jerusalem manage to be both workmanlike and picturesque. Members of the Narragansett tribe still live in Charlestown, which was for centuries the burial ground of Narragansett sachems. Today the Royal Indian Burial Ground on Narrow Lane off Route 2 is closed to visitors, but you may observe costumed dancing and ritual at the annual Narragansett gathering in early August.

Its hook permanently baited with an alluring lighthouse, **Point Judith** juts into Block Island Sound, attracting the fishing and ferry boats that ceaselessly churn up these waters. This busy port hums with anticipation as fishermen set sail hoping for a record-breaking catch and holidaymakers board the Block Island ferry dreaming of tranquility. Block Island at least never disappoints its faithful.

A shorefront beach house along East Matunuck State Beach.

◆ WATCH HILL *map page 281, A-6*

If Newport's mansions reek of new money, the Victorian seaside resort of Watch Hill suggests the older, more discreet variety. On this western tip of Rhode Island, graceful rather than flamboyant houses perch on rolling hills, overlooking some of the state's most beautiful beaches. The 1938 hurricane was so charmed with the summer cottages then dotting **Napatree Point** that it swept them away in one enthusiastic blast, bequeathing today's walkers a shoreline of unparalleled beauty. One of the best places in the region to watch the autumn hawk migration, Napatree also affords delightful views of Watch Hill lighthouse.

Returning to the town, you cannot miss the immense **Ocean House Hotel** on Bluff Avenue, a Victorian leviathan built in 1868. You will also be pulled up short on Bay Street by the **statue of Ninigret,** sachem of the Niantics, and by the **Flying Horse Carousel,** America's oldest, built in 1867 and still turning. A summer visit may be enjoyable, but a late autumn or even winter walk on **Misquamicut State Beach,** east of Watch Hill, is far more than that. Understandably popular with families in good weather, Rhode Island's largest state beach is exquisite even on turbulent afternoons, when the seven-mile expanse of drifting sand is pounded by thundering surf and the seagulls seem unusually moody.

The Ocean House Hotel on Watch Hill. (above)
Watch Hill lighthouse at sunset. (opposite, photo by Carol Glover)

RHODE ISLAND

◆ WESTERLY *map page 281, A-5*

When traveler and diarist Madam Knight stopped in Westerly in 1704, she was certainly appalled. "The family were the old man, his wife, and two children," she wrote of her visit to one habitation, "all and every part being the picture of poverty….An Indian like animal came to the door on a creature very much like himselfe in mien and feature, as well as ragged clothing." Dwellings and fortunes improved when this became a vigorous textile-producing and granite-quarrying center from the 18th century onwards. Victorian and Greek Revival mansions still line many of the side streets, and the exquisite 18-acre **Wilcox Park and Arboretum** has formed the fragrant heart of the town since 1898.

NAMING OF NARRAGANSETT

I went to bed, tho' pretty hard, Yet neet and handsome. But I could get no sleep, because of the Clamor of some of the town tope-ers in next Room, Who were entred into a strong debate concerning ye Signifycation of the name of their Country, (*viz.*) *Narraganset.* One said it was named so by ye Indians, because there grew a Brier there, of a prodigious Highth and bigness, the like hardly ever known, called by the Indians Narragansett; And quotes an Indian of so Barberous a name for his Author, that I could not write it. His Antagonist Replyed no—It was from a Spring it had its name, which hee well knew where it was, which was extreem cold in summer, and as Hott as could be imagined in the winter, which was much resorted too by the natives, and by them called Narragansett, (Hott and Cold,) and that was the originall of their places name—with a thousand Impertinances not worth notice, which He utter'd with such a Roreing voice and Thundering blows with the fist of wickedness on the Table, that it peirced my very head. I heartily fretted, and wish't 'um tongue tyed; but with as little succes as a freind of mine once, who was (as shee said) kept a whole night awake, on a Jorny, by a country Left. and a Sergent, Insigne and a Deacon, contriving how to bring a triangle into a Square.

—Madam Knight, *The Journal of Madam Knight*, 1704

■ BLOCK ISLAND

inset map page 281, B-6

Getting there: Block Island is reached by ferry from Point Judith: 401-783-4613; in summer from Newport and Providence: 203-442-7891; and from New London, CT, 401-783-4613.

Twelve miles off the Rhode Island coast and measuring just 11 square miles, this dollop of land nibbled and occasionally chewed by the Atlantic Ocean is one of New England's greatest wonders. You can see everything in a day, particularly in spring or autumn, when the summer crowds have retreated. But be prepared to feel as if you might stay

Passengers on the Block Island Ferry.

forever. It is not simply the sound of the wind on an October night battering the shuttered Victorian hotels that surround the harbor, or the complete darkness that swallows the road ahead and sharpens your hearing. It is the island's apparently infinite store of surprises. *Block Island Tourism: 800-383-2474 or 401-466-5200.*

Walking the **Clay Head Trail** (off Corn Neck Road), for example, you proceed along a honeysuckle-scented lane toward the distant artillery barrage of surf and suddenly emerge on a rock-strewn cove bounded by red cliffs. Admiring the 150-foot-high Mohegan Bluffs from **Southeast Lighthouse,** which has the most powerful beam on the eastern seaboard, you are startled by the resonant hiccup of an American bittern camouflaged in the reeds below. Even the wide, sandy strip of

(following pages) Mohegan Bluffs Natural Scenic Area.

RHODE ISLAND

Crescent Beach, on the island's eastern shore, astonishes you with the variety of sandpipers nervously avoiding the waves.

Over 20 percent of Block Island's land is protected from development, and approximately 40 rare species thrive here. Hike through **Rodman's Hollow** or across the **Lewis-Dickens Farm Nature Preserve,** both on Cooneymous Road. The harbor seals who sunbathe regularly in Cow Cove (near Settler's Rock) and the loons giggling on Chaqum Pond are easily spotted.

There are other humans, of course, on Block Island, and social as well as natural pleasures. The tiny **Airport Diner** on Center Road is a good place to enjoy off-season banter as you relish a fine breakfast. And at the magnificently ramshackle **Spring House Hotel** on Spring Street, the staff putting the elegant giant to sleep for the winter will happily fill you in on local history or gossip. There is also a turbulent history. Named Manisses (Manitou's Little Island) by the native Narragansetts, Block Island saw its first English settlement in 1661, was repeatedly besieged during the French and Indian Wars, and was terrorized by deserters and criminals during the Revolutionary War. None of which is imaginable as you stand on what feels like the edge of the world, looking back at the edge of the continent.

Thelma Fay has been conducting tours of Block Island in her taxi for 50 years. (above)

View of Block Island from the Coast Guard Station toward Charleston Beach. (opposite)

FOOD & LODGING

■ ABOUT LODGING IN SOUTHERN NEW ENGLAND

Lodging in Massachusetts, Connecticut, and Rhode Island is an even mix of large hotels (mostly in the cities), motels (along the interstate highways and on Cape Cod), B&Bs, and country inns. The latter may have served travelers for the past two centuries, their floorboards worn and comfortably creaky. Or they may be spanking new with Laura Ashley sheets and six layers of lace-edged pillows on the king-size canopy bed. As you would expect, the smaller the place, the more personal the hospitality. And you can expect breakfast in most New England B&Bs to last you until teatime.

For a list of chain hotels in Southern New England, please see the chart on page 375. To find out which towns have listings for accommodations and/or restaurants in this book, please see the chart on pages 375 and 376 and the map opposite.

■ ABOUT DINING IN SOUTHERN NEW ENGLAND

No longer the bastion of chicken pot pie and baked beans, New England has come a long way in the past decade. Well-known chefs choose Boston and Providence for their restaurants, which serve a growing audience of appreciative foodies. Seafood is impeccably fresh and, except in the plentiful clam-shacks, rarely deep fried. In keeping with national trends, chefs in finer restaurants value ingredients raised or caught locally, in season—blueberries, corn, and tomatoes in late summer, apples and squash in fall, oysters in winter. Look in cities for ethnic neighborhoods: Italian food in Boston's North End or Providence's Federal Hill, Cantonese in Boston's Chinatown. Search out festivals celebrating local harvests of everything from cranberries to quahogs (clams native to Narragansett Bay and Long Island Sound).

Lodging rates, per room, double occupancy:
$ = under $50; $$ = $50–100; $$$ = $100–150; $$$$ = over $150

Restaurant prices, entree excluding drinks, tax, tips:
$ = under $10; $$ = $10–20; $$$ = over $20

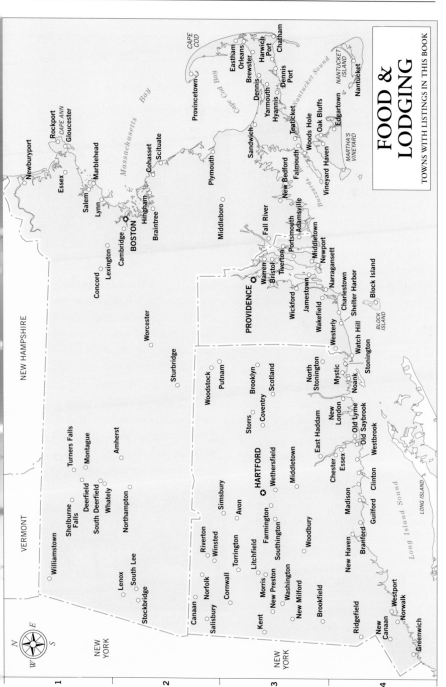

FOOD & LODGING

TOWNS WITH LISTINGS IN THIS BOOK

MASSACHUSETTS FOOD & LODGING

Amherst, MA *map B-2*

☆ **Lord Jeffrey Inn.** 413-253-2576;
✗ 30 Boltwood Ave. $$-$$$
This brick inn, built in 1926, looks as if it has been facing Amherst Common forever and the public areas feel like an old faculty club. Traditional American food is served in **Boltwood's Tavern**, where you should choose a table looking onto the garden; $$. More formal meals are served in the **Windowed Hearth**, $$$. The bedrooms are pleasant and the views of the Common and Amherst College soothing. Eight suites, 40 rooms, restaurant and bar.

✗ **Antonio's.** 413-253-0808;
31 North Pleasant St. $
Some of the best pizza in the valley, with imaginative daily specials. The noise level is high and seating limited during term.

✗ **Pasta E Basta.** 413-256-3550;
26 Main St. $
This friendly, inexpensive place is a student favorite but the Italian food is good enough to tempt non-academic diners. There's no waiter service or reserved seating. Order at the counter, set your own table or grab a counter stool, and enjoy the sometimes frenetic atmosphere.

Boston, MA *map E-2*

☆ **Beacon Hill Bed & Breakfast.**
617-523-7376 ; 27 Brimmer St. $$$
Six-story brick rowhouse built in 1869 overlooks the Charles River, facing Cambridge. All three rooms have a fireplace and private bath.

BOSTON HARBOR HOTEL

☆ **Boston Harbor Hotel.** 617-439-7000 or 800-752-7077; 70 Rowes Wharf $$$$
Probably the most gorgeous location in Boston, this hotel and its surrounding landscape feel like part of the life of the city. Ask for a harbor view.

☆ **Copley Inn.** 617-236-0300 or 800-232-0306; 19 Garrison St. $$
This traditional brownstone B&B offers 21 guest rooms with kitchenettes and private baths. Near Copley Place.

ELIOT AND PICKETT HOUSES

☆ **Eliot & Pickett Houses.** 617-248-8707;
6 Mt. Vernon Place (off Joy St.) $$

With 20 guestrooms in two brick town-houses, this B&B is steps from the State House at the pinnacle of Beacon Hill.

Eliot Suite Hotel. 617-267-1607 or 800-44-ELIOT; 370 Commonwealth Ave. $$$-$$$$
This European-style hotel's 93 suites attract many European travelers as well as musicians playing at Symphony Hall.

FOUR SEASONS HOTEL

THE ELIOT SUITE HOTEL

Fairmont Copley Plaza Hotel.
617-267-5300 or 800-527-4727;
138 Saint James Ave. $$$-$$$$
This newly restored, beautiful Edwardian-era grande dame anchors one end of Copley Square and features one of the coolest jazz bars in the city.

Four Seasons Hotel. 617-338-4400 or 800-332-3442; 200 Boylston St. $$$$
Chic, cosmopolitan, but not stiff. Always battling the Ritz to be named Boston's best. Great restaurants complement good rooms, some with excellent Public Garden views.

463 Beacon Street Guest House.
617-536-1302; 463 Beacon St. $$
This turn-of-century brownstone is a poorly kept secret among Boston B&Bs, but it remains a great deal. Most rooms have kitchenette and private bath.

HARBORSIDE INN

Harborside Inn. 617-723-7500;
185 State St. $$-$$$
Located in a former spice warehouse built in 1858, this 54-room hotel with exposed brick-and-granite walls and Victorian-style furnishings opened in 1998 as a modest boutique hotel in the Financial District.

Le Meridien Boston. 617-451-1900 or 800-543-4300; 250 Franklin St. $$$$ Set in the glorious architecture of the former Federal Reserve Bank in the Financial District, this Meridien rises above many in North America. Outstanding restaurants.

LE MERIDIEN BOSTON

Lenox Hotel. 617-536-5300 or 800-225-7676; 710 Boylston St. $$$$ Freshly renovated 1900 landmark hotel one block from Copley Square features fireplaces in the more expensive rooms.

NEWBURY GUEST HOUSE

Newbury Guest House. 617-437-7666 or 800-437-7668; 261 Newbury St. $$ It's hard to believe that such nice rooms are available at these prices on Back Bay's toniest street, but they are. Breakfast included.

REGAL BOSTONIAN HOTEL

Regal Bostonian Hotel. 617-523-3600 or 800-343-0922; Faneuil Hall $$$$ Offers a surprisingly plush and sheltered retreat from the bustling marketplace next door. Check out the display of archaeological treasures that were uncovered when the hotel was built.

THE RITZ-CARLTON

The Ritz-Carlton, Boston. 617-536-5700 or 800-241-3333; 15 Arlington St. $$$$

The Ritz chain sends its management employees and concierges-in-training here to learn how it's done. The epitome of formal elegance, down to the white-gloved elevator operators.

⛫ **Swissôtel Boston**. 617-451-2600 or 800-621-9200; One Avenue de Lafayette $$$$
Stunning hotel with impeccable service and excellent kitchen amid downtown shopping, Financial District, and the last remnants of the Combat Zone.

✗ **Anago**. 617-266-6222; Lenox Hotel, 65 Exeter St. (at Boylston) $$-$$$
Food here is luscious: house-smoked sturgeon, roasted duck with späetzle and figs. Portions are generous, but leave room for the great pastries. Prices are lower than they are at most Boston restaurants of this caliber.

✗ **Aujourd'hui**. 617-351-2072; Four Seasons Hotel, 200 Boylston St. $$$$
The formal, top-flight French cuisine here is impeccable—just make sure your cards aren't maxed out. Window tables overlook the Public Garden. **The Bristol Lounge** shares Aujourd'hui's chef, but it's less expensive and less formal.

✗ **Bay Tower**. 617-723-1666; 60 State St. $$$-$$$$
The view from the 33rd story has always been unbeatable, and the chef's menus are as swanky as the room. Look for classy treats like roasted sea bass dressed with osetra caviar or a duck risotto with fig sauce. The raised lounge offers an even better view of Boston Harbor.

✗ **Biba**. 617-426-7878; 272 Boylston St. $$$-$$$$
Lydia Shire and Susan Regis (1998 James Beard Foundation best Boston chef) share the top toques at this colorful room where creative food pairings are impeccably presented. Eclectic dishes (scallops with Tuscan black cabbage and black lentils) are balanced by wonderfully simple, traditional ones (corn and lobster chowder). At **Pignoli** (617-338-7500), on the flip side of the same building, Shire and Regis concoct a northern Italian–accented menu.

✗ **China Pearl**. 617-426-4338; 9 Tyler St. $-$$
China Pearl draws the largest crowds in Chinatown for dim sum, with lines stretching down the stairs and into the street on weekends. During the noon peak, as many as 60 varieties of these bite-sized plates are available in the two huge red-pink-gold dining rooms.

✗ **Clio**. 617-536-7200; Eliot Hotel, 370A Commonwealth Ave. $$$$
One of Boston's star restaurants, Clio is decorated in leopard-skin and beige. All the dishes have finesse: seared scallops on the half shell dabbed with osetra caviar, side dishes of vegetables with shavings of white truffle. But elegance and excellence do have a price, both in waiting time and final tally.

✗ **Durgin-Park**. 617-227-2038; 5 Faneuil Hall Marketplace $-$$
Long before tourism was invented, Durgin-Park was serving such traditional New England fare as baked beans,

broiled cod, and Indian pudding to those who worked in and near the markets. Yes, it's a huge tourist draw, but there's nothing phony about it.

✕ **Galleria Italiana.** 617-423-2092; 177 Tremont St. $$$-$$$$
It has some serious competition, but this classy Abruzzi restaurant offers the best Italian dining in Boston. The menu lists just a few antipasti, a few salads, a few pastas, a few meat and fish dishes—all of them brilliant and small enough so you'll order every course.

✕ **Hamersley's Bistro.** 617-423-2700; 553 Tremont St. $$$-$$$$
Gordon Hamersley's oversized bistro is hugely popular: book ahead for a weekend table. The lemon roast chicken is fantastic, as is the rest of the French provincial fare. Dine outdoors on the plaza in warm weather. Inside, it gets loud when it's full.

✕ **Icarus Restaurant.** 617-426-1790; 3 Appleton St. $$$
The kitchen here cooks with French soul, Asian style, and American strut. Even better, Icarus maintains genial fine-dining along with a range of healthy meals: you can get grilled sweetbreads on frisée with blood oranges, or a low-salt, low fat "Square Meal" (on a square plate, no less) as well as a vegetarian "Green Plate."

✕ **Julien.** 617-451-1900; Le Meridien, 250 Franklin St. $$$$
Contemporary French cuisine without gimmicks doesn't get much better than

here, where the heavy dishes of Escoffier receive up-to-date light treatment. The setting is imposing (the old Federal Reserve bank) but the wingback chairs and soft lighting make it almost intimate. As the more "casual" of the Meridien's restaurants, **Cafe Fleuri** is still elegant, with a dramatic high glass ceiling that bathes the café in light by day. The menu is distinctly French, but the special attraction is a high-end Sunday brunch buffet.

✕ **L'Espalier.** 617-262-3023; 30 Gloucester St. $$$$
This Back Bay townhouse converted to an elegant restaurant is the most romantic spot in the city. Dining here often marks an event—a marriage proposal, a megamillion-dollar deal. Prix-fixe menu most nights. The vegetarian tasting menu is a tour de force.

✕ **Library Grill at the Hampshire House.** 617-227-9600; 84 Beacon St. $$$
A romantic spot with Edwardian decor and a lively New American menu. The Sunday jazz brunch is a particular delight, especially if you can snag a table by the windows overlooking the Public Garden. Many of the diners here walk from home, as the Library Grill caters to the real Beacon Hill.

✕ **Maison Robert/Ben's Café.** 617-227-3370; 45 School St. $$$$/$$
The Robert family introduced modern French dining in Boston 30 years ago, and young chef Jacky Robert continues the tradition at this formal dining room

and more casual bar-café with outdoor seating. The oldtimers buried next door at King's Chapel may be turning in their graves as Jacky injects new blood into the classic French tradition. Gourmets on a budget might consider the prix-fixe at **Ben's Café.**

✕ **Maurizio's.** 617-367-1123; 364 Hanover St. **$$-$$$**
Chef-owner Maurizio Loddo is nothing short of brilliant. His Sardinian upbringing shows in wonderful fish dishes such as a thick swordfish steak stuffed with olives, pine nuts, basil. The place is small but they take reservations. Make one.

✕ **New Shanghai Restaurant**
617-338-6688; 21 Hudson St. **$$**
Chef C. K. Sau aims to make New Shanghai the equal of any fancy room in Hong Kong, where he trained, and with white linens and an airy look, this restaurant definitely stands out. Non-Chinese chefs from all over Boston come here to be inspired.

✕ **No Name Seafood.** 617-338-7539; 15 Fish Pier **$-$$**
No Name has a simple formula: Buy the fish off the boat and either fry or bake it. Consider whiling away a rainy afternoon here with ice-cold beer and a hot bowl of the fish chowder, which has a little bit of everything that came off the boats that day. The barroom seediness (though very clean) is part of the charm.

✕ **Oak Room.** 617-267-5300; Fairmont Copley Plaza, 138 Saint James Ave. **$$$$**
For a truly lavish steak dinner at truly lavish prices, this is the place. The Edwardian room boasts a molded plaster ceiling, intricate dark woodwork, and blood red drapery. All portions are overwhelming.

✕ **Olives.** 617-242-1999; 10 City Square, Charlestown **$$$-$$$$**
Olives is Boston's most famous restaurant of the moment, and the kitchen delivers the goods with Italian-influenced New American cuisine. Pastas are hardly conventional—viz. an anchovy-potato mini-lasagna with a crusted tuna steak and a veal stock reduction. You'll almost certainly wait. And you won't be able to converse over the din.

✕ **Rebecca's.** 617-742-9747; 70 Charles St. **$$-$$$**
Chef-owner Rebecca Caras helped bring Boston out of the culinary Dark Ages a generation ago. Her New American restaurant with an Italian accent has evolved into a comfortable neighborhood restaurant in a rather demanding neighborhood. Look for lamb, rabbit, duck, and fish; if you're broke, you can get a burger, even at dinner.

✕ **Ritz-Carlton Hotel Dining Room, Bar, Café.** 617-536-5700; 15 Arlington St. **$$$-$$$$**
The Bar, with a fireplace and windows on the Public Garden, is an elegant choice for lunch or light supper. **The Café** has perked up with a full-scale reinterpretation of its traditional American fare with dishes like smoked salmon in brioche topped with frisée. The cav-

ernous **Dining Room** has changed more glacially (in keeping with the pace of dining here) but shows glimmers of entering the 20th century at the dawn of the 21st. Still, where else will a tuxedoed waiter bone your Dover sole tableside?

✕ **Rowes Wharf Restaurant.**
617-439-3995; 70 Rowes Wharf $$$-$$$$
The chef here grows, forages, hooks, and/or hunts many of the ingredients himself, then prepares them with loving care. The rack of lamb with a Roquefort crust is as heavy as food gets, yet the kitchen also prepares a ginger-braised scrod in carrot-vermouth broth. The room feels like a library—except that it overlooks Boston Harbor.

✕ **Salamander.** 617-225-2121;
One Athenaeum St. $$$-$$$$
The open kitchen with surges of flame and flashes of steel suggests chef-owner Stan Frankenthaler's penchant for the dramatic. Frankenthaler delights in complex combinations of flavors and textures. Great sandwiches are available for lunch, and the bar area serves a lighter menu in the evening.

✕ **Tapeo.** 617-267-4799; 266 Newbury St. $$
As the name suggests, Tapeo specializes in tapas, and manages to do them with striking authenticity. A dandy spot to sit with a dry sherry and nibble on tortilla española or grilled prawns. Sit at the blue-tiled bar or by the fireplace in the pretty dining room.

✕ **Truc.** 617-338-8070; 560 Tremont St. $$ -$$$
The kitchen here turns out high-end traditional French bistro fare (at bistro-plus prices), which is rare in Boston. If you're hankering for a classic coq au vin or crème brulée, Truc's for you.

✕ **The Vault.** 617-292-9966;
105 Water St. $$$-$$$$
The two dozen wine selections by the glass might tip you off that this dramatically appointed dining room is owned by wine merchants. Expect relatively straightforward delectable meat and fish dishes, such as pan-roasted chicken breast over artichokes.

Brewster/Dennis Area, MA *map F-3*

⌧ **The Corsair.** 508-398-6600;
41 Chase Ave., Dennis Port $-$$$
Two-story motor inn on private beach, with pools indoors and out.

⌧ **The Cross Rip.** 508-398-6600;
33 Chase Ave., Dennis Port $-$$$$
Family-sized rooms with kitchenettes, some with whirlpool tubs, surrounding pool on private ocean beach.

⌧ **Edgewater Beach Resort.**
508-398-6922; 95 Chase Ave.,
Dennis Port $-$$
Motel complex on private beach with indoor and outdoor pools, putting green, balconies, sauna, fitness center. Also family-sized rooms and suites with kitchens.

ISAIAH HALL B&B

⊞ **Isaiah Hall B&B.** 508-385-9928; 152 Whig St., Dennis $$-$$$
Eleven-room inn with relaxed atmosphere. A nice place to gather in the evening with other guests.

⊞ **The Lighthouse Inn.** 508-398-2244; Lighthouse Rd., West Dennis $$$
Shingled cottages surround the main house, in an old-fashioned beach resort, where families are welcome. Along with a working lighthouse are tennis courts, lawn games, heated pool, and private beach. Breakfast included.

⊞ **Michael's Cottages.** 508-896-4025; 618 Main St. (Route 6A), Brewster $$
Efficiency and standard rooms; cottages.

✕ **Cobie's.** 508-896-7021; 3260 Main St. (Route 6A), Brewster $
A Cape Cod institution for fried clams, lobster and crab rolls, ice cream. Eat at picnic tables on the deck or carry-out, 11 to 9 daily, May through Labor Day.

✕ **Gina's-By-the-Sea.** 508-385-3213; 134 Taunton Ave., Dennis $-$$
Casual beach house where children are welcome, servings generous. Basic Italian dishes and seafood.

✕ **Red Pheasant.** 508-385-2133; 905 Main St. (Route 6A), Dennis $$-$$$
The dining room here has a colonial decor with candlelight, but the menu is strictly up-to-date. Don't miss the scallops, as they're a work of art.

Cambridge, MA *map E-2*

⊞ **Cambridge Center Marriott.** 617-494-6600; Broadway at Third St. $$$-$$$$
A little out of the way unless you're doing business at MIT, but the Red Line can take you to downtown Boston or Harvard Square in minutes.

A CAMBRIDGE HOUSE BED & BREAKFAST

⊞ **A Cambridge House Bed & Breakfast.** 617-491-6300 or 800-232-9989; 2218 Massachusetts Ave. $$-$$$
This grand turn-of-the-century home is elegantly decorated in Waverly fabrics and wall coverings and filled with antiques and period furnishings.

CHARLES HOTEL

🏨 Charles Hotel in Harvard Square.
617-864-1200 or 800-882-1818
One Bennett St. **$$$-$$$$**
Great location. Wonderful public spaces and great restaurants ameliorate the spareness of the very modern rooms. Top jazz club in the city.

🏨 A Friendly Inn at Harvard Square.
617-547-7851; 1673 Cambridge St. **$$**
A well-kept and pleasant B&B behind the city high school and library and five minutes on foot from Harvard Yard.

🏨 Isaac Harding House. 617-876-2888;
288 Harvard St. **$$-$$$**
In 1997, a handsome renovation of a historic mid-Cambridge house produced this superb, fully accessible B&B halfway between Harvard and Central Squares.

🏨 Royal Sonesta. 617-491-3600;
5 Cambridge Pkwy. **$$$-$$$$**
Spectacular views of Charles River and skylines of Beacon Hill and Back Bay. Near the Museum of Science.

🏨 Sheraton Commander Hotel.
617-547-4800; 16 Garden St. **$$$-$$$$$**
Fits old-style Harvard types like a velvet smoking jacket. This Cambridge grande dame on Cambridge Common has undergone extensive renovation, though some rooms and halls are rather small.

✕ Cafe Celador. 617-661-4073;
5 Craigie Circle **$$$**
The flavors of Catalonia accent the Mediterranean menu here. In winter, the braised rabbit risotto can lift your spirits. Best bargain is the three-course, pre-theater prix fixe.

✕ Casablanca. 617-876-0999;
40 Brattle St. **$$-$$$**
The menu at this Harvard Square legend has been transformed into a sophisticated take on Moroccan–North African cuisine, as in grilled sea scallops with pistachio-basmati-lentil pilaf. The casual bar in back is louder and offers excellent burgers for the less adventurous.

✕ Chez Henri. 617-354-8980;
One Shepard St. **$$$**
As urban chic and timeless as the little black dress, Chez Henri is a French bistro with a Cuban accent that shows in the signature duck tamales. But there's nothing Cuban about the grilled venison with honey-glazed shallots. You'll wait to get in (no reservations for parties under 6), but there's a terrific prix fixe under $30.

✕ Giannino. 617-576-0605;
20 University Rd. **$$$**
Giannino is hidden from view behind the Charles Hotel, but lovers of hearty Abruzzi cuisine find it soon enough. Plating is simple and elegant and portions are huge. The braised and roasted meats are the real stars, like an osso buco rich as Croesus.

✕ **Harvest.** 617-868-2255, 44 Brattle St. $$$

This sleek and elegant restaurant re-opened in 1998, and it's every bit as popular with Cambridge's in-crowd as it used to be. The New American cuisine served here is extremely innovative, and always tasty. Make a reservation.

✕ **Rialto.** 617-661-5050; The Charles Hotel, One Bennett St. $$$-$$$$

The award-winning kitchen here is known for all-American interpretations of Southern European dishes: quail is prepped in a pepper marinade, then roasted and served with figs, watercress, and preserved oranges. Thick velvet banquettes give the room a swank feel.

✕ **Up Stairs at the Pudding.** 617-864-1933; 10 Holyoke St. $$-$$$$

Harvard's unofficial restaurant, this eatery over the Hasty Pudding Theatre offers a lovely Sunday brunch and superb lunches on the rooftop deck. It's also a fine dinner venue. Don't miss the lobster bouillabaisse if it's available.

Chatham, MA *map F-3*

☗ **Captain's House Inn.** 508-945-0127; 369 Old Harbor Rd. $$$

Large, inviting rooms in the mansion, carriage house, and cottage, with luxurious decor and furnishings. Includes a delightful afternoon tea with scones. You can use the inn's bicycles to pedal the half-mile to the village or to the ocean.

☗ **Chatham Wayside Inn.** 508-945-5550 or 800-391-5734; 512 Main St. $$$

Traditional gracious village inn with restaurant; some rooms have balconies, patios, canopy beds, whirlpool tubs, and/or fireplaces.

CHATHAM WAYSIDE INN

☗ **The Seafarer of Chatham.** 508-432-1739 or 800-786-2772; 209 Main St. $$

Attractive motel with nice grounds, coffee and tea in rooms, attention to detail.

☗ **Wequassett Inn.** 508-432-5400 or 800-225-7125; Pleasant Bay Rd. $$$$

A premier resort with cottages nicely spaced on 23 acres of wooded waterfront. Facilities abound: tennis, croquet, private beach, mini-bars, in-room coffee, daily papers, private golf course.

✕ **Andiamo Restaurant.** 508-432-1807; 2653 Main St. $-$$

Casual Italian and continental dining, dinner only.

✕ **Cape Sea Grille.** 508-432-4745; 31 Sea St., Harwich Port $$

Inventive and stylish New American menu, with accent on seafood. It's no longer a secret, so make reservations.

✕ **Pate's Restaurant.** 508-945-9777;
1260 Main St. $$
Open-hearth grilling. The Caesar salad is
locally renowned. Dinner only, daily.

✕ **Vining's Bistro.** 508-945-5033;
595 Main St. $$
Creative salads, vegetables, and pasta
combinations. Known for wood-grilled
chicken; dinner only.

Concord, MA *map D-1*

⊞ **The Colonial Inn,** 978-369-9200;
✕ 48 Monument Square $$$-$$$$
Country inn decor, with dining room
serving traditional New England fare.

⊞ **The Concordian Motel.**
978-263-7765; 71 Hosmer St.
(off Hwy. 2), Acton $
Family-friendly, spotless and a real bar-
gain. Some rooms have terraces, all have
cable television, VCR and dataport; pool
has grill and picnic tables for guests.

⊞ **The Hawthorne Inn.** 978-369-5610;
462 Lexington Rd. $$$-$$$$
Attractive B&B less than a mile from vil-
lage green, in a home built in the 1870s.

✕ **Guida's.** 978-371-1333; 84 Thoreau St.
$$-$$$
Near-perfect fusion of Portuguese and
New American cuisines, with careful at-
tention to detail. Look for traditional
Iberian dishes using the freshest New
England seafood and local farm produce.

✕ **Papa Razzi.** 978-371-0303;
768 Elm St. $$
Italian through and through, with a long
menu of Northern specialties, interesting

pizzas and pasta dishes. The setting is
Euro-sleek. The breads are baked in
wood-fired brick oven.

Deerfield, MA *map B-1*

⊞ **The Deerfield Inn.** 413-774-5587 or
800-926-3865; 81 Old Main St. $$$$
Ideally situated in the middle of historic
Deerfield, this 1884 inn with modern
annexes is so tasteful that it covers the
televisions with TV coZies. The atmosphere is restful and hushed, the dining
room menu and wine list impressive,
and afternoon tea a pleasant treat.

THE DEERFIELD INN

⊞ **Sunnyside Farm Bed and Breakfast.**
413-665-3113; 21 River Rd., Whately $
Eight miles south of Deerfield in agricultural surroundings, this unpretentious inn is furnished with family heir-
looms as well as antiques. Hearty country breakfasts, too. Five rooms with two
shared bathrooms. No credit cards.

✕ **Sienna.** 413-665-0215; 6 Elm St.,
South Deerfield $$$
The menu at this small, critically ac-
claimed restaurant changes constantly but
has a distinct flavor of France mixed with

California. The atmosphere is quite formal. Reservations neccesary. Dinner only.

Eastham/Orleans, MA *map F-3*

THE OVER LOOK INN

The Over Look Inn. 508-255-1886 or 800-356-1121; 3085 County Rd. (US 6), Eastham **$$**
Victorian mansion with real character and lovely gardens; Scottish dishes highlight breakfast.

The Whalewalk Inn. 508-255-0617; 220 Bridge Rd., Eastham **$$$**
Antiques, restful surroundings, and gardens. Rooms and suites, fine breakfasts.

The Cheese Corner. 508-255-1699; 56 Main St., Orleans **$**
Sandwiches, soups, chowder, salads, and excellent breads. You can eat in at the cafe tables or carry out.

Essex, MA *map E-1*

Essex River House Motel. 978-768-6800; 132 Main St. (Route 133) **$-$$**

Modest, comfortable rooms in village location; ideal for families. Closed in winter.

George Fuller House. 978-768-7766; 148 Main St. (Route 133) **$$-$$$**
Seven-room bed-and-breakfast in an attractively restored historic home. The hosts are very congenial.

Periwinkles. 978-768-6320; 74 Main St. (Route 133) **$-$$**
Family favorite with fresh, nicely presented seafood and local brews.

Woodman's Lobster Pool. 978-768-6451; 129 Main St. (Route 133) **$-$$$**
Frying Ipswich clams since 1914, it's a Cape Ann institution.

Fall River, MA *map E-3*

Abbey Grill. 508-675-9305; 100 Rock St. **$$**
In a former church hall in the historic Highlands neighborhood; dining room of the International Institute of Culinary Arts, meaning you can look forward to creative cooking. Reservations suggested.

Eagle Restaurant. 508-677-3788; 35 North Main St. **$-$$**
Dowtown Fall River's oldest restaurant, opened in 1929, is a reliable pasta-seafood-steak kind of place.

Regatta. 508-679-4115; 392 Davol St. **$$**
Right on the riverfront park's shoreline, with a huge bar and an umbrella-shaded deck that allows broadside views of

Battleship Cove's war vessels. The menu lists enough selections to suit everyone's taste. Reservations suggested.

✗ **Sagres.** 508-675-7018; 181 Columbia St. **$$**

Thanks to Fall River's strong Portuguese, Azorean, and Cape Verdean identity, you're in luck if you like tasty Portuguese food. Reservations suggested.

✗ **Waterstreet Café.** 508-672-8748; 36 Water St. **$**

Pleasantly casual, conveniently situated on the fringe of Fall River's riverfront park, also close to popular Battleship Cove. Reservations not necessary.

Falmouth Area, MA
map E-3

⊞ **Admiralty Inn.** 508-548-4240 or 800-341-5700; 51 Teaticket Hwy. (Route 28), Falmouth **$$**.

Motel-style rooms around a pool on well-kept grounds. It's close to the center of town, but not to the beach.

⊞ **The Cape Wind.** 508-548-3400 or 800-267-3401; 334 Maravista Ave., Teaticket **$$-$$$$**

Secluded on spacious lawns and surrounded by trees with shaded picnic grove, these motel-style units are large and nicely decorated.

⊞ **Green Harbor.** 508-548-4747; 134 Acapesket Rd., East Falmouth **$$**

Motel rooms with kitchenettes and balconies overlooking the water. Large pool; paddleboats to take on the harbor.

⊞ **Shoreway Acres Resort Inn.** 508-540-3000 or 800-352-7100; 59 Shore St., Falmouth **$-$$**

Rooms are spread through an unusual mix of three old sea-captain's houses and more modern buildings set amid gardens. Guests can play lawn games or use the sauna.

✗ **Betsy's Diner.** 508-540-0060; 457 Main St., Falmouth **$**

A classic pleated-chrome diner where the kitchen doesn't hold back on its servings of Yankee pot roast, clam chowder, and crab cakes.

✗ **Fishmonger Cafe.** 508-548-9148; 56 Water St., Woods Hole **$$**

Serving three healthy and creatively prepared meals everyday except Monday. This is fusion cuisine at its best, and the menu is full of almost surprising combinations. Heavy emphasis on seafood.

✗ **Peking Palace.** 508-540-8204; 452 Main St., Falmouth **$$**

Uncommon Mandarin dishes join the more common Cantonese and Szechuan ones. Definitely a cut above average. Open daily for lunch and dinner.

✗ **The Quarterdeck.** 508-548-9900; 164 Main St., Falmouth **$-$$**

Cozy and dark, almost rustic decor, with a friendly, lively atmosphere. Highly creative and eclectic dishes, with an Iberian flair. Good wine list, reasonably priced. Lunch and dinner.

✗ **The Regatta of Falmouth By-the-Sea.** 508-548-5400; Clinton Ave., Falmouth Harbor **$$-$$$**

Haute cuisine with an attention to every detail of food preparation, table setting, and service. Sauces are superlative.

Gloucester, MA *map E-1*

☷ **Best Western Bass Rocks Ocean Inn.** 978-283-7600; 107 Atlantic Rd., $$-$$$
The main ebuilding is an old mansion with antiques and large rooms. The motel-style annex rooms have balconies with views of the sea and of the twin lighthouses nearby. Closed in winter.

☷ **Cape Ann Motor Inn.** 978-281-2900; 33 Rockport Rd. $$
Clean, well-run motel; some units have kitchenettes. Closed in winter.

☷ **Captain's Lodge Motel.** 978-281-2420; 237 Eastern Ave. (Route 127) $$
Spacious rooms surround courtyard; kitchenettes in some units. Coffee shop on the premises.

☷ **The White House.** 978-525-3642; 18 Norman Ave., Magnolia $$
A 16-room bed-and-breakfast in a posh neighborhood away from the bustle of central Gloucester.

✕ **L'Amante.** 978-282-4426; 197 East Main St. $$
Northern Italian cuisine: pastas, veal, steaks. The menu changes frequently, and there is an appealing, largely Italian wine list.

✕ **The Rudder.** 978-283-7967; 73 Rocky Neck Ave. $-$$
Bordering on rowdy, the lively atmos-phere is as much a part of the Rudder's charm as the reliably good traditional seafood dishes are.

Hyannis, MA *map F-3*

✕ **Sam Diego's.** 508-771-8816; 950 Iyanough Rd. (Route 132) $
No frills Tex-Mex in a light-hearted at-mosphere. All the usuals, plus 100 per-cent American burgers.

Lenox, MA *map A-2*

☷ **Blantyre.** 413-637-3556;
✕ 16 Blantyre Rd. $$$$
A mock-Scottish castle on 88 acres, Blantyre allows you—at substantial cost—to live in the Gilded Age. Rooms in the main house are huge and the fur-nishings appropriately grandiose, while accommodation in the carriage house is modest by comparison but still luxuri-ous. The menu has a French (not Scot-tish) accent. Rstaurant: $$$$ Closed November to May. Ten suites, 13 rooms, restaurant, pool, hot tub, sauna, tennis courts, croquet.

☷ **The Village Inn.** 413-637-0020;
✕ .16 Church St. $$$-$$$$
Lenox's oldest inn, open since 1775, has fireplaces in several rooms, and antiques everywhere. The dining room offers tra-ditional food such as a Yankee pot roast, as well as lighter seafood alternatives; $$$. With 32 guest rooms, restaurant, and bar.

⊟ **Wheatleigh.** 413-637-0610;

✕ Hawthorne Rd. **$$$$**

Built in 1893 and standing on 22 acres, this mock-Florentine palazzo has elegant, lofty rooms, and a main dining room that features "contemporary classical" dishes. Low-fat, vegeterian, and standard tasting menus are offered; nonvegetarian menus often include wild game, **$$$$ The Grill Room** provides more casual dining, **$$**. With 19 rooms, restaurant, bar, pool, tennis courts, and exercise and conference rooms.

WHEATLEIGH

✕ **Cafe Lucia.** 413-637-2640;

80 Church St. **$$**

The decor in this fashionable restaurant is more modern than traditional Italian and the same is true of the imaginative menu, which nonetheless includes fine basics like homemade ravioli with tomatoes, garlic, and basil. Reservations are necessary, especially during Tanglewood.

Lexington, MA *map D-1*

⊟ **Sheraton Lexington Inn.**

781-862-8700 or 800-325-3535,

727 Marrett Rd., **$$$-$$$$**

Big hotel with colonial decor and all the amenities; some rooms have terraces. The best act in town.

✕ **Lemon Grass Grille.** 781-862-3530,

1710 Massachusetts Ave. **$-$$**

Above average Thai dishes and an accomodating waitstaff. Beware of dishes labeled "hot." They mean it.

Lynn, MA *map E-1*

⊟ **Diamond District Breakfast Inn.**

781-599-4470 or 800-666-3076;

142 Ocean St. **$$$-$$$$**

Sandy beaches are just down the street from this 1911 industrialist's mansion. Fireplaces in some rooms, the grounds are nicely kept. Full breakfasts.

Marblehead, MA *map E-1*

⊟ **The Harbor Light Inn.** 781-631-2186;

58 Washington St. **$$$**

Oriental rugs soften guests' footfalls in this antique-furnished restoration. A sense of serenity pervades this place, which is well-suited to a town with such distinguished history.

THE HARBOR LIGHT INN

☴ **Seagull Inn.** 781-631-1893; 106 Harbor Ave. $$-$$$$
Three-suite bed-and-breakfast where your dog will be welcome, too. Shaker-style furniture (made by one of the owners) and ocean views gives the guest rooms an airy feel.

☴ **Spray Cliff on the Ocean.**
781-631-6789; 25 Spray Ave. $$$
Upscale three-story bed-and-breakfast with seven rooms and sea views. The decor is simple and No children, please.

✕ **Maddie's Sail Loft.** 781-631-9824; 15 State St. $-$$.
Yachters congregate here for hearty, well-prepared food. The dining room gets pretty boisterous.

Martha's Vineyard, MA
map E-3, E-4

☴ **Admiral Benbow Inn.** 508-693-6825; 520 New York Ave., Oak Bluffs $$-$$$.
Six-room B&B near the harbor, furnished with antiques. Warm atmosphere.

☴ **Captain Dexter House.** 508-627-7289; 100 Main St., Vineyard Haven $$
Impeccably restored sea captain's home furnished in antiques, with canopy beds, oriental rugs. Within walking distance from ferry landing.

☴ **Colonial Inn of Martha's Vineyard.**
508-627-4711; 38 North Water St., Edgartown $$-$$$.
Rambling vintage inn with spacious, bright rooms, efficiencies, and apart-ments. All of the guest rooms have been renovated and now feature air conditioners, modems, cable TV.

COLONIAL INN

☴ **The Look Inn.** 508-693-6893; 13 Look Inn St., Vineyard Haven $$
Restored 1806 farmhouse with shared baths, comfortable rooms, and continental breakfasts.

☴ **The Ship's Inn.** 508-693-2760; 18 Kennebec Ave., Oak Bluffs $-$$
Some rooms have private entrances, all are comfortable, with upbeat decor.

☴ **Shiretown Inn,** 508-627-3353; North Water St., Edgartown $-$$$
National Historic Register property with pleasant rustically styled rooms and a garden. Near the harbor.

☴ **Vineyard Harbor Motel.** 508-693-3334; Beach Rd., Vineyard Haven $$
Motel two blocks from ferry landing, with private beach. Some units have kitchenettes.

✕ **Black Dog Bakery.** 508-693-2867; Water St., Vineyard Haven $
True, the nationally ubiquitous Black

Dog Bakery T-shirt may irritate you, but it's still worth stopping here for the delicious breads and pastries. The **Black Dog Tavern** on Beach Street Extension serves full dinners as well as very good, simple chowders. Reservations are not taken. 508-693-9223 $$

✗ **O'Brien's Serious Seafood and Grill.**
508-627-5850; 137 Upper St.,
Edgartown $$
Dine by candlelight or in a rose garden on well-prepared seafood, meats, or pasta entrees. Closed in winter.

✗ **The Scottish Bakehouse.**
508-693-1873; 977 State Rd.,
Vineyard Haven $
A bakery-restaurant, serving breakfast, lunch, and tea. Scones, shortbread, meat pies, and breads. Closed Wednesday.

✗ **Zapotec.** 508-693-6800;
10 Kennebec Ave., Oak Bluffs $$
Innovative Mexican food is served in an upbeat, colorful dining room.

Middleboro, MA *map D-1*

▣ **On Cranberry Pond Bed-and-Breakfast.**
508-946-0768; 43 Fuller St. $$
Literally on the edge of a cranberry bog and a pond, with walking trails and winter skating. Large rooms are well decorated and the hospitality makes you right at home immediately.

▣ **Zachariah Eddy House.** 508-946-0016;
51 South Main St. $$
Victorian home of local gentry restored to preserve its unusual architecture. A

wide porch overlooks the shaded yard; breakfast is served here in nice weather.

ZACHARIAH EDDY HOUSE

Montague, MA *map B-1*

✗ **Montague Book Mill.** 413-367-9206;
440 Greenfield Rd. $-$$
Just outside the pretty village of Montague, a rambling old mill overlooking the Sawmill River houses not only thousands of second-hand books, but also a pleasant coffee shop (and an unrelated, formal restaurant). Lunch specials at the Book Mill have a health-food but not penitential flavor.

Nantucket, MA *map F-4*

▣ **The Beachside Resort at Nantucket.**
508-228-2241 or 800-322-4433;
30 North Beach St. $$-$$$$
Hotel with 90 well-furnished rooms, close to Main Street shops and restaurants. Outdoor heated pool, tennis courts nearby.

Jared Coffin House. 508-228-2400 or 800-248-2405; 29 Broad St. $$-$$$

A set of several distinguished homes in the historic district, a short walk from ferry landing, each restored with period features intact and furnished with antiques. The menu at Jared's may sound like it's filled with traditional Yankee fare, but classic dishes take on new life here, thanks to the kitchen's updated interpretations. Restaurant: $$-$$$.

Nantucket Inn. 508-228-6900 or 800-321-8484; 27 Macy's Lane $$-$$$$

Upscale resort, some units with fireplaces, cathedral ceilings. Indoor pool and free boat shuttle to town.

Periwinkle Guest House. 508-228-9267 or 800-588-0087; 9 North Water St. $-$$$$

Cozy inn with king and queen beds, continental breakfast, in the heart of the old town, close to ferry landing.

The Pineapple Inn. 508-228-9992; 10 Hussey St. $$$$

Restored 1838 sea captain's mansion furnished with antiques, and marble baths in the bathroom. This inn provides lots of creature comforts. Closed in winter.

Sherburne Inn. 508-228-4425; 10 Gay St. $-$$$

Well-kept 1835 home in historic district, close to ferry landing. Home-baked pastries are served with the continental breakfast.

Wauwinet Inn. 508-228-0145 or 888-303-3661, 120 Wauwinet Rd. $$$$

Situated on a ridge between Nantucket Sound and the ocean, this historic inn offers 25 rooms and five cottages. Broad lawns surround the main building, and both harbor and ocean beaches are close at hand. Topper's Restaurant boasts elegant ambiance and sophisticated cuisine. Restaurant: $$$$

WAUWINET INN

Boarding House. 508-228-9622; 12 Federal St. $$-$$$.

New American cuisine, with Asian and Mediterranean accents. You can sit in the intimate dining room, on the patio, or in the bar area, which gets a little rowdy on summer evenings.

Brotherhood of Thieves. no phone; 23 Broad St. $$

Casual and always busy, a popular spot for sandwiches or heartier meals. Lunch and dinner daily; there's live music some evenings.

The Sea Grille. 508-325-5700; 45 Sparks Ave. $-$$

Seafood dishes of all sorts, nicely prepared, in an attractive setting.

New Bedford, MA *map E-3*

✕ **Davey's Locker.** 508-992-7359;
1480 East Rodney French Blvd. **$$**
Overlooking Clark's Cove, this eatery is primarily a seafood restaurant, but patrons can also order steaks, chicken, ribs. Reservations are recommended.

✕ **Freestone's City Grill.** 508-993-7477;
41 William St. **$$**
The historic district's standout restaurant, in a rock-solid recycled 19th-century bank building. Casual atmosphere. The kitchen offers fish chowder, grilled seafood, char-grilled hamburgers, and serious salads. Reservations suggested.

Newburyport, MA *map E-1*

▥ **The Clark Currier Inn.** 978-465-8363;
45 Green St. **$$-$$$**
This former shipbuilder's home was built in 1803 and has been beautifully restored. Rooms are furnished with antiques. The inn is conveniently located, and offers an afternoon tea.

▥ **The Garrison Inn.** 978-499-8500;
11 Brown Square **$$-$$$$**
Comfortable inn with 24 rooms, some wheelchair accessible.

✕ **The Bayou.** 978-499-0428; 50 State St.
$-$$
Spicy Creole and down-home southern dishes, rare in Yankeedom, along with New England seafoods.

✕ **Nasturtiums.** 978-463-4040;
27 State St. **$$**
Creative and lively New American menu with delightful mixing of flavors. Dinner nightly, lunch Thursday through Sunday.

✕ **Scandia Restaurant.** 978-462-6271;
25 State St. **$$**
Eclectic cuisine with a European bias. Lots of seafood; salmon dishes are positively inspired. Elegant weekend brunch. Very small, so make a reservation.

✕ **Ten Center Street.** 508-462-6652;
10 Center St. **$$-$$$**
Traditional Yankee cooking for lunch and dinner; hunker down next to the roaring fireplace.

Northampton, MA
map B-2

HOTEL NORTHAMPTON

▥ **Hotel Northampton.** 413-584-3100,
✕ 36 King St. **$$-$$$**
This brick hotel in the town center has cozy rooms, some with four-poster beds or balconies overlooking the street, and a traditional dinner menu in its **Wiggins Tavern**. More casual fare is available in the **Coolidge Park Cafe. $$-$$$**

⌂ **Knoll Bed-and-Breakfast.** 413-584-8164; 230 N. Main St., Florence $$-$$$
This small, unpretentious guest house is a quiet retreat offering a four-poster bed in each room and an eclectic mixture of furnishings. Four rooms with two shared baths. No credit cards.

✕ **Eastside Grill.** 413-586-3347; 19 Strong Ave. $$
Definitely part of the new Northampton, this chic restaurant, serving entrees such as oysters and pan-seared fish, is also pleasant for a casual drink.

✕ **Jake's.** 413-584-9613; 17 King St. $
A favorite with locals, this old Northampton institution serves no-frills lunches in a pleasantly creaky coffeeshop setting.

✕ **Northampton Brewery.** 413-584-9903; 11 Brewster Court $-$$
This microbrewery serves bar food and a variety of beers. The roof deck is open in warm weather, and there's live music on Sunday evenings.

Plymouth, MA *map E-2*

⌂ **Governor Bradford Motor Inn.** 508-746-6200 or 800-332-1620; 98 Water St. $
Overlooks the harbor, outdoor swimming pool.

⌂ **John Carver Inn.** 508-746-7100 or 800-274-1620; 25 Summer St. $-$$
Nice restaurant and a swimming pool.

⌂ **Pilgrim Sands Motel.** 508-747-0900 or 800-729-SAND; 150 Warren Ave. (Route 3A) $-$$

Tidy, nicely kept motel with a private beach for guests.

✕ **Cafe Nanina.** 508-747-4503; 14 Union St. $$
Northern Italian specialties in a bright dining room overlooking the wharves.

✕ **Iguana's.** 508-747-4000; 170 Water St. $-$$
Home of burritos and enchiladas, along with char-broiled steaks and ribs.

✕ **Isaac's.** 508-830-0001; 114 Water St. $$
For seafood dining with views of Plymouth Harbor. Dinner reservations recommended.

✕ **The Weathervane.** 508-746-4195; 6 Town Wharf $
Good for seafood; overlooks the harbor.

Provincetown, MA
map F-2

Lodging prices and crowds drop after the summer high season, but many places remain open.

⌂ **Bradford-Carver House.** 508-487-4966 or 800-826-9083; 70 Bradford St. $$-$$$.
Set of three carefully restored buildings, with each room or suite a different decor, all of them stylish. Pool and gardens in courtyard.

⌂ **Brass Key Guest House.** 508-487-9005 or 800-842-9858; 67 Bradford St. $$-$$$
Congenial hosts, pool; breakfast available on request.

⌂ **Cape Colony Inn.** 508-487-1755; 280 Bradford St. $-$$
Clean motel with pool and free movies.

Harborside Realty. 800-838-4005; 162 Commercial St.
Cottage, condo, and apartment rentals by the week or longer.

The Masthead Resort. 508-487-0523 or 800-395-5095; 31-34 Commercial St. $$-$$$
Motel, cottages, apartments, all well-furnished, some with antiques. Set in gardens along 450 feet of private beach, with freeboat moorings and launch service. Open year-round.

Surfside Inn. 508-487-1726; 543 Commercial St. $$.
Modern motels right on the beach. There's a coffee shop on the property and restaurants nearby. Within walking distance from town.

✕ **Dancing Lobster.** 508-487-0900; 463 Commercial St. $$
Mediterranean-inspired menu, filled with creative dishes.

✕ **Martin House.** 508-487-1327; 157 Commercial St. $$.
New England fare accented with influences from all over the world. Dine outdoors in good weather.

Rockport, MA *map E-1*

Addison Choate Inn. 978-546-7543 or 800-245-7543; 49 Broadway $$
Historic home turned bed-and-breakfast, with elegant rooms and congenial hosts. Fine breakfasts.

ADDISON CHOATE INN

Peg Leg Inn. 800-346-2352; 18 Beach St. $-$$$
Stay in one of the charming rooms in the main house or in a cottage overlooking the sea. Original art in public rooms, genial innkeepers. Breakfast is included. Closed in winter.

Pleasant Street Inn. 978-546-3915 or 800-541-3915; 17 Pleasant St. $$
Victorian home nicely converted to a B&B, close to harbor. The tower room has its own cupola.

Seaward Inn and Cottages. 978-546-3471 or 800-648-7733; 44 Marmion Way $$
Inn rooms and cottages, some with kitchen, set on five acres. Swimming pond, bicycles. Breakfast included.

Yankee Clipper Inn. 978-546-3407 or 800-545-3699; 96 Granite St. $$-$$$
Well-kept rooms overlook lawns and gardens stretching to the sea. Each room is different, many with antiques, some with sitting rooms. Breakfast included. Katherine Anne Porter wrote *Ship of Fools* while staying here.

A note on dining in Rockport:
Rockport is a "dry" town, where wine and beer cannot be sold, even in restaurants. Nick into Gloucester for a bottle before you head for dinner here.

✗ **The Greenery.** 978-546-5130 **$$**
Contemporary American cuisine such as grilled seafood, delicious pastas, and fresh salads. Breakfast is served on weekends; open April through November.

✗ **Peg Leg Restaurant.**
978-546-3038; 18 Beach St. **$-$$**
Specializes in seafood, often old favorite dishes, but with a creative approach; excellent chowders, good service. The chef also offers many healthy alternatives.

Salem, MA *map E-1*

🏨 **Hawthorne Hotel at Salem Common.**
978-744-4080 or 800-SAY-STAY;
18 Washington Square West
(Route 1A) **$$-$$$**
Restored historic hotel nestled close to Pickering Wharf. Rooms are individually decorated; many have four-poster beds. Full hotel facilities with restaurant, bar, pool privileges at nearby YMCA.

🏨 **Inn at Seven Winter Street.**
978-745-9520; 7 Winter St. **$$-$$$**
Elegant Victorian mansion with fine period details and antique furnishings. Some rooms have decks, fireplaces, whirlpools, canopied beds. No children, please.

🏨 **The Salem Inn.** 978-741-0680;
7 Summer St. **$$-$$$$.**

Actually three historic inns that share a single check-in and breakfast room in the **West House,** a set of brick attached townhouses built in the Federal period. **Craven House** and **Peabody House** are both well-restored colonial homes. All are close to Salem's prime attractions.

THE SALEM INN

✗ **Lyceum Bar & Grill.** 978-745-7665;
43 Church St. **$$.**
Elegant decor in a historic building, with a menu featuring New American and international cuisine. Known especially for creative grilled meats, seafood, and vegetables dishes.

✗ **Roosevelt's.** 978-745-9608;
300 Derby St. **$$**
Informal and family-friendly, with a Teddy Roosevelt theme and American menu, featuring the standards but with updated style and flourish. Animal trophies hang on the walls.

MASSACHUSETTS
FOOD & LODGING

Sandwich, MA *map F-3*

⌂ **The Belfry Inne.** 508-888-8550;
8 Jarves St. $$-$$$
Victorian "painted lady" renovated lavishly with balconies, fireplaces, skylights, and other features to give each room individual character.

⌂ **The Dan'l Webster Inn.** 508-888-3622
or 800-444-3566; 149 Main St. $$-$$$
Modern, well-maintained hotel with traditional rooms, four-poster beds, fireplaces, whirlpool baths. Swim in pool or at nearby beach. Four restaurant in the inn are local favorites.

⌂ **Isaiah Jones Homestead.**
508-888-9115; 165 Main St. $$-$$$
Impeccably dressed in Oriental rugs and period furniture, some rooms with fireplaces and whirlpool tubs. Candlelight breakfast is big enough for a dinner.

⌂ **Shady Nook Inn and Motel.**
508-888-0409; 14 Route 6A $-$$
Attractive motel made less plain by its setting in terraced rockgardens; heated pool, free movies.

✗ **The Beehive Tavern.** 508-833-1184;
406 Route 6A $.
Friendly, fun and frugal, possibly the best food value on the Cape. Lobster pie is a specialty, as is their ice cream.

✗ **Dunbar Tea Shop.** 508-833-2485; One Water St.
The small tea room behind the tealover's shop is a lunchtime and afternoon delight. Open year-round; hours are longer in summer and fall, so call ahead.

Scituate Area *map E-2*

⌂ **The Allen House.** 781-545-8221;
18 Allen Place, Scituate $$-$$$
Hospitable B&B in a Victorian home overlooking the harbor. Breakfasts are monumental.

⌂ **Kimball's By-the-Sea.** 781-383-6650;
124 Elm St., Cohasset $$
A pleasant motor inn with interior corridors, right at Cohasset's harbor.

✗ **The Barker Tavern.** 781-545-6533; 21 Barker Rd., Scituate $$-$$$
Possibly New England's oldest eatery, built in 1634, the tavern specializes in New England standby dishes and does them exceedingly well.

✗ **Spazio.** 781-849-1577; 200 Quincy Ave. (Route 53), Braintree $$
Hard to spot, but well worth seeking out for inspired Mediterranean dishes, where the flavors of North Africa, the Aegean, and Sicily blend seamlessly.

✗ **Tosca.** 781-740-0080; 14 North St., Hingham $$-$$$
You won't be alone in singing arias in praise of this outstanding Italian oasis on the South Shore. Detail is everything, and the chef pays close attention to each nuance, whether the dish is a rabbit ragout or a heavenly risotto.

Shelburne Falls Area, MA *map B-1*

⌂ **Penfrydd Farm.** 413-624-5516;
Box 100A, Colrain $$$

An ideal country retreat, this quiet renovated farmhouse sits in the middle of a 160-acre working farm and, particularly in autumn, seems to invite the surrounding forest in through its skylights.

☵ **Davenport's Maple Farm.** 413-625-2866; 111 Tower Rd. (follow signs for Hwy. 2), Colrain $
Outstanding hearty breakfasts on the farm in a sublime setting. Breakfast only, weekends only. Opens the first weekend before March 1 for six weekends. Pancake breakfasts for about five bucks.

Stockbridge, MA *map A-2*

HISTORIC MERREL INN

☵ **Historic Merrel Inn.** 413-243-1794 or 800-243-1794; 1565 Pleasant St., South Lee $$$$
Once a private residence and a stagecoach stop, this 200-year-old building contains the only intact "birdcage" colonial bar—semicircular with enclosing slats—in America. Tastefully decorated.

☵ **Red Lion Inn.** 413-298-5545; 30 Main St. $$$$

Opened in 1773, this large, welcoming inn dominates Main Street and over the years has gradually spilled over into a number of annexes. The comfortable rooms have a delightful mixture of formal and country furnishings. New England specialties are served in the dining room and, during the summer, in the gardens. Bar food is also available. With 26 suites, 96 rooms with bath, 15 rooms sharing five baths, two restaurants, bar, pool, exercise, conference rooms.

RED LION INN

Sturbridge, MA *map C-2*

✕ **Whistling Swan.** 508-347-2321; 502 Main St. $$-$$$
Located in a clapboard house west of Old Sturbridge Village, this restaurant serves the most elaborate food in town. The dishes in the more casual **Ugly Duckling Loft**, housed in a converted barn, also incorporate the best ingredients, but in high-end renditions of pub fare—fish-and-chips, burgers, salads. Live music some nights. $-$$

Turner's Falls, MA
map B-1

✕ **Shady Glen Diner.** 413-863-9636;
7 Avenue A **$-$$**
"The Shady," as regulars call it, is one of
the region's best diners. The turkey in
your turkey club sandwich has been
roasted in the kitchen, and the pies are
outstanding.

Williamstown, MA
map A-1

⌂ **River Bend Farm.** 413-458-5504;
643 Simonds Rd. **$$$**
An artfully restored farmhouse, tastefully
furnished with antiques of a rural rather
than a formal nature. Some rooms have
four-poster beds or rope beds with feath-
er mattresses. Four rooms with two
shared baths. No credit cards.

THE WILLIAMS INN

⌂ **The Williams Inn.** 413-458-9371 or
800-828-0133; On the Green **$$$**
A modern hotel that nonetheless seems
at home on the town common. The
rooms are large and luxurious while the
atmosphere in the lounge is more collegiate than corporate.

✕ **Mezze Bistro.** 413-458-0123;
84 Water St. **$$-$$$**
Definitely more New York than New
England, this chic restaurant and bar is a
favorite late-night venue of actors during
the Williamstown Theatre Festival. The
food is predictably fashionable but undeniably good. Dinner only. Closed September to May.

✕ **Wild Amber Grill.** 413-458-4000;
101 North St. **$-$$**
The New American menu at this unpretentious restaurant changes frequently
but is reliably good whatever the combinations of beef, poultry, seafood, and
vegetables. Sunday brunch is available
from 11 to 2. Closed on Tuesdays.

Worcester, MA *map C-2*

✕ **Restaurant at Tatnuck Bookseller
Marketplace.** 508-755-5640; 3353
Chandler St. (Route 122)
Set in the city's largest bookstore, this ca-
sual cafe offers three meals every day.
Known for fresh ingredients, lots of veg-
etables, and chocolate desserts.

Yarmouth Area, MA
map F-3

⌂ **Blueberry Manor.** 508-362-7620;
438 Main St. (Route 6A), Yarmouthport
$$-$$$
Originally a 1700s sea captain's home,
the house was later added on to. Guest
rooms are furnished with antiques.

⌶ **Captain Farris House.** 508-760-2818 or 800-350-9477; 308 Old Main St., South Yarmouth **$$$**
Historic property lovingly restored, with modern comforts discreetly added. Most rooms have whirlpool baths, fireplaces, sundecks. Three-course breakfasts.

⌶ **The Mariner Motor Lodge.** 508-771-7887; 573 Main St. (Route 28), West Yarmouth **$-$$**
Indoor and outdoor pools, miniature golf, picnic tables, and a grill. The lodge is designed for families, with free movies, refrigerators, and inside corridors.

⌶ **Olde Schoolhouse B&B.** 508-778-9468; 22 Lewis Rd., West Yarmouth **$$**
Greek Revival–style schoolhouse featuring stylish rooms with four-poster beds, quilts, some with whirlpool baths. Near the beach and shopping.

⌶ **One Centre Street Inn.** 508-362-8910; One Centre St., Yarmouthport **$$-$$$**
A former parsonage with elegant rooms, a gracious air, and colorful gardens. Guests are welcome to use the inn's bicycles.

ONE CENTRE STREET INN

⌶ **Red Mill Motel.** 508-398-5583; 793 Main St., South Yarmouth **$**
Plain but comfortable, with some efficiencies and a swimming pool.

⌶ **Tidewater Motor Lodge.** 508-775-6322; 135 Main St. (Route 28), West Yarmouth **$-$$**
Large motel units with refrigerators, around outdoor pool and play area.

⌶ **The Wedgewood Inn.** 508-362-5157; 83 Main St. (Route 6A), Yarmouthport **$$$-$$$$**
Greek Revival/Federal–style home from 1812, with working fireplaces in most rooms. Rooms have canopy beds, antiques, and abundant hospitable details. Gardens and memorable breakfasts.

✕ **Abbicci.** 508-362-3501; 43 Main St. (Route 6A), Yarmouthport **$$**
Creative dishes based in Northern Italian cuisine, and the breads are superb. Attractive setting. Reservations are advised.

✕ **Captain Parker's.** 508-771-4266; 668 Main St. (Route 28), West Yarmouth **$$**
Casual seafood restaurant with children's menu, Sunday brunch.

✕ **Clancy's.** 508-775-3332; 175 Main St. (Route 28), West Yarmouth **$-$$**
Family favorites like fish-and-chips, sandwiches. Bar has entertainment, too.

CONNECTICUT FOOD & LODGING

Avon, CT *map B-3*

⊞ **Avon Old Farms Hotel.** 860-677-1651;
✕ Route 10 and US 44 **$$**
A big (161-room) country hotel on a
20-acre hillside site. Outdoor pool with
snack bar and locker rooms, gym. Varied
dining spaces include **Seasons Restau-
rant**, a bright open room with views of
fields and trees. The menu changes sea-
sonally, and the work of local artists is
displayed on the walls; **$$$**.

Branford, CT *map B-4*

✕ **Le Petit Cafe.** 203-483-9791;
225 Montowese St. **$$$**
A true Lyonnais bistro in Branford, run
by Jacques Pepin's niece and her hus-
band. A set menu, reasonably priced,
features rustic French dishes served in
heavy rustic crockery. Only 15 tables.

Brookfield, CT *map A-3*

✕ **Christopher's.** 203-775-4409; US 7 **$$**
Ask for harvest potato soup, followed by
seafood, steak, or veal. A quaint spot for
traditional American cooking.

Brooklyn, CT *map C-3*

✕ **Golden Lamb Buttery.** 860-774-4423;
499 Wolf Den Rd. **$$$$**
A 1,000-acre farm is the site of this
restaurant serving huge portions of excellent traditional American food. You
can even take a hayride before dinner.

Canaan, CT *map A-2*

✕ **The Cannery Café.** 860-824-7333;
85 Main St. **$$**
Don't be misled by the modest storefront;
this is a popular American-style bistro.

✕ **Collins Diner.** 860-824-7040;
US 44 at US 7 **$-$$**
One of five classic American diners list-
ed on the National Register of Historic
Places. The authentic diner experience.

Chester, CT *map B-4*

⊞ **The Inn at Chester.** 860-526-9541 or
✕ 800-949-7829; 318 West Main St. **$$$**
A modernized 42-room country inn on
the edge of Chester village; the main
building dates from 1776. Contempo-
rary Yankee cooking in the **Post &
Beam** dining room; **$$-$$$**.

✕ **Fiddler's.** 860-526-3210; 4 Water St. **$$**
Well-known regionally for mesquite
grilling and a good variety of fresh-
caught local seafood.

✕ **Restaurant du Village.** 860-526-5301;
59 Main St. **$$$**
The village's haute-cuisine eatery, with a
French-Alsatian accent. Reservations
suggested—only 40 seats.

Cornwall, CT *map A-3*

✕ **Brookside Bistro.** 860-672-6601;
Route 128 **$$**
French bistro fare, indoors or outside on
the deck alongside the Mill Brook.

Note: Map coordinates refer to the map on page 327.

Coventry, CT *map C-3*

✕ **Bidwell Tavern.** 860-742-6978;
260 Main St. $-$$
A vintage tavern built in 1822, serving
meat and seafood, plus tasty Bidwell
burgers. Live entertainment most
evenings.

East Haddam, CT *map C-3*

⌂ **Bishopsgate Inn.** 860-873-1677;
Norwich Rd. $$
An 1818 shipbuilder's homestead with
six fireplaces, six nicely furnished guest
rooms. Full breakfasts served.

⌂ **Gelston House.** 860-873-1411;
✕ 8 Main St. $$-$$$
Right next to the Goodspeed Opera
House; known for the fresh and creative
American-international fusion cuisine.

Essex, CT *map C-4*

COPPER BEECH INN

⌂ **Copper Beech Inn.** 860-767-0330;
46 Main St., Ivoryton $$-$$$
Built for one of the village's former ivory
merchants and named for the enormous
copper beech tree standing out front. A
classy restaurant for French cuisine.
Reservations suggested.

⌂ **The Griswold Inn.** 860-767-1776;
✕ 36 Main St. $$-$$$.
Essex wouldn't be Essex without the
"Gris," claimed to be the state's earliest
three-story structure. Currier & Ives
steamboat prints adorn the **Covered
Bridge** dining room, where the atmos-
phere is comfortable and the food
straightforward American. Dinner reser-
vations required. $$

Farmington, CT *map B-3*

⌂ **Barney House.** 860-674-2796;
11 Mountain Spring Rd. $$
A 19th-century B&B mansion with ten-
nis courts and five acres of private land
for recreation. All seven guest rooms
overlook a formal garden and Victorian
greenhouse.

✕ **Apricots.** 860-673-5405;
1593 Farmington Ave. $$$,
Attractive views of the Farmington River
enhance the dining experience upstairs;
downstairs, the pub-like dining room
more crowded, noisier. The eclectic
menu borrows from regional American
and French traditions; lunch is more reasonably priced. Reservations suggested.

✕ **Brannigan's Restaurant & Gathering.**
860-621-9311; 176 Laning St.,
Southington $$
Primarily a barbecue place where the
specialty is baby back ribs. Seafood,

chicken and charbroiled steaks, too, plus hefty desserts. Reservations suggested.

Greenwich, CT *map A-4*

✕ **La Maison de Indochine.**
203-869-2689;
107-109 Greenwich Ave. $$-$$$
An up-market choice for Vietnamese specialties for lunch or dinner.

✕ **Le Figaro Bistro de Paris.**
203-622-0018; 372 Greenwich Ave. $$$
A French favorite in the heart of downtown Greenwich. Attractively appointed dining room, delicious bistro fare—a bit pricey, though. Reservations advised.

✕ **Manero's.** 203-869-0049;
559 Steamboat Rd. $$
A solid, popular, reasonably priced meat-and-potatoes establishment.

✕ **Restaurant Jean-Louise.**
203-622-8450; 61 Lewis St. $$$-$$$$
Befitting the sophistication of Greenwich, this intimate spot excels in nouvelle French dishes. Reservations advised.

✕ **Thataway Café.** 203-622-0947;
409 Greenwich Ave. $-$$
A huge terrace for casual al fresco dining, with a menu ranging from hamburgers to full-course meals.

Guilford, CT *map B-4*

✕ **Bistro on the Green.** 203-458-9059;
25 Whitfield St. $$
Facing one of the largest village greens in New England, and housed in an airy room with a brick patio. A popular,

casual place for a snack or meal, and just the ticket for a long weekend breakfasts. Original art adorns the walls.

✕ **Cilantro.** 203-458-2555;
85 Whitfield St. $
An up-market deli, aromatic bakery, coffee roastery, and specialty food store with made-to-order sandwiches and pleasant window-side tables.

Hartford, CT *map B-4*

▣ **Goodwin Hotel.** 860-246-7500 or
✕ 800-922-5006; 1 Haynes St. $$-$$$.
An 1881 Queen Anne–style beauty, this hotel was built as a townhouse for zillionaire J. P. Morgan. It's the only nonchain hotel downtown. Fine cuisine is served downstairs in Mr. Morgan's namesake restaurant, **Pierpont's.** Reservations necessary; $$-$$$.

✕ **Chuck's Steak House.** 860-241-9100;
1 Civic Center Plaza $$
Centrally located in the huge Hartford Civic Center.

✕ **Hartford Brewery Ltd.** 860-246-BEER;
35 Pearl St. $
Features roast beef, pot roast, and three dozen ales, stouts, and porters.

✕ **Max Downtown.** 860-522-2530;
185 Asylum St. $$$
Downtown's classiest eatery. Reservations required.

✕ **No Fish Today.** 860-244-2100;
80 Pratt St. $$
In a historic brick building; recommendable for Italian specialties and, despite the name, seafood.

Kent, CT *map A-3*

Constitution Oak Farm. 860-354-6495; 36 Beardsley Rd. $$
On 200 acres, an ex-dairy farm where the house dates from the 1830s. Four cozy guest rooms.

Fife & Drum Restaurant & Inn. 860-927-3509; 53 North Main St. $$
Eight guest rooms, center-of-town convenience, sizeable wine list in the barnwood restaurant; $$-$$$.

Stroble's Baking Company. 860-927-4073; 14 North Main St. $
Open the door and your olfactory senses will be overwhelmed by the aroma of buttered baguettes and apricot tarts, specialties of this village landmark.

The Villager. 860-927-3945; 28 North Main St. $
Hugely popular for burgers and milkshakes, plus sizeable wake-up breakfasts.

Litchfield, CT *map A-3*

TOLLGATE HILL INN

Tollgate Hill Inn & Restaurant. 860-567-4545 or 800-445-3903; US 202 and Tollgate Rd. $$$
Two 18th-century buildings amid a grove of white birch trees. Hearty meals are served in the original tavern. $$-$$$.

Litchfield Inn. 860-567-4503; 432 Bantam Rd. (US 202) $$-$$$.
A colonial-type inn with two dozen rooms and **Bistro East** restaurant. $$.

LITCHFIELD INN

La Cupola. 860-567-3326; 637 Bantam Rd. (US 202) $$-$$$
Sited in a stone house overlooking Bantam Lake. Tempting Italian cuisine.

West Street Grill. 860-567-3885; 43 West St. $$-$$$
Overlooking the village green; great for celebrity-watching. Contemporary American cuisine draws large crowds, so make reservations.

Madison, CT *map B-4*

The Inn at Lafayette. 203-245-7773; 725 Boston Post Rd. $$$
Housed in a 19th-century church building, this inn offers five guest rooms and a convenient town-center location. **Cafe Allegre** restaurant: $$$

Madison Beach Hotel. 203-245-1404;
94 West Wharf Rd. $$-$$$
A gray-shingled Victorian, nicely restored and featuring beach frontage in a secluded Madison neighborhood. All-American meals are served in the **Wharf Restaurant**; $$-$$$.

TIDEWATER INN

Tidewater Inn. 203-245-8457;
949 Boston Post Rd. $$-$$$
This white stucco B&B inn, dating from 1880, opens onto English-style flower gardens. Just a mile from Hammonasset Beach State Park.

Middletown, CT *map B-3*

Harbor Park Restaurant.
860-347-9999; 80 Harbor Dr. $$
Originally the Middletown Yacht Club's 1915 haven, located on Harbor Park alongside the Connecticut River. Meat and seafood.

Atticus Books & Cafe. 860-347-1194;
45 Broad St. $
In addition to breads and pastries, big salads and hearty soups are available at this bakery. The tables are set amid stacks of children's books.

Eleanor Rigby's. 860-343-1730;
360 Main St. $
A popular, very casual city-center delicatessen and cafe. Homemade soups and muffins, great salad bar.

O'Rourke's Diner. 860-346-6101;
728 Main St. $
Straight out of 1947, a classic American diner complete with art deco stainless-steel wall coverings, wooden booths, Formica-topped counters, glass bricks, and a neon sign.

Tuscany Grill. 860-346-7096;
600 Plaza Middlesex (on College St.)
$$-$$$
Housed in a former opera house, this chic restaurant serves sophisticated pastas, pizzas, and more.

Cornerstone's. 860-344-0222;
98 Washington St. $$-$$$
American menu, stylish atmosphere.

Morris, CT *map A-3*

Deer Island Gate. 860-567-4622;
Route 209 $$
On the shore of Bantam Lake, a largely German restaurant, with such hearty fare as sauerbraten with red cabbage always on the menu.

Mystic, CT *map C-4*

The Inn at Mystic. 860-536-9604 or
800-237-2415; US 1 and Route 27 $$$
Five-room Georgian colonial inn, listed on the National Register of Historic Places. Lauren Bacall and Bogey stayed here during their honeymoon. Includes

the praiseworthy **Flood Tide Restaurant.** Reservations required; $$-$$$.

OLD MYSTIC INN

Old Mystic Inn. 860-572-9422;
52 Main St. $$
A circa-1784 house and carriage house alongside the Mystic River, now an eight-room B&B. Some rooms have fireplaces, some have whirlpool tubs; all have tasteful and comfortable decor.

RED BROOK INN

Red Brook Inn. 860-572-0349;
2800 Gold Star Hwy. $$-$$$
Two historic colonial dwellings, both filled with antiques, on 17 acres in the quiet end of town.

Steamboat Inn. 860-536-8300;
73 Steamboat Wharf $$

Ten waterfront rooms with fireplaces and whirlpools. Continental breakfast.

Whaler's Inn. 860-536-1506 or 800-243-2588; 20 East Main St. $$
A four-building complex with a total of 41 guest rooms, close to everything in the heart of town.

Bravo Bravo. 860-536-3228;
20 East Main St. $$-$$$
Downtown's top choice for Italian food. **Cafe Bravo,** on the waterfront terrace, is more casual and wonderful in warm weather. Reservations required.

S&P Oyster Company. 860-536-2674;
1 Holmes St. $$
Dine while viewing the Mystic River and Mystic's 1922 bascule drawbridge.

Seamen's Inne. 860-536-9649;
105 Greenmanville Ave. $$
Just a short walk from the ever popular Mystic Seaport maritime museum; hearty meals plus the social Samuel Adams Pub.

New Haven, CT *map B-4*

Three Chimneys Inn. 203-789-1201;
1201 Chapel St. $$
Be pampered in this Victorian mansion reborn as a 10-room B&B. Just one block from Yale University.

Louis' Lunch. 203-562-5507, 261-263 Crown St. $
The story goes that Louis Lassen invented the hamburger here in 1895. His descendants still broil the thick but low-fat patties vertically, then serve them on toast with onions, cheese, tomatoes.

CONNECTICUT
FOOD & LODGING

✕ **Scoozi Trattoria & Wine Bar.**
203-776-8268; 1104 Chapel St. $$-$$$
A trendy pasta place. The abbacchio Siciliana—braised lamb shank with sundried tomato–calamata olive sauce and Tuscan white beans—is exemplary. Ditto the tagliatelle boscaiola—wide ribbons of pasta with wild mushrooms, sun-dried tomatoes, marsala, basil, and garlic.. Reservations required.

✕ **Union League Café.** 203-562-4299;
1032 Chapel St. $$
With its casual bistro ambience and French country cuisine, this restaurant is popular with Yale professorial types. The Edwardian interior features dark wood and stained glass. Reservations advised.

New London, CT *map C-4*

⬚ **Lighthouse Inn.** 860-443-8411;
✕ 6 Guthrie Place $$-$$$
Waterfront accommodations in a circa 1900 pink stucco mansion with a private beach and elegant restaurant. Dinner $$$. Reservations suggested.

New Milford, CT *map A-3*

✕ **Rudy's.** 860-354-7727;
122 Litchfield Rd., New Milford $$
A kitschy but fun Swiss-German restaurant complete with waitresses in dirndls.

New Preston/ Washington, CT *map A-3*

⬚ **The Birches Inn.** 860-868-1735;
✕ 233 West Shore Rd., New Preston $$$$

Very upscale and perfectly positioned for lake views; features a private beach and critically acclaimed restaurant; $$-$$$.

THE BIRCHES INN

⬚ **Boulders Inn.** 860-868-0541 or
✕ 800-552-6853; East Shore Rd.
(Route 45), New Preston $$$-$$$$
Classy but casual lodgings in an 1875 Victorian mansion with Lake Waramaug and Pinnacle Mountain views. On the premises is a delightful restaurant. Reservations suggested; $$$.

BOULDERS INN

⬚ **Hopkins Inn.** 860-868-7295;
✕ 22 Hopkins Rd., New Preston $$$
A Federal-style country inn and Swiss-Austrian restaurant overlooking Lake Waramaug. Restaurant: $$-$$$.

☈ **Mayflower Inn.** 860-868-9466;

✕ 118 Woodbury Rd., Washington $$$

An exemplary New England country inn, the Mayflower is a century old and set on 28 acres with a duck pond and hillside gardens. There are also a health spa and a fine restaurant. Reservations required. Restaurant: $$$-$$$$.

✕ **G. W. Tavern.** 860-868-6633;

20 Bee Brook Rd., Washington Depot $$

American and Brit favorites, from meat loaf and chicken pot pie to fish-n-chips.

✕ **Le Bon Coin.** 860-868-7763; US 202, New Preston $$$-$$$$

In an old white house in a charming village, the very finest French cuisine you're liable to find in this part of Connecticut. Reservations required.

✕ **The Pantry.** 860-868-0258;

Titus Rd., Washington Depot $

A restaurant, deli, bake shop, and heaLth-food store; handy for picnic supplies.

Noank, CT *map C-4*

☈ **The Palmer Inn.** 860-572-9000;

25 Church St. $$

The very essence of a Yankee B&B in a picturesque coastal village. Built by a shipwright in 1907, it now offers six guest rooms.

✕ **Abbott's Lobster in the Rough.**

860-572-9128; 117 Pearl St. $$

An oceanside setting for New England shore dinners (clam chowder, boiled lobster, "steamer" clams, corn on the cob).

✕ **Fisherman Restaurant.** 860-536-1717;

937 Groton Long Point Rd. $$

A casual place overlooking the village's Fisher's Island Sound.

✕**Seahorse Tavern.** 860-536-1670;

65 Marsh Rd. $$

Fresh seafood, also steaks in a little eatery on the town dock.

Norfolk, CT *map A-2*

☈ **Mountain View Inn.** 860-542-6991;

✕ 67 Litchfield Rd., Norfolk $$$

An elite seven-room country inn in a building dating from 1875; gourmet fireside dining. Reservations required; $$$.

Norwalk Area, CT *map A-4*

☈ **Inn at National Hall.** 203-221-1351;

✕ 2 Post Rd. West, Westport $$$$

Historic 19th-century inn with 15 rooms alongside the Saugatuck River. Indulge in a gourmet meal with impeccable service at the inn's posh **Miramar Restaurant**, 203-222-2267. Reservations suggested; $$$.

☈ **Roger Sherman Inn.** 203-966-4541;

✕ 195 Oenoke Ridge, New Canaan $$$

This 1783 mansion is today a plush inn and local landmark. The updated but still rich menu features classic continental cuisine. $$$

(See picture next page.)

ROGER SHERMAN INN

✕**Amberjacks.** 203-853-4332;
99 Washington St., South Norwalk $$
Right in the midst of SoNo's "restaurant
row," this spot gets lively and sometimes
noisy. Creative, contemporary prepara-
tions of fresh seafood, pastas.

✕ **Blue Water Café.** 203-972-1799;
15 Elm St., New Canaan $-$$
This long-time local favorite is the place
for fresh fish and creative pasta selections.

✕ **Brewhouse Restaurant.** 203-853-9110;
13 Marshall St., Norwalk $
Conveniently close to Norwalk's Maritime Center nautical museum, a casual
New England brewpub.

✕ **Jeremiah O'Donovan's.** 203-838-3430;
138 Washington St., Norwalk $
The very essence of an old-time saloon,
complete with pressed-tin ceiling and
photos of pugilists covering the walls.
Good inexpensive food, too.

✕ **Silvermine Tavern.** 203-847-4558,
194 Perry Ave., Silvermine $$-$$$
Order from an eclectic menu while seat-
ed (fickle New England weather permitting) on a terrace overlooking a waterfall
and duck pond. In the placid suburb of
Silvermine, north of downtown Norwalk. Reservations suggested.

Old Lyme, CT *map C-4*

BEE & THISTLE INN

▣ **Bee & Thistle Inn.** 860-434-1667 or
✕ 800-622-4946; 100 Lyme St $$
This establishment, comparably genteel,
began its existence as a riverside resi-
dence built in 1756. Today the inn and
its restaurant regularly garner many
awards, including a consistent ranking as
most romantic. $$

▣ **The Inn at Harbor Hill Marina.**
860-739-0331; 60 Grand St., Niantic $$
Eight waterview guest rooms in an
1870s building. Continental breakfast is
included.

▣ **Old Lyme Inn.** 860-434-2600 or 800-
434-5352; 85 Lyme St. $$
Thirteen guest rooms in a genteel 1850s
Victorian mansion.

✕ **The Shack.** 860-739-8898;
Flanders Rd., East Lyme $-$$
Down-home cooking; all-you-can-eat
fish fry daily. Worth finding it for plump
Niantic Bay scallops.

Old Saybrook, CT *map C-4*

⛢ **Captain Dibbell House.** 860-669-1646;
21 Commerce St., Clinton **$$**
An antique-filled B&B in a circa-1866
Victorian house with four guest rooms.

SAYBROOK POINT INN

⛢ **Saybrook Point Inn.** 860-395-2000 or
✕ 800-243-0212; 2 Bridge St.
Posh waterfront lodgings complete with
spa facilities, pools, and a marina, plus
Mediterrean/Northern Italian cuisine in
the **Terra Mar Grille**. **$$-$$$**

✕ **Dock 'n' Dine.** 860-388-4665;
Saybrook Point **$$**
Right on land's end, with wraparound
windows look out onto the Connecticut
River flowing into Long Island Sound.

✕ **Pat's Kountry Kitchen.** 860-388-4784;
70 Mill Rock Rd. East **$$**
Home cooking in a cheerful homespun
setting; great pies.

✕ **Saybrook Fish House.** 860-388-4836;
99 Essex Rd. **$$**
Worth a stopover for good, affordable
seafood lunches and dinners.

✕ **Wine & Roses.** 860-388-9646;
150 Main St. **$$-$$$**
A winner of a restaurant in a shingle-
sided building. Eclectic, imaginative
menu. Don't miss the exotic dessert:
wontons filled with bananas and white
chocolate. Reservations suggested.

Putnam Area, CT *map C-2*

✕ **The Harvest.** 860-928-0008;
37 Putnam Rd., Pomfret **$$-$$$**
Fine dining in a 1785 homestead; an
eclectic international menu.

✕ **The Vine Bistro.** 860-928-1660;
85 Main St., Putnam **$$**
In midst of Putnam's cluster of antique
shops; down-to-earth American food.

Ridgefield, CT *map A-4*

⛢ **The Elms Inn.** 203-438-2541;
500 Main St. **$-$$**
Dates from 1799 and is appropriately
filled with antiques. Twenty comfortable
rooms. Continental breakfast included.

STONEHENGE INN

(See following page.)

☂ **Stonehenge Inn.** 203-438-6511;
✕ 35 Stonehenge Rd. **$$**
A New England country inn in a gorgeous natural setting, on spacious grounds. The **Stonehenge** dining room overlooks a swan pond and features updated French country cuisine; try the rack of lamb. Reservations required. **$$$**

Salisbury, CT *map A-2*

☂ **Interlaken Inn.** 860-435-9878;
74 Interlaken Rd. (Route 112),
Lakeville **$$**
Accommodations include duplex suites with fireplace; amenities include fitness center and tennis courts, heated outdoor pool, swimming and boating on Lake Wononskopomuc.

☂ **Under Mountain Inn.** 860-435-0242;
✕ 483 Under Mountain Rd. (Route 41) **$$$**
An 18th-century white-clapboard farmhouse with seven guest rooms, plus an English-style pub and English specialties (such as steak and kidney pie) for dinner. Reservations suggested. **$$**

☂ **The White Hart.** 860-435-0030;
✕ Village Green **$$**
Landmark 1867 village inn; traditional American specialties are served in the **American Grill. $$$ The Garden and Tap Room** tavern/restaurant offers a more casual atmosphere and a more contemporary menu. **$$**

Scotland, CT *map C-3*

✕ **Olde English Tea Room.**
860-456-8651; 3 Devotion Rd.,
Routes 14 and 97 **$**
Pearl Dexter uses several rooms in her home for tea: one houses her teapot collection; another, tea-related tchochkes; and a third, a tearoom. Light lunches and high teas are available; go for a tea with scones, tea sandwiches, etc.

Simsbury, CT *map B-3*

☂ **Simsbury 1820 House.** 860-658-7658
✕ 731 Hopmeadow St. **$$**
This historic house is set on the crest of a hill overlooking the heart of old Simsbury. Gifford Pinchot, America's first forester, built this home, which has been restored to its old glory. The 32 guest rooms are embellished with English antiques. The dining room offers New American cuisine, with an emphasis on seasonal ingredients. Restaurant **$$.**

Stonington, CT *map C-4*

☂ **Randall's Ordinary.** 860-599-4540;
✕ 41 Norwich Westerly Rd. (Hwy. 2),
North Stonington **$$-$$$**
Accommodations in a colonial wayside inn and a converted 1819 dairy barn; costumed waiters serve hearth-cooked meals. **$$-$$$.** Reservations required.

✕ **Noah's.** 860-535-3925; 113 Water St. **$-$$**
A friendly, laid-back place frequented by

residents and visitors. Real home cooking with an emphasis on locally caught fish.

✕ **One South.** 860-535-0418;
201 North Main St. $-$$
Lots of atmosphere: wonderful pasta dishes, locally caught fish, and the best burger in the area.

✕ **Water Street Cafe.** 860-535-2122;
142 Water St. $-$$
Chef Walter Houlihan, who hails from the Ambassador Grill in New York, is an artist with his contemporary American cuisine. The tiny space, popular with locals, is set up as a bar with a few tables.

Storrs, CT *map C-3*

⊟ **Altnaveigh Inn.** 860-429-4490;
957 Storrs Rd. (Route 195) $
Six guest rooms in a 1734 wayside inn; close to the University of Connecticut.

THE FITCH HOUSE

⊟ **The Fitch House.** 860-456-0922;
563 Storrs Rd. (Route 195), Mansfield $-$$
This colonnaded Greek Revival mansion was built in 1836; now it's a three-room

B&B. Breakfast is often served in the solarium. Furnished with antiques; one room has a fireplace.

Torrington, CT *map A-3*

⊟ **Yankee Pedlar Inn.** 860-489-9226;
✕ 93 Main St. $$
A completely refurbished 1891 inn with Hitchcock furnishings. Convenient location. The **Conley Pub & Restaurant** downstairs offers deliciously updated renditions of traditional American cuisine; $$.

Westbrook, CT *map B-4*

⊟ **Captain Stannard House.**
860-399-4634; 138 South Main St. $$
An 1850 sea captain's manse has been reborn as a village B&B.

⊟ **Water's Edge Inn & Resort.**
✕ 860-399-5901 or 800-222-5901;
1525 Boston Post Rd. $$$
Overlooking Long Island Sound from its spread atop a bluff, this resort's amenities include a spa and fitness center and haute-cuisine restaurant. Dinner $$$

✕ **Aleia's.** 860-399-5050; 1687 Boston Post Rd. $$-$$$
Delightfully airy decor, especially for meals served on the canopied deck. Try the gourmet-caliber pasta and seafood dished. Reservations required.

✕ **Lenny & Joe's Fish Tale.** 860-669-0767;
86 Boston Post Rd. $$
A perpetually busy place, renowned all along the coast for its fried clams.

Wethersfield, CT map B-3

⊞ **Chester Bulkley House.** 860-563-4236; 184 Main St. $$
Nestled in the historic village of Old Wethersfield, this circa-1830 Greek Revival beauty has been converted to an economical B&B with five guest rooms.

Winsted Area, CT map B-2

OLD RIVERTON INN

⊞ **Old Riverton Inn.** 860-379-8678;
✕ 436 East River Rd. (at Route 20), Riverton $-$$
Welcoming guests since 1796, alongside the Farmington River, located on what once was the post road between Hartford and Albany. Wonderfully antique dining room.

✕ **The Tributary.** 860-379-7679; 19 Rowley St., Winsted $$
Housed in a mid-19th-century warehouse on the banks of the Mad River. Economical huge meals.

Woodbury, CT map B-3

⊞ **Curtis House.** 203-263-2101;
✕ 506 Main St. South $$-$$$
Connecticut's oldest inn, dating at least back to at least 1736, with canopy beds in its 18 guest rooms. Good old American cuisine for lunch and dinner; $$-$$$

CURTIS HOUSE

✕ **Carole Peck's Good News Café.** 203-266-4663; 694 Main St. South $$-$$$
For terrific, innovative gourmet food in a restaurant, bar, and art gallery.

Woodstock, CT map C-2

⊞ **The Inn at Woodstock Hill.**
✕ 860-928-0528; 94 Plaine Hill Rd., South Woodstock $-$$.
Listed on the National Register of Historic Places, a country estate with 22 antique-furnished guest rooms, on a 14-acre property. Plus an excellent American and continental restaurant. $$$

RHODE ISLAND FOOD & LODGING

Block Island, RI *map D-4*

A note on lodging in Block Island:
Most B&Bs and inns require a minimum stay, especially on weekends, and many places close just after Columbus Day. Summer rates are shown; spring and fall are often much lower.

☎ **Gables Inn.** 401-466-2213; Dodge St. $-$$$
A pair of Victorian homes with small comfortable rooms, shared baths, and homey welcome. Breakfast included. Near ferry landing.

☎ **Hotel Manisses.** 401-466-2421 or
✗800-626-4773; One Spring St. $$-$$$$
The island's showpiece, barely saved from ruin and now updated with tasteful decor and modern amenities. Large breakfast buffet. **Manisses Restaurant** ($$-$$$), which serves a classic menu, is tops. Wheelchair accessible.

HOTEL MANISSES

☎ **National Hotel.** 401-466-2901 or 800-225-2449; Water St. $-$$$
Good traditional hotel with full services, updated rooms; directly opposite ferry landing in the center of town. Just a short walk from a beautiful beach.

☎ **Rose Farm Inn.** 401-466-2021; 105 Roselyn Rd. $$-$$$
Sea views, large rooms in older home or in posh new quarters with balconies overlooking the spacious grounds. Full breakfast included.

☎ **Seacrest Inn.** 401-466-2882; 207 High St. $$
Nothing lavish, but clean, comfortable, well-kept and one of the most convenient locations, a few steps from the ferry landing. Perfect for families, with secure play yard. Continental breakfast is included.

☎ **1661 Inn.** 401-466-2421 or 800-626-4773; Spring St. $$-$$$$
Affiliated with the Hotel Manisses, this inn is more casual, but also beautifully decorated and maintained, with some suites for families. A full breakfast buffet is included.

☎ **Spring House Hotel.** 401-466-5844 or 800-234-9263; Spring St. $$$-$$$$
This 140-year-old hotel has magnificent porches, a creakily elegant interior, and one of the island's loveliest views. Open from May to October.

Note: Map coordinates refer to the map on page 327.

✗ **Eli's.** 401-466-5230; 456 Chapel St. **$**.
Always crowded, except in winter (it's
open year-round), serving up creative
Italian dishes in deceptively casual surroundings. There's nothing casual about
the kitchen's work, however.

✗ **Finn's Seafood Restaurant.**
401-466-2473; Water St. **$-$$**
The menu is full of fresh fish and shellfish of every stripe, and not all of it's
fried. Casual, often crowded and usually
noisy indoors, with outside dining on
deck overlooking the harbor.

✗ **Winfield's.** 401-466-5856;
Corn Neck Rd. **$$**
New American cuisine with an Italian
accent and a casual upbeat atmosphere.
Look for lobster over fettuccine and
game entrees.

Bristol Area, RI *map D-3*

⊞ **Nathaniel Porter Inn.** 401-245-6622;
✗ 125 Water St., Warren **$$**
An 18th-century classic on Warren's wa-
terfront is a good choice for overnight
accommodations and meals in the can-
dlelit dining room. Dinner **$$-$$$**.

⊞ **Rockwell House Inn.** 401-253-0040;
610 Hope St. **$$**
Right in the picture-perfect center of
town, this 19th-century Greek Revival
"wedding-cake" edifice contains four
guest rooms; huge breakfasts are price-
inclusive.

ROCKWELL HOUSE INN

✗ **Café la France.** 401-253-0360;
483 Hope St. **$**
The town's premier sandwich emporium
also thrives as an ice-cream parlor, coffee
house, and pastry shop.

✗ **The Lobster Pot.** 401-253-9100;
119 Hope St. **$$$**
A pricey-but-worth-it seafood restaurant
with the bonus of Bristol Harbor pano-
ramics on Narragansett Bay.

✗ **Redlefsen's Rotisserie & Grill**
401-254-1188; 425 Hope St. **$$**
Combined Danish-German atmospher-
ics, and food specialties in the same vein.

✗ **South Shore Grill.** 401-782-4780;
210 Salt Pond Rd, Charlestown **$$- $$$**.
A South County gem of a seafood
restaurant, overlooking a cove and "rub-
bing shoulders" with the Point Judith
Yacht Club.

Jamestown, RI *map D-3*

☂ **Bay Voyage.** 401-423-2100 or 800-225-3522; 150 Conanicus Ave. $$-$$$
This appealing family-type resort hotel on Conanicut Island features across-the-bay views of Newport and Rose Island. A fine dining room, too.

✕ **Oyster Bar & Grill.** 401-423-3380; 22 Narragansett Ave. $$
Fresh seafood is the draw in this casual, unfancy little eatery.

✕ **Trattoria Simpatico.** 401-423-3731; 13 Narragansett Ave. $$$
The very best Italian restaurant in the Newport/Conanicus Island vicinity. Reservations suggested.

Middletown, RI *map D-3*

✕ **Tommy's Deluxe Diner.** 401-847-9834; 159 East Main Rd. (Route 138) $
An all-original 1941 gem serving not only traditional New England food, but also Greek and Portuguese specials. Three meals a day.

Narragansett, RI *map D-4*

☂ **The Village Inn.** 401-783-6767 or
✕ 800-843-7437; One Beach St. $$
A modern gray-shingled stalwart is biggest and best in town for beachfront lodgings. Indoor pool and Jacuzzi. A tavern/restaurant and casual café are also on-site; $-$$.

✕ **Coast Guard House.** 401-789-0700; 40 Ocean Rd. $$-$$$
Great for ocean views while dining in an 1888 life-saving station. Lunches, dinners, and stupendous Sunday buffets. .

Newport, RI *map D-3*

☂ **Admiral Benbow Inn.** 401-848-8000 or 800-343-2863; 93 Pelham St. $$-$$$
Listed on the National Register of Historic Places, the Admiral Benbow is located two blocks from the harbor. The 15 rooms are decorated in antiques, and all have private baths. An excellent continental breakfast is included in the rates. Open year-round.

ADMIRAL BENBOW INN

☂ **Elm Tree Cottage.** 401-849-1610 or 800-882-3356; 336 Gibbs Ave. $$$-$$$$.
This is the real thing: a Newport mansion from the Gilded Age, where the Duke and Dutchess of Windsor often stayed. Rooms and suites, all beautifully decorated, sumptuous breakfast.

🏠 **Francis Malbone House.**
401-846-0392; 392 Thames St. $$-$$$.
It's like staying in a museum where you
can sleep in the beds and lounge in the
chairs. Friendly people, great breakfasts.

THE VICTORIAN LADIES

🏠 **The Victorian Ladies.** 401-849-9960;
63 Memorial Blvd. $$-$$$
Victorian lace never overwhelms these
elegant rooms that blend a rich, tailored
look with frivolity. Gardens are beautiful
as well. Within walking distance to
mansions, beach, shopping, restaurants.

🏠 **Villa Liberte.** 401-846-7444;
22 Liberty St. $$$.
Art deco rooms have a bold contempo-
rary look, and checkered walls to match
the inn's colorful past; easy walk to
restaurants, mansions, shopping.

A note about dining in Newport:
Many restaurants along Thames Street
do not accept reservations, so savvy din-
ers browse the posted menus, then have
their names put on the waiting list while
they stroll along the harbor and return
at the suggested time. A few do reserve,
as do most restaurants elsewhere in

town, but strolling along restaurant row
in the evening is a Newport tradition.

✕ **The Alva.** 401-846-6200;
41 Mary St. $$-$$$
In circa-1909 Vanderbilt Hall; a sophis-
ticated restaurant for indoor or patio
dining. Recommendable: steak, oyster
and Guinness stew, also classic lobster
thermador. Open for lunch, dinner, and
English tea time. Reservations suggested.

✕ **The Black Pearl.** 401-846-5264;
Bannister's Wharf $$-$$$
The best-known and most popular
dockside restaurant in town; more ex-
pensive in the Commodore Room than
in the black-painted tavern. Specialties
include rack of lamb and brochette of
shrimp and sea scallops. Reservations
not taken.

✕ **Brick Alley Pub & Restaurant.**
401-849-6334; 140 Thames St. $-$$
A favorite for locals and visitors, this
place is loaded with funky antiques and
its menu includes steaks, ribs, chicken,
and pasta; there's also a massive salad
bar. Reservations suggested.

✕ **Café Zelda.** 401-849-4002;
528 Thames St. $$
A relaxing restaurant for soup-salad-
sandwich lunch or steak-and-seafood
dinner, augmented by a fine vintage
from the wine cellar. Lunch $, dinner $$.
Reservations suggested.

✕ **Christie's.** 401-847-5400;
Christie's Landing $$-$$$
Can't be beat for Newport Harbor views;
on two floors with picture windows over-

looking the wharf. Ocean-fresh specialties include lobster, baked halibut, and
terrific Nantucket Bay scallops, shrimp,
and lobster in a puff pastry. Lunch and
dinner. Reservations suggested.

✕ **Elizabeth's Cafe.** 401-846-6862;
404 Thames St. $$-$$$
In Elizabeth Burley's charming rendition
of an antique-filled Welsh parlor, feast
on epic stuffed sourdough bouillabaise.
Reservations required.

✕ **Gary's Handy Lunch.** 401-847-9480;
462 Thames St. $.
Handy indeed if you're looking for a
budget midday meal. Soups, burgers,
fries, meatloaf, American chop suey, and
blue-plate specials pretty well sum up
the daily fare.

✕ **La Forge Casino Restaurant.**
401-847-0418; 186 Bellevue Ave. $$-$$$
A Newport institution since 1954; this
restaurant's pink and green Victorian
porch is directly alongside the International Tennis Hall of Fame's Horseshoe
Piazza grass court. Dine in the Irish-style
pub or semi-formally (on continental
fare) on the covered porch. Evening
reservations required.

✕ **Lucia.** 401-846-4477;
186 Thames St. $$
The accent's on northern Italian at this
little upstairs trattoria. Crescentina
(stuffed fried pizza) and ergazzone
(spinach pie) are among the recom-
mendables. Dinner reservations are sug-
gested.

✕ **Music Hall Café.** 401-848-2330;
250 Thames St. $$
Specializes in Southwestern and Tex-
Mex cuisine.

✕ **Ocean Coffee Roasters.** 22 Washington
Square; 401-846-6060 $
Espresso drinks and a tempting array of
sandwiches, scones, bagels, and muffins.
In addition, the blackboard lists soups
and chili, fruit and cheese plates, plus
vegetarian pizza and super-duper focac-
cia pizza. No reservations necessary.

✕ **The Place.** 28 Washington Square;
401-847-0125
A wine bar with vegetarian specials is the
chic, pricey portion of **Yesterday's**, an
upscale luncheon pub with 26 brands of
micro-brewed beer. Restaurant $$, pub
$. Dinner reservations suggested.

✕ **Restaurant Bouchard.** 401-846-0123;
505 Thames St. $$$$.
Unmatched locally for French haute cui-
sine.

✕ **The Rhumbline.** 401-849-6950;
62 Bridge St. $$
In a colonial house in Newport's historic
Point neighborhood. An eclectic international menu ranges from Austrian
Wienerschnitzel to Thai pork and lin-
guine. Dinner only.

✕ **White Horse Tavern.** 401-849-3600;
Marlborough and Farewell Sts. $$$$
Newport's priciest restaurant. The set-
ting is quite legitimately colonial—the
White Horse has been in business since
1687. Splurge on beef Wellington, rack

of lamb, or Chateaubriand. For a grand finale, savor the White Horse's dessert sensation: triple chocolate silk pie. Dinner only. Reservations required.

Providence, RI *map D-3*

🛏 **Day's Hotel.** 401-272-5577 or 800-325-2525; 220 India Point $$-$$$
Family-friendly, with well-maintained rooms and a good cafe. In-town location is on waterfront and bicycle trail.

🛏 **Mill Street Inn.** 401-849-9500 or 800-392-1316; 75 Mill St. $$-$$$
This 19th-century mill building is now an all-suite hotel.

🛏 **Old Court Bed and Breakfast.** 401-751-2002; 144 Benefit St. $$.
An 1863 mansion in the heart of the city; antiques furnish rooms in a variety of styles. Espresso or cappuccino with breakfast.

🛏 **Providence Biltmore.** 401-421-0700; 11 Dorrance St. $$$.
A dazzling restoration has breathed new life into an old charmer, done up in crystal, gilt, and marble. Large rooms, modern amenities, next to the Convention Center.

🛏 **Westin Providence.** 401-598-8200 or 800-228-3000; One West Exchange St. $$$-$$$$
Striking architecture is the keynote of downtown's skyline, lobby rotunda is simply grand. Rooms match the opulence of the building, with all of the amenities and nice views.

✕ **Al Forno.** 401-273-9760; 577 Main St. $$$
The city's best-known restaurant, acclaimed for its eclectic menu and excellent wood-grilled food. Reservations are not taken, so be prepared to wait.

✕ **Angelo's Civita Farnese.** 401-461-7495; 141 Atwell's Ave. $
The heart of Little Italy, geographically and spiritually, Angelo's is a no-frills, family-run restaurant serving unfussy, fresh pasta dishes and daily specials.

✕ **Café Nuovo.** 401-421-2525; One Citizens Plaza $$
Indoor-outdoor seating overlooking downtown's Riverwalk while dining on Caribbean, Asian, and Southwestern cuisine. Reservations advised.

✕ **Federal Reserve.** 401-277-0307; 60 Dorrance St. $$
A recycled bank lobby, complete with turn-of-the-century vault, sets the tone for contemporary New England dining. Reservations advised.

✕ **L'Epicureo.** 401-454-8430; 238 Atwell's Ave. $$$
Once Joe's butcher shop, now one of the city's most elegant restaurants, specializing in fresh pasta dishes, wood-grilled steaks, and veal.

✕ **Hemenway's.** 401-351-8570; One Providence Washington Plaza $$
International seafood galore in the restaurant, plus an oyster bar. Reservations suggested.

✗ **New Rivers.** 401-751-0350;
7 Steeple St. **$$-$$$**
A stylish, elegant bistro atmosphere for fusion cuisine with worldwide influences.

✗ **Union Station Brewery.** 401-274-2739;
36 Exchange Terrace **$**
Downtown brewpub serving inexpensive meals accompanied by the house brand of beer and ale.

Tiverton Area, RI *map D-3*

Note:

For lodgings near Tiverton, look just over the bridge in Portsmouth or in nearby Fall River, Massachusetts, where you'll find several moderately priced chain hotels.

⊞ **Brown's-Bed and-Breakfast.**
401-683-0155; 502 Bristol Ferry Rd., Portsmouth **$-$$.**
Cheerful, homey, and hospitable, with views over well-kept lawns to Narragansett Bay. Portuguese breakfast breads.

⊞ **Founder's Brook Motel.** 401-683-1244 or 800-334-8765; 314 Boyds Lane, Portsmouth **$$**
Suites are sized for families, with kitchen facilities and big closets; at the foot of Mount Hope Bridge.

✗ **Abraham Manchester's.** 401-635-2700;
Route 81, Adamsville **$-$$**
The atmosphere is rustic and the portions gigantic, but the menu is sophisticated and creative.

✗ **Evelyn's Nannaquaket Drive In.**
401-624-3100; 2335 Main Rd., Tiverton **$**

Generous portions of mostly fried seafood; fresh clams. Tables overlook the water.

✗ **Flo's Drive-In.** no phone; Park Ave., Portsmouth **$**
Just across the bridge from Tiverton, a basic clam shack where natives go for the best fried clams. Picnic tables overlook the water.

Wakefield, RI *map D-3*

⊞ **Admiral Dewey Inn.** 401-783-2090;
668 Matunuck Beach Rd. **$$-$$$**
Posh accommodations, ideal for summertime vacationers, in a beach village on the south coast.

ADMIRAL DEWEY INN

⊞ **Larchwood Inn.** 401-783-5454;
521 Main St. **$$**
A converted mansion in the town center now functions nicely as an old-fashioned inn and New England–style restaurant with a surprisingly wide-ranging international wine list. The atmosphere may be a bit stodgy, but a well-worn, comfortable feel permeates the guest rooms and public spaces. Dinner **$$$**.

Watch Hill, RI *map D-4*

🏨 **Ocean House Hotel.** 401-348-8161;
2 Bluff Ave. **$$$**
This elegant Victorian hotel offers a private beach, ample porches, pretty gardens, and a restaurant with views of the ocean.

OCEAN HOUSE HOTEL

✕ **Olympia Tea Room** 401-348-8211;
74 Bay St. **$-$$**
A Watch Hill landmark since 1916; old-fashioned wooden booths. Menu choices balance Yankee classic dishes with South American and Caribbean surprises.

Westerly, RI *map D-4*

🏨 **Breezeway Motel.** 401-348-8953;
70 Winnapaug Rd., Westerly **$$-$$$**
Plain, but very well-kept rooms surrounding a pool, sundeck, play area, and picnic tables. Perfect for families.

🏨 **The Villa.** 800-722-9240 or
401-596-1054; 190 Shore Rd.
(Route 1A) **$$-$$$$**

Stunning rooms, some with private garden, fireplace, or whirlpool tub. Grand gardens with fountain, swimming pool, terrace, outdoor hot tub. Includes breakfast and sweets on arrival.

THE VILLA

🏨 **Winnapaug Inn.** 401-348-8350 or
800-288-9906; 169 Shore Rd.
(Route 1A) **$$-$$$**
A resort hideaway alongside a golf course and a mile from Misquamicut's big sandy beach. Recreation facilities include swimming pool.

✕ **Maria's Gourmet Italian.**
401-322-0444; Old Post Rd. (US 1),
Shelter Harbor **$-$$**
Traditional Sicilian dishes blend with northern Italian, in a friendly, lively atmosphere.

Wickford, RI *map D-3*

✕ **Duffy's Tavern.** 401-294-3733;
235 Tower Hill Rd. **$$**
A super-casual place for chowder, clam cakes, or complete seafood meals.

INDEX OF LISTINGS IN THIS BOOK

CHAIN LODGINGS IN SOUTHERN NEW ENGLAND
Toll-Free Numbers

Best Western 800-528-1234

Comfort Inn 800-228-5150

Day's Inn 800-325-2525

Doubletree 800-528-0444

Hampton Inn 800-426-7866

Hilton 800-445-8667

Holiday Inn 800-465-4329

Hyatt 800-233-1234

Marriott 800-228-9290

Radisson 800-333-3333

Residence Inn (Marriott). .800-331-3131

Sheraton 800-325-3535

Suisse Chalet 800-258-1980

Westin 800-228-3000

MASSACHUSETTS FOOD & LODGING BY REGION

Town	Page	Map	Town	Page	Map	Town	Page	Map
BOSTON AREA			*SOUTH SHORE, cont'd*			*SOUTH SHORE, cont'd*		
Boston	328	E-2	Dennis	334	F-3	Vineyard Haven	343	E-4
Cambridge	335	E-2	Dennis Port	334	F-3	Woods Hole	340	F-3
Concord	338	D-1	Eastham	339	F-3	Yarmouth	352	F-3
Lexington	342	D-1	Edgartown	343	E-4			
			Fall River	339	E-3	*INTERIOR*		
NORTH SHORE			Falmouth	340	E-3	Amherst	328	B-2
Essex	339	E-1	Harwich Port	337	F-3	Deerfield	338	B-1
Gloucester	341	E-1	Hingham	350	E-2	Lenox	341	A-2
Lynn	342	E-1	Hyannis	341	F-3	Montague	344	B-1
Marblehead	342	E-1	Martha's Vnyd.	343	E-4	Northampton	346	B-2
Newburyport	346	E-1	Middleboro	344	E-3	Shelburne Falls	350	B-1
Rockport	348	E-1	Nantucket	344	F-4	South Deerfield	338	B-1
Salem	349	E-1	New Bedford	346	E-3	South Lee	351	A-2
			Oak Bluffs	343	E-4	South Lee	351	A-2
SOUTH SHORE, CAPE			Orleans	339	F-3	Stockbridge	351	A-2
COD & ISLANDS			Plymouth	347	E-2	Sturbridge	351	C-2
Braintree	350	E-2	Provincetown	347	F-2	Turners Falls	352	B-1
Brewster	334	F-3	Sandwich	350	F-3	Whately	338	B-1
Chatham	337	F-3	Scituate	350	E-2	Williamstown	352	A-1
Cohasset	350	E-2	Teaticket	340	E-3	Worcester	352	C-2

Note: Map coordinates refer to the map on page 327.

CONNECTICUT FOOD & LODGING BY REGION

Town	Page	Map	Town	Page	Map	Town	Page	Map
CENTRAL & EASTERN			*NORTHWEST*			*COAST, cont'd*		
			Canaan	354	A-2	Madison	357	B-4
Avon	354	B-3	Cornwall	354	A-3	Mystic	358	C-4
Brooklyn	354	C-3	Kent	357	A-3	New Canaan	361	A-4
Chester	354	B-4	Litchfield	357	A-3	New Haven	359	B-4
Coventry	355	C-4	Morris	358	A-3	New London	360	C-4
East Haddam	355	B-3	Norfolk	361	A-2	New Milford	360	A-3
Essex	355	C-4	Riverton	366	B-2	Noank	361	C-4
Farmington	355	B-3	Salisbury	364	A-2	North Stonington	364	C-3
Hartford	356	B-4	Torrington	365	A-3	Norwalk	361	A-4
Middletown	358	B-3	Washington	360	A-3	Old Lyme	362	C-4
New Preston	360	A-3	Woodbury	366	B-3	Old Saybrook	363	C-4
Putnam	363	C-2				Ridgefield	363	A-4
Scotland	364	C-3	*COAST*			Stonington	364	C-4
Simsbury	364	B-3	Branford	354	B-4	Storrs	365	C-3
Southington	355	B-3	Brookfield	354	A-3	Westbrook	365	B-4
Wethersfield	366	B-3	Clinton	363	C-4	Westport	361	A-4
Woodstock	366	C-2	Greenwich	356	A-4	Winsted	366	B-2
			Guilford	356	B-4			

RHODE ISLAND FOOD & LODGING BY TOWN

Town	Page	Map	Town	Page	Map	Town	Page	Map
Adamsville	373	E-3	Narragansett	369	D-3	Wakefield	373	D-3
Block Island	367	D-4	Newport	369	D-3	Warren	368	D-3
Bristol	368	D-3	Portsmouth	373	D-3	Watch Hill	374	D-4
Charlestown	368	D-4	Providence	372	D-3	Westerly	374	D-4
Jamestown	369	D-3	Shelter Harbor	374	D-4	Wickford	374	D-3
Middletown	369	D-3	Tiverton	373	D-3			

Note: Map coordinates refer to the map on page 327.

I N D E X

■ ABOUT THE AUTHOR

Anna Mundow has lived and traveled in New England since 1983. A native of Ireland, she is a correspondent for the *Irish Times* and a book critic for the *New York Daily News.* She is also a regular contributor to *Newsday* and to the *Boston Globe,* and she has appeared as a commentator on BBC Radio, Monitor Radio, and WGBH television. Mundow's writing has appeared in a variety of other publications, from the *Los Angeles Times* and *Mirabella* to *Boston Magazine* and the *Manchester Guardian.*

■ ABOUT THE PHOTOGRAPHER

DAVID GROSSMAN

James Marshall began making photographs as a teenager in his basement darkroom. Since 1978 he has traveled extensively throughout Asia, North America, and Europe, covering events and documenting cultures. Along the way, he produced and edited *Hong Kong: Here be Dragons; A Day in the Life of Thailand;* and *Planet Vegas: A Portrait of Las Vegas.* After nearly 20 years in New York and Connecticut, in 1997 he moved to the coast of Maine, where he especially enjoys the fish chowder.

Food & Lodging Contributors: In addition to writing the Compass guide to *Boston,* Cambridge-based writers Patricia Harris and David Lyon are restaurant critics for *Boston Sidewalk* and contribute to *Yankee Magazine, Boston Globe,* and *Travel Holiday.* Boston resident Tom Bross is a freelance writer who writes for *TravelAmerica, Historic Traveler,* and *AAA Today.* Barbara and Tim Stillman-Rogers have been writing guides to New England together for the past dozen years.

COMMENTS, QUESTIONS, OR SUGGESTIONS? *Write:* **Compass American Guides,** 5332 College Ave., Suite 201, Oakland, CA 94618 *E-mail:* compassk@a.crl.com